HARALD HARDRADA

IN MEMORY OF KNAP

HARALD HARDRADA

THE WARRIOR'S WAY

JOHN MARSDEN

SUTTON PUBLISHING

First published in the United Kingdom in 2007 by
Sutton Publishing Limited · Phoenix Mill
Thrupp · Stroud · Gloucestershire · GL5 2BU

British Library Cataloguing in Publication Data
A catalogue record for this book is available from the British Library.

ISBN hardback 978-0-7509-4290-4
ISBN paperback 978-0-7509-4291-1

Typeset in Sabon.
Typesetting and origination by
Sutton Publishing Limited.
Printed and bound in England.

Contents

Author's Note and Acknowledgements

A book written in English for a non-academic readership and yet drawing on source material originally set down in Old Norse, Byzantine Greek, Russian, Anglo-Saxon and Latin does require a note as to its policy in the naming of names. As there appears to be no standard form of English spelling of early Scandinavian names, I have used whichever form seems the most appropriate in the historical context and the least intimidating for an English reader. Similarly, the title of 'earl' is spelled in that English form where it occurs in England, but in its original Old Norse form as *jarl* in a Scandinavian context. Sometimes names and terms are also given in their original spelling – set in italics and usually in parentheses – so it might be helpful to explain that the Norse character ð is pronounced 'th' (as in ra*the*r). I should also mention my specific use of the term *viking* in its original sense of 'sea-raider' as distinct from the modern usage of 'Viking' as a generic term for anyone (or anything) associated with early medieval Scandinavia.

Notes have been kept to a minimum and most often used to acknowledge references to or quotations from the work of others, but there are two such authors to whom I owe a more prominent acknowledgement because Sigfús Blöndal's *The Varangians of Byzantium* in the English edition revised and translated by Benedikt S. Benedikz was the work which played a greater part than any other in developing my interest in the man who forms the subject of this book. A more personal acknowledgement is due to my friend John Hamburg of Carrollton, Kentucky, whose unfailing enthusiasm for the same subject played its own part in encouraging this attempt at a biography of Harald Hardrada.

J.M.

Maps

LAPPS

OB-UGRIANS

U R A L   M O U N T A I N S

River Pechora

GULF of FINLAND

Staraja
Ladoga

CHUDS

Novgorod

River Volga

Bulghar

VOLGA
BULGARS

River Dvina

RUS

River Dnieper

LAND

Kiev

River Dniester

SEA of AZOV

CASPIAN
SEA

RY

PECHENEGS

KHAZARS

BLACK   SEA

ARMENIA

BULGARIA

Bosphorus

Constantinople

ASIA MINOR

River Euphrates

AEGEAN SEA

A

CRETE

CYPRUS

HOLY LAND

MAP 1

MAP 2

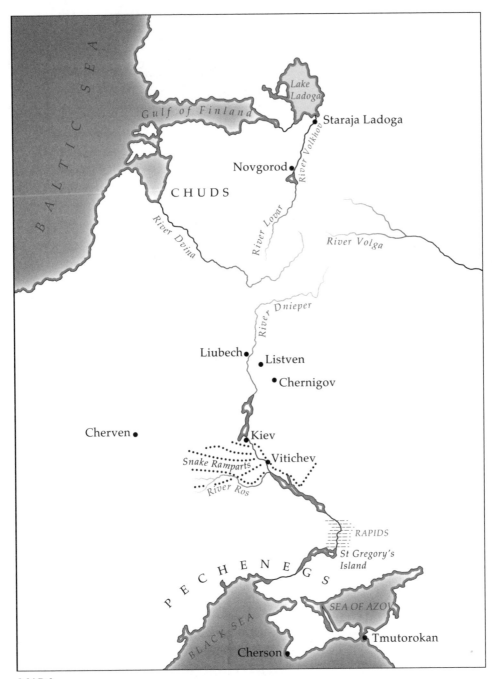

MAP 3

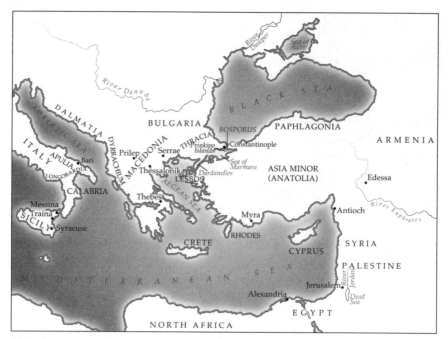

MAP 4

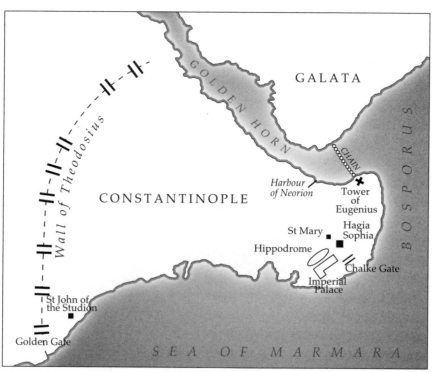

MAP 5

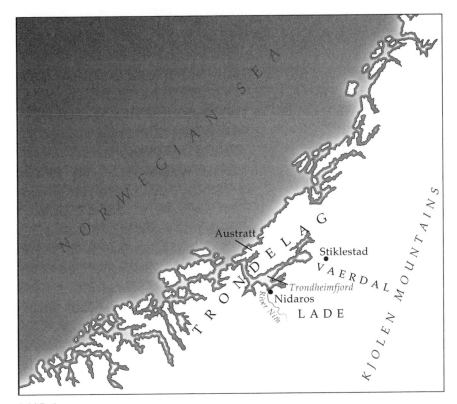

MAP 6

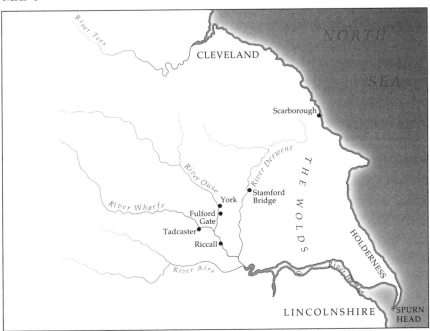

MAP 7

xiii

Sagas, Skalds and Soldiering

AN INTRODUCTION TO A MILITARY BIOGRAPHY

When he is remembered only as a Norwegian king slain in battle at Stamford Bridge in Yorkshire, where his invading army was crushed just three days before the arrival of the conquering Normans, the place of Harald Hardrada in the mainstream of English history amounts to little more than that of the 'third man' of the undeniably memorable year 1066. He spent no more than eighteen days on English soil, after all, and the subsequent events of that fateful autumn have left him overshadowed, first by the English Harold and ultimately by William the Norman, thus obscuring his reputation – acknowledged by historians ancient and modern – as the most feared warrior of his world and time.

If Stamford Bridge is set into a wider context than that of Anglo-Saxon England, however, it comes into a very different focus as the last of innumerable conflicts fought out along a warrior's way that had ranged across most of Scandinavia and eastward by way of Russia to the far-flung empire of Byzantium through the three and a half decades since a sturdy youngster stood with his half-brother, the king and future saint Olaf, in the blood-fray at Stiklestad in the west of Norway. The most comprehensive accounts of that great arc of warfaring are found in the thirteenth-century collections of sagas of the Norwegian kings, of which the most respected is the one known as *Heimskringla* and reliably attributed to the Icelander Snorri Sturluson. His version of Harald's saga is described by the editors of its standard modern English translation as 'a biography which in Snorri's hands becomes the story of a warrior's progress. Essentially it is the life and career of a professional soldier, starting with a battle

1

– the battle of Stiklestad where Harald, aged fifteen, is wounded and his brother the king killed – and ending in battle, thirty-six years later, at Stamford Bridge.'[1]

It was that observation which first suggested Harald Hardrada to me as the subject for a military biography, most especially because of its use of the term 'professional soldier'. While there are warrior kings aplenty throughout the history of the early medieval period, and not least in the northern world, Harald can be said to stand almost, if not entirely, alone among them in having spent all the years of his young manhood on active service as a professional soldier – and, quite specifically, in the modern understanding of the term.

Within a year of his escape from the field of Stiklestad, he had crossed the Baltic and found his way into Russia where he reappears among the Scandinavian mercenary fighting-men employed by the Russian princes to whom they were known as *Varjazi* or 'Varangians'. In that capacity and apparently as a junior officer, he is known to have taken part in a major campaign against the Poles, but assuredly also came up against the subject peoples of the northern forests and the steppe warriors to the south along the Dnieper. Some three years later he arrived in Constantinople, not yet twenty years old but already a battle-hardened commander of his own warrior company, to enter imperial service with the Varangian mercenaries of Byzantium.

During nine years of service under three emperors, Harald saw action at sea in the Mediterranean against Saracen corsairs and on land against their shore bases in Asia Minor, led his troop on escort duty to the Holy Land and took part in the Byzantine invasion of Arab-held Sicily, before being despatched against rebellions in the south of Italy and in Bulgaria. His accomplishments in the Sicilian and Bulgarian campaigns earned him promotion to the emperor's personal Varangian bodyguard in Constantinople where he was almost unavoidably – although very probably not innocently – caught up in the whirlpool of Byzantine politics. Subsequently falling from imperial favour, he was briefly imprisoned before escaping in time to play his own grisly part in the downfall of an emperor amid the bloodiest day of rioting ever seen in the city.

Shortly afterwards Harald's ambitions turned back towards his homeland and, despite having been refused imperial permission of leave, he launched his ships in a daring departure from Constantinople to begin the long journey north.

From the Black Sea he made his way up the Dnieper and back into Russia, assuredly bringing military intelligence to the Grand Prince in Kiev whose daughter he was to marry before moving north to assemble the great wealth he had acquired in the east and is said to have sent on to Novgorod for safe-keeping. So it was that Harald provided himself with the personal treasury which was later to assume legendary proportions in the hands of the saga-makers but still must have been more than sufficient to fund the force of ships and fighting-men that he would need to challenge his nephew Magnus' sovereignty over Norway and Denmark. By the spring of 1046 he was back in Scandinavia, forging a short-lived alliance with the claimant to Danish kingship and raiding around Denmark on a campaign of intimidation. Before the end of the year, the Danish ally had been discarded and the nephew had accepted his uncle into an uneasy joint kingship, which was to extend only until the following autumn when the sudden death of Magnus left Harald in sole possession of the Norwegian kingdom.

Thus, within less than eighteen months of his return from the east, the professional soldier had emerged in his perhaps more familiar guise of warrior king, and one whose reign was to be almost entirely taken up with conflict – seventeen years of sporadic war on the Danes, interspersed with bitter suppression of recalcitrant Norwegian factions and their Swedish allies, leading finally to the doomed invasion of England – all in seemingly voracious pursuit of dominion, vengeance and conquest.

Even that drastically abbreviated synopsis can leave scarcely any doubt of Harald Hardrada's potential as the subject of a military biography. Indeed, it might be thought to preclude the possibility of any account of his life not dominated by warfaring, and yet the approach to be taken here will still be at some degree of variance from the customary biographical format. While, of course, it will seek to offer a realistic portrait of the man himself – and of other remarkable individuals who played influential roles in his story – its first intention will be a reconstruction in some detail of the extraordinary military career by which he acquired his awesome reputation. Beyond that central concept, however, there lies a broader scope of interest, because to trace the course of Harald's warrior's way would seem to offer an exceptional, even unique, opportunity for exploration of the wide spectrum of warrior cultures – from Bulgar rebels to Norman mercenaries and Pecheneg steppe warriors to Anglo-Saxon housecarls – which he encountered across the greater extent of Scandinavian expansion at its high peak in the first half of the eleventh century.

From that perspective, Harald's mercenary soldiering in the east might be seen as an especially fitting education for a man said to have wanted to become a warlord since infancy. If the teenage years in Russia can be taken to represent a privileged apprenticeship and the wide-ranging experience in Byzantine service his time as a journeyman, taken together they assuredly informed, and in some measure shaped, his return to the northland as a warrior king. Thus the subject and structure of this book are also intended as 'the life and career of a professional soldier . . . beginning with a battle, the battle of Stiklestad . . . and ending in battle, thirty-six years later at Stamford Bridge', and so Snorri Sturluson's version of Harald's saga would seem to offer itself as my first choice of working template. Such a choice, however, raises all the scholarly doubt as to whether a saga set down in Iceland some two hundred years after the events it describes can be taken as reliable historical evidence for an eleventh-century Norwegian king. There was a time, even as recently as the earlier decades of the twentieth century, when the *konunga sögur* (or 'kings' sagas') – and especially those forming Snorri's *Heimskringla* cycle – were accorded all the respect due to impeccable sources of historical record, but modern scholarship has cast so much doubt on their reliability as to greatly diminish the esteem in which they were formerly held.

The historian's raw material for an understanding of the past is its surviving written record, so the first measure of any document's historical value must usually be its proximity in time and place to the events it describes, and yet in the case of Harald Hardrada the most closely contemporary documentary record cannot be considered any better than uneven. While his invasion of England is properly entered in the *Anglo-Saxon Chronicle* for 1066, his earlier presence in Russia would seem to have entirely escaped the notice of the Kievan monks who were setting down the annals now known as the *Russian Primary Chronicle* within a decade of his death, and yet his service with the Varangians of Byzantium is fully confirmed by a generous notice in a Byzantine document dated to the last quarter of the eleventh century.

As to the early sources originating in the Scandinavian and Baltic world, the most closely contemporary is the work of a German churchman, Adam of Bremen, whose *History of the Archbishops of Hamburg-Bremen* was written in Latin and completed by 1075. Adam's account of Harald, while hardly much better than fragmentary, is almost unrelentingly hostile, and understandably so when its author had derived so much of his information by way of personal contact with Harald's discarded Danish ally and subsequent lifelong enemy, Svein Estridsson. Nonetheless, Adam of Bremen does offer his own acknowledgement of Harald's warlike reputation when he refers to him as the 'thunderbolt of the north' and, on occasion, can also supply interesting detail to be found in no other source.

The earliest history actually written by a Scandinavian does not appear until at least a hundred years after that of Adam of Bremen from whose work its author, known as Saxo Grammaticus, evidently borrowed material. Saxo's *Gesta Danorum* (or 'Acts of the Danes') is another Latin history, although one more probably written by a lay clerk than a monk, because Saxo was of a Danish warrior family, a background which may well account for the unswerving loyalty he shows to Svein Estridsson; it would also account for the rather different light he might be thought to throw upon the saga record of warfare between Svein and Harald. The first historian of the Norwegian kings generally believed to have been himself a Norwegian was a contemporary of Saxo known only as 'Theodoric the Monk' whose Latin *Historia*, written around the year 1180, is dedicated to the archbishop of Nidaros (now Trondheim). It is a work which shows extremely scant respect for Norway's royal house and is thus thought likely to have provoked the ruling Norwegian king Sverri Sigurdsson, himself the subject and patron of the first saga set down in writing, to encourage the composition of a history more sympathetic to his ancestors and one which would serve as a counter to Theodoric's *Historia*.

This was to become the work now known as *Ágrip* or 'Summary', an abbreviation of *Ágrip af Nóregs konunga-sögum* ('Summary of the sagas of the Norwegian kings'), a title applied only in the last few centuries, and which reflects the incomplete state of the sole surviving manuscript copy while doing less than justice to the landmark significance of the long-lost original. Probably composed as early as the 1190s, and by an Icelander living in Norway, *Ágrip* is the oldest surviving history of Norwegian kings written in the Old Norse vernacular and was extensively used as a source by saga-makers in the thirteenth century, although they were certainly working from a fuller and better text than that preserved in the surviving manuscript. Of no less importance here, though, is its anonymous author's use of material from the oral tradition to expand upon that found in the Latin histories, because it is just this approach which points the way, followed in subsequent decades by the authors of the more expansive saga histories – and especially those bearing on Harald Hardrada.

Variant versions of Harald's saga are found in the three oldest collections of *konunga-sögur* – the *Morkinskinna*, the *Fagrskinna* and *Heimskringla* – while another, sometimes known as the 'Separate' *Harald's saga*, is found in a later manuscript volume known as the *Flateyjarbók*. Reference will be made to all of these saga sources throughout the following pages and so this might be a useful point at which to introduce them.

Of the four named above, only the *Flateyjarbók* survives as an original manuscript, the largest of all Icelandic parchments, of which the core was set down by two known Icelandic scribes in the later fourteenth century. A number of further folios, including the text of the 'Separate' *Harald's saga*, had been added by an unknown hand when it reappeared in a later ownership on the island of Flatey (hence its name, meaning 'The Book of Flatey') in the second half of the fifteenth century. The three earlier saga collections have all been dated to the first few decades of the thirteenth century, even though none survive as original manuscripts but only as copies of various dates and in no less various conditions.

The collection called *Morkinskinna* ('mouldy vellum') was written around the year 1275 by Icelandic scribes reworking an older text – now lost, but referred to as the 'Oldest *Morkinskinna*' – which has been dated to at least fifty years earlier, with one scholarly estimate even placing its composition as precisely as the period 1217–22. It was this original text of *Morkinskinna*, containing sagas of the kings reigning between 1035 and the latter half of the twelfth century, which appears to have been the source of later sections in *Fagrskinna* and in *Heimskringla* and so might be taken to represent the earliest of the thirteenth-century collections unless, of course, all three were drawing upon an unknown common source.

Fagrskinna ('fair vellum') is a title applied through the last few hundred years to a work surviving only in copies deriving from an early thirteenth-century original which is thought to have been written earlier in Nidaros, or the surrounding Trondelag region, and probably by an Icelandic author. Apparently known in medieval times as *Nóregs konunga tal* ('List of the Kings of Norway'), it is a collection of kings' sagas beginning in the ninth century with Halfdan the Black, father of Harald *hárfagri* ('fair-hair'), and extending to the year 1177, which was probably also the terminal point of the original *Morkinskinna* as it certainly was of the third *konunga sögur* collection – and the one of first importance here – which is, of course, the *Heimskringla* attributed to Snorri Sturluson.

I have been using the cautious term 'attributed to' in this context because there is no confirmation of the author's identity in any of the numerous medieval manuscripts of the work – most of them dating from the fourteenth century – even though the great weight of later evidence recognising him as Snorri Sturluson (and the total absence of any suggested rival claimant) puts the question almost entirely beyond doubt. Although there is no known original manuscript, there is one single leaf surviving from a copy set down before 1275 and believed to be the closest to Snorri's original on the evidence of its full text, which is preserved in at least three good transcripts. The title *Heimskringla* ('the world's orb'), which is derived from the work's opening line ('The orb of the world on which mankind dwells . . .') and has been applied since the seventeenth century, has a cosmic resonance well befitting the scope of its cycle of sixteen sagas extending from the mythic origins and legendary ancestry of the Norwegian royal house through to the last quarter of the twelfth century.

Snorri Sturluson himself was one of the most prominent figures in the Iceland of his time, a man of wealth and power as well as literature and learning. Although born into one of the most powerful Icelandic kindreds around the year 1179, he was to acquire much of his wealth and land through marriage, while also seeking to extend his influence by marrying his daughters into other important Icelandic families. He made two extended visits to the Scandinavian mainland where he is said to have been honoured with the title of *jarl*, as well as twice holding the presidential post of lawspeaker in the *Althing*, the Icelanders' parliament. In his later years, however, Snorri fell victim to a poisonous blend of family feud and political intrigue when offence caused to his resentful in-laws and to the Norwegian king Hakon Hakonsson resulted in an attack on his home by an armed band led by one of his sons-in-law. They found Iceland's most eminent man of letters, sixty-two years of age and utterly defenceless, taking refuge in his cellar and there they murdered him on a September night in the year 1241. Other than that lightly sketched outline, Snorri Sturluson's remarkable life story lies beyond the scope of these pages and yet there are some aspects with such significant bearing upon his authority as Harald Hardrada's saga-maker as to demand due notice here.

When his father, Sturla Thordason of Hvamm, died Snorri was only five years old and was passed into the foster-care of Jon Loptsson, the most cultivated of Icelandic chieftains, whose home at

Oddi was the foremost cultural centre in Iceland at a time when Icelanders could genuinely boast the pre-eminent literary culture of the Scandinavian world. There can be little doubt that the civilised ambience of Oddi, and especially its fine library, offered an exceptional stimulus to the literary inclinations of a youngster who might well be thought to have inherited a gift for poetry by way of his mother's descent from the warrior-poet Egil Skalla-Grimsson, who is now best known as the hero of the famous *Egil's saga*, another work often attributed to Snorri's authorship. In fact, there can be no question of Snorri's accomplishment and learning in the art of the *skáld* (the Old Norse term for a 'court-poet'), not only because one work of which he is firmly identified as author is the outstanding medieval treatise on skaldic verse known as the *Snorra Edda* (although more usually in the English-speaking world as the *Prose Edda*), but because his own youthful praise-poetry sent to the Norwegian court made so great an impression that he was invited to visit Norway. He was to take up that invitation in 1218 and spent the next two years on the Scandinavian mainland, much of that time in the service of Jarl Skuli, who held the office of regent to the young king Hakon Hakonsson.

The decade following his return from Norway in 1220 represented a period of peace in Icelandic society, a lull before the storm of internecine violence that erupted in the later 1230s. Snorri was already a man of great wealth, perhaps even the richest in Iceland, and settled on the farm at Reykjaholt to which he had moved from his wife's estate in 1206. There he would undoubtedly have built up his own library and there too he apparently had the assistance of an amanuensis, so it was at Reykjaholt that he is thought to have written most, if not all, of his surviving works – not only *Heimskringla*, but also his *Edda* and, quite possibly, *Egil's saga* too – between the years 1220 and 1230. The key item of evidence supporting this unusually precise dating is a passage found in *Íslendinga saga* ('Saga of the Icelanders', a history of his own Sturlung kindred written within living memory of Snorri's lifetime by his nephew, Sturla Thordason) which tells how another nephew, Sturla Sigvatsson, spent the winter of 1230–1 at Reykjaholt where he 'had saga-books copied from the works which Snorri had composed'.

While the writing of *Heimskringla* can be convincingly placed at Reykjaholt in the 1220s, the gathering together of all the history and tradition upon which it draws must have represented the work of a lifetime for a man who had by then entered into his fifth decade. It was a pursuit upon which Snorri had probably first embarked in his foster-home at Oddi and continued throughout the following years, especially when his travels around Norway and Sweden during the first sojourn on the Scandinavian mainland would have allowed visits to historic sites associated with Norwegian kings and introduced him also to oral traditions which were to inform his sagas.

As to his documentary sources, Snorri's own prologue to *Heimskringla* acknowledges a debt to an earlier historian, the esteemed Icelander Ari Thorgilsson, and to his 'lives of the kings', presumably a saga-history but a work now long since lost. He does, however, make passing reference to other written sources which have survived into modern times and of these an early version of *Orkneyinga saga* – known to Snorri as *Jarls' saga* – will be of special importance here by reason of its bearing on Harald Hardrada. Meticulous scholarly research into the text of *Heimskringla* has identified further documentary sources, notably *Ágrip* and *Morkinskinna*, upon which he appears to have drawn but does not mention by name. There is, however, another body of historical record, quite independent of the narrative histories, and this is the wealth of skaldic verse which represented a key primary source for the saga-maker, having been used first by the author of *Ágrip*, to a greater extent by those who composed *Morkinskinna* and *Fagrskinna*, but most extensively of all by Snorri in *Heimskringla*.

These court-poets known as *skálds*, almost all of them firmly identified as Icelanders, had been in richly rewarded attendance on Norwegian kings since the time of Harald Fair-hair in the later ninth century. Usually informed at first hand and sometimes even themselves eye-witness to the events they described, their poetry can be taken to represent an immediately contemporary source of history. Before the battle of Stiklestad, Olaf insisted on his skalds sheltering within a shield-wall in order that they should see the conflict and survive to commemorate its deeds in verse for posterity. So too, Thjodolf Arnorsson, who was Harald Hardrada's favourite among his own court-poets, fought beside his king at Stamford Bridge and is thought to have been slain in the battle or to have died soon afterwards of wounds suffered there. *Heimskringla* contains very many more examples of the first-hand authority of skaldic verse, as Snorri himself confirms in his prologue when he acknowledges having 'gathered the best of our information from what we are told in these poems which were recited before the chieftains themselves or their sons'.

The contemporaneity of such information thus lies almost entirely beyond dispute, and yet reasonable doubt might still be cast on its objectivity when, as Snorri admitted, 'it is the way of the court-poet to lavish greatest praise on those for whom the poems were composed'. Even so, he was still able to 'regard as the truth everything which is found in those poems concerning their expeditions or their battles . . . because none would dare tell the king of deeds which everyone present would know to be nonsense and untruth. To do so would have been mockery, not praise.' Clearly, then, the skald addressing his praise-poetry to the king in the company of a warrior nobility, at least some of whom could have witnessed the events he was celebrating, might be expected to aggrandise or exaggerate, but he certainly could not lie.

The art of the skald was highly sophisticated in terms of poetic form as well as being a style of writing dominated by the kenning, a compound word-form found throughout the early medieval literatures of the northern world and characterised by idiomatic imagery often alluding to pagan tradition. While such allusions are often elaborate to the point of obscurity for the modern reader, there are more straightforward illustrative examples of the kenning such as the skald Thjodolf's calling Harald Hardrada 'feeder of ravens' to signify his battle prowess and likewise referring to his warships as 'ocean dragons'. Scarcely less complex than the most elaborate kennings were the strict forms of stanza, metre and rhyme which defined the structure of skaldic verse and also served to protect it from the corruption which afflicted the folk-tale and similar material preserved in oral tradition. Such was evidently Snorri's own opinion expressed in his prologue to *Heimskringla*, where he suggests that 'these poems are the least likely to be distorted, if properly composed and sensibly interpreted'.

Interpretation was of crucial importance when skaldic verse was used as a source of history, as is demonstrated by examples of misconstrued skaldic references leading to erroneous conclusions found elsewhere in the saga literature. Snorri's own extensive knowledge of the art of the skald is so impressively confirmed by his *Edda* that his interpretation of skaldic verse as historical record must be accounted more reliable than that of other saga-makers, and especially so in his meticulous identification of the skalds whose work he quotes and in his subtle indications as to the authority of their evidence. It is a sphere of expertise of most especial value for *Harald's saga*, as Snorri himself implied when he wrote of 'a great deal of information about King Harald found in the verses which Icelandic poets presented to him and to his sons. Because of his own great interest in poetry, he was one of their very best friends.' Not only was Harald the patron of poets, but he was also a skald in his own right and some number of his verses are preserved in Snorri's saga. 'No king of Norway was a better poet', in the opinion of the eminent authority Gabriel Turville-Petre, 'and none showed a deeper appreciation of the art than Harald did, nor expressed his views in more forthright terms.'[2]

While Snorri recognised the legacy of skaldic verse as the most reliable of his sources, he makes a point of emphasising his caution in selecting information about Harald from elsewhere in the oral tradition: 'Although we have been told various tales and heard about other deeds . . . many of his feats and triumphs have not been included here, partly because of our lack of knowledge and partly because we are reluctant to place on record stories which are not substantiated.'

As well as the evidence he had gleaned from the skalds and earlier saga-makers, Snorri Sturluson was singularly fortunate in his access to an important source bearing on Harald Hardrada within his own family, because he himself was directly descended from a daughter of Halldor Snorrason who had been one of Harald's two principal lieutenants throughout his years as a Varangian in Byzantine service. A formidable character in his own right – and one who will make further appearances in these pages – Halldor is recognised by the most authoritative modern work on the subject as 'the Icelandic Varangian who is most popular in Norse sources, being in this respect close to King Harald himself . . . [and] almost certainly the source for the bulk of the Icelandic tradition in respect of the King's Varangian career'.[3] Halldor returned to Norway with Harald and apparently remained for a time at court after his accession to the kingship, but relations between the two were not often the most harmonious and eventually Halldor made his way home to Iceland where he earned great renown as a tale-spinner, principally on the strength of his adventuring in the east. His stories may even have been worked into a saga, albeit one which survived only in oral tradition and was probably never set down in writing, although Halldor himself is the subject of two tales preserved in the *Morkinskinna* and *Flateyjarbók* manuscript collections. It was probably inevitable that Halldor's original stories should have become corrupted during more than a century of oral transmission, even had they not been greatly elaborated already in the course of Halldor's own repeated retellings, and yet Snorri's family connection can still be said to have provided him with privileged access to material for his *Harald's saga* which had its origin – even if no more than that – in genuinely first-hand recollections of Harald Hardrada's Varangian years.

The word *saga* is sometimes translated into English as 'history'; however, for all the care with which Snorri Sturluson claims to have handled his sources, the *Harald's saga* in *Heimskringla* still cannot really be read as history in the modern sense of the term. It does offer the most comprehensive medieval account of three and a half decades of Harald's career and yet its narrative, inevitably uneven over so wide a compass, sometimes falling short on plausibility and on occasion quite inaccurate on points of detail, must be constantly checked against other records, most especially those bearing on Russian, Byzantine and Anglo-Saxon contexts. While its principal authority as an historical document must rest upon its preservation of the closely contemporary skaldic poetry – a total of more than ninety strophes (eight-line stanza form) or half-strophes from a dozen different skalds – it also deserves credit for its preservation of other evidence, ultimately deriving from oral tradition and however degraded, which might otherwise have been entirely lost to history.

In many respects, Snorri's sagas bear a resemblance to medieval hagiographies (or lives of saints), which themselves derive from oral traditions preserved in monastic communities. Indeed, his *Olaf Tryggvason's saga* and *Olaf the Saint's saga* in *Heimskringla* were almost certainly informed by lives of those two fiercely evangelistic warrior kings written in the Icelandic monastery of Thingeyrar, and his *Harald's saga* might be recognised as their secular counterpart with the similar intention of preserving a reputation held high in the folk memory of his own time. If such was his purpose, then Snorri can surely be said to have succeeded because the portrait of Harald Hardrada which emerges from the pages of his saga quite unmistakably reflects the reputation of the most feared warrior of the northern world.

In his obituary of Harald in the closing pages of the saga, Snorri writes of having 'no particular accounts of his youth until he took part in the battle of Stiklestad at the age of fifteen'. Now that is a puzzling statement indeed because there is one anecdote, however historically dubious, which is specifically concerned with Harald in early childhood and must have been known to Snorri when it was included in his *Olaf the Saint's saga*, the longest of all sixteen in the *Heimskringla* collection and almost certainly written before *Harald's saga*. Moreover, a fairly full account of Harald's parentage, ancestry and background can be pieced together, principally from *Olaf the Saint's saga* but also from other sagas in the *Heimskringla* collection, and might be usefully surveyed to conclude this introduction.

First of all, though, there is a question of nomenclature. Thus far, as also in the title, I have used the name-form 'Harald Hardrada' simply because it is probably the one most immediately recognisable to an English-speaking readership and even though no form of 'Hardrada' is found applied to Harald in any of the skaldic poetry or other closely contemporary sources and so would seem not to have been used in his own time. 'Hardrada', while often taken to mean 'the hard ruler', represents the anglicised form of the Norse term *harðráði*, literally 'hard counsel' although perhaps better translated as 'ruthless'. As to how Harald might have been known to his contemporaries, it is hardly unexpected to find Adam of Bremen calling him *malus* ('evil' or 'wicked'), although rather more curious is the cognomen *har fagera* applied to him by the northern recension of the *Anglo-Saxon Chronicle*. If *har fagera* represents an Old English corruption of *hárfagri*, the cognomen borne by Harald's celebrated ancestor Harald Fair-hair, it is hardly likely that a late eleventh-century Anglo-Saxon chronicler would have confused the Norwegian king killed in England as recently as 1066 with a namesake who had died some hundred and twenty years earlier, but perhaps it is just possible that he took *hárfagri* to have been a family surname.

The earliest known association of *harðráði* with Harald in a Scandinavian source occurs in the verse treatise *Háttalykill* attributed to Orkney/Icelandic authorship in the mid-twelfth century, but it is there applied to him and to other warlords simply as an adjective. Its application to Harald as a specifically personal byname does not appear until more than a century later when, as Turville-Petre explains, 'Norwegians and Icelanders of a much later age developed the suitable nickname *harðráði* . . . [which] seems to creep into chapter-headings and regnal lists probably during the latter half of the thirteenth century'.[4]

What can be said with confidence is that Harald was not known to Snorri Sturluson as *harðráði* because, while other saga titles in *Heimskringla* – such as *Olaf the Saint's saga* and *Magnus the Good's saga*, to name those of Harald's half-brother and nephew as just two examples – incorporate bynames established and current in the early thirteenth century, his own saga is headed with the straightforward patronymic as *Harald Sigurdsson's saga*, which will conveniently serve here to introduce the subject of his parentage. Harald's father was Sigurd Halfdansson, a great-grandson of Harald Fair-hair and king of Ringerike in the Uppland region north of Oslofjord. Sigurd's very practical interest in farming earned him the less than kingly nickname of *syr* (or 'sow' because he 'nosed about rooting up the ground') from the saga-makers. While Sigurd Syr appears on occasion as the full equal of his peers and a respected voice often tempered with wise caution, other anecdotes in Snorri's *Olaf the Saint's saga* seem to delight in portraying him as the harassed second husband of the formidable Ásta Gudbrondsdottir, the wife who bore him two daughters and three sons, of whom the youngest was Harald.

Ásta had formerly been married to Harald Gudrodsson, called *Grenske* ('of Grenland', a district south of Westfold), another great-grandson of Harald Fair-hair and ruler of the southern part of Norway on behalf of the Danish king Harald Gormsson, called 'bluetooth'. Harald Grenske is said to have been killed in Sweden towards the end of 994 or early in the following year (although saga accounts of the circumstances are historically untrustworthy), leaving Ásta to return to her parents as a widow pregnant with his son, the future king and saint Olaf, to whom she gave birth in the summer of 995.

Thus when she remarried shortly afterwards, Ásta brought with her a stepson to be raised by Sigurd Syr until the twelve-year-old Olaf Haraldsson – already possessed of great strength, accomplished with bow and spear, brimming over with self-confidence and fired with great ambition according to his saga in *Heimskringla* – was given by his mother into the charge of an experienced viking warrior who took him raiding around the Baltic. The saga, fully supported by skaldic verses, records his fighting in no fewer than five battles in Sweden, Finland and Holland before he eventually arrived in England as one of the huge raiding force led by Thorkell the Tall which descended on Kent in the August of 1009.

After some three years of warfaring in England, including the battle of Ringmere and the siege of Canterbury, Olaf crossed the

Channel to Normandy, effectively a Scandinavian colony which had begun as a viking base on the Seine in the later ninth century and became thoroughly gallicised into a French province within seventy years, yet still offering a haven to northmen at large in Europe into the eleventh century. There he entered the service of Duke Richard II, evidently as a mercenary fighting-man according to saga accounts of his campaigning corroborated by the eleventh-century Norman historian William of Jumièges, who also records the duke's having stood as sponsor for Olaf's baptism into the Christian faith at Rouen in 1013. Even though William's account of Olaf's conversion discredits the sagas' claim for his having been baptised by Olaf Tryggvason in very early childhood, his entry into the faith can be recognised now as an event of the greatest significance for his Norwegian homeland as well as for his own place in history, because less than two years later he was back in Norway fiercely determined to complete the campaign of conversion left unfinished by Olaf Tryggvason. Yet to do so he would first need to fulfil another ambition and reclaim the sovereignty of the unified kingdom lost some fifteen years before when Olaf Tryggvason, facing defeat at the battle of Svold, had flung himself overboard from his beleaguered warship.

The kingdom which had fallen from the hand of Olaf Tryggvason thus became a fruit of victory shared between the victors: the Danish king Svein Haraldsson, called 'forkbeard', his Norwegian son-in-law Erik Hakonsson, jarl of Lade (*Hlaðir*, near Trondheim), and the Swedish king Olaf Eriksson who apparently owed some form of allegiance to Svein of Denmark. By the time of Olaf Haraldsson's return to his homeland – certainly by 1015, although possibly in the autumn of 1014 – there had been a shift in the political balance of the tripartite lordship imposed on Norway some fifteen years earlier. Svein Forkbeard had died in England in the first weeks of 1014, barely a month after winning the English crown, and the subsequent attention of his son Cnut became firmly fixed on winning his father's English conquest for himself. Olaf of Sweden had already passed responsibility for much of his Norwegian interest to Jarl Svein, the brother of Erik of Lade who by this time had joined Cnut in assembling an invasion fleet which would soon be on its way to England, leaving his Norwegian lordship in the care of his son Hakon.

Thus it was the young Jarl Hakon whom Olaf encountered, took by surprise and made captive, when he arrived off the west coast of Norway with two *knorr* (oceangoing merchant craft as distinct from warships) and 120 warriors. Having secured Hakon's submission and surrender, Olaf released the young jarl unharmed and allowed his departure to join his father in the service of Cnut in England, before setting out on his own progress eastward through Norway seeking support for his cause. In fact, as just one among numerous descendants of Harald Fair-hair, Olaf cannot be said to have had any outstanding claim to the kingship of Norway, but his burly physique (he was known as 'Olaf the Stout' in his lifetime) and warfaring experience, his sheer self-assurance and persuasive oratory would have offered him as an impressive candidate for kingship. He was almost certainly also in possession of a substantial treasury, accumulated in the course of his viking career and not least from sharing in payments of *danegeld* with which Anglo-Saxon England regularly bought off Scandinavian raiding armies in the tenth and eleventh centuries.

Nonetheless, he was to find opinion in Norway sharply divided between himself and Hakon's uncle, Jarl Svein, who had already fled inland to marshal his own support, and so Olaf turned south to Ringerike where he sought the advice and assistance of Sigurd Syr, who solemnly warned his stepson of the formidable powers whom he sought to challenge. Nonetheless, Sigurd was still ready to help his stepson and brought together an assembly of provincial kings and chieftains of the Upplands which was eventually won over by Olaf's oratory and acclaimed him king. As men of central Norway began flocking to his standard, Olaf made his way north into the Trondelag, heartland of the jarls of Lade, and even there opposition had not the strength to withstand him, at least until Jarl Svein launched a counter-attack on Nidaros which drove Olaf back to the south. There he mustered his forces and assembled a warfleet for the inevitable decisive battle which was fought off Nesjar, a headland on the western shore of Oslofjord, on Palm Sunday in the year 1016.

The victory went to Olaf and with it the kingship of all Norway; the defeated Jarl Svein fled east into Sweden, where he died of sickness the following autumn, and the jarls Erik and Hakon became otherwise engaged with Cnut who was now king in England. In the customary way of victorious warrior kings, Olaf bestowed generous gifts on his supporters, and especially upon the stepfather who had not only helped bring the Uppland kings to Olaf's cause but also, according to the saga, brought with him 'a great body of men' when he joined his stepson's forces in the decisive battle. It seems likely that Olaf's gift-giving to Sigurd Syr was to be the last meeting of the two men, because when the saga next tells of Olaf at Ringerike, some two years after the victory at Nesjar, it mentions that Sigurd had died the previous winter. In fact, that account of Olaf's visit to his mother is of particular significance here because it represents the very first appearance of Harald Hardrada in the *Heimskringla* cycle.

In celebration of her son's homecoming, the proud Ásta prepared a great banquet for Olaf who 'alone now bore the title of king in Norway' and after the feast brought her three young sons (by Sigurd) to meet their royal half-brother. The saga account of that meeting, while hardly to be considered other than an apocryphal anecdote, does at least have the ring of plausibility when it tells how the king sought to test the character of the three young princes by pretending to become suddenly and thunderously angry. While Guthorm the eldest and Halfdan the second son drew back in fear, the reaction of Harald the youngest was simply to give a tug to his tormentor's beard. If, as the saga claims, Olaf really did respond to Harald's bold gesture by telling the three-year-old that 'You will be vengeful one day, my kinsman', history was to prove him no poor judge of character.

The following day, as Olaf walked with his mother around the farm they saw the three boys at play, Guthorm and Halfdan building farmhouses and barns which they imagined stocking with cattle and sheep, while Harald was nearby at the edge of a pool floating chips of wood into the water. When asked what they were, Harald said these were his warships and Olaf replied: 'It may well be that you will have command of warships one day, kinsman.'

19

Calling the three boys over to him, Olaf asked each in turn what he would most like to own. 'Cornfields' was Guthorm's choice, while Halfdan chose 'cattle' and so many as would surround the lake when they were watered, but when it came to Harald's turn he had no hesitation in demanding 'housecarls', the fighting men who formed a king's retinue. 'And how many housecarls would you wish to have?' asked the king. 'As many as would eat all my brother Halfdan's cattle at a single meal!' came the reply. Olaf was laughing when he turned to Ásta saying, 'In this one, mother, you are raising a warrior king', and, indeed, there is good reason to believe that such had been her intention from the first. The saga relates more than one anecdote bearing on Ásta's ambitions for her sons and it would seem likely that it was she rather than her husband Sigurd who had chosen the name given to their youngest boy. If so, then her choice carries its own remarkable significance because the name *Haraldr* derives from the Old Norse term *her-valdr*, 'ruler of warriors'.

Some dozen years had passed before there is any saga reference to Harald meeting again with Olaf, although this time it was to be in very different circumstances because much had changed since 1018. Driven from power in Norway, Olaf had found refuge in Russia and it was from there that he returned in 1030 in a doomed attempt to reclaim his kingdom by the sword. News of his coming had apparently reached Ringerike even before he had passed through Sweden and the first to meet him as he approached the border was his half-brother Harald – now fifteen years old and described by the saga as 'so manly as if he were already full-grown' – who brought some seven hundred Upplanders to join Olaf's modest army on its westward advance into the Trondelag.

Ahead of them in Værdal lay the battle which was to mark the beginning of Harald Hardrada's warrior's way when the sun turned black in the summer sky above Stiklestad . . . .

I

Stiklestad

Norway, 1030

In the greater historical scheme of things, the presence of the young Harald Sigurdsson at Stiklestad might be thought to represent little more than a footnote to the epic drama centred upon the death in battle of the king who was soon to become Norway's national patron saint. Such might even be the inference of the saga record when the first chapter of *Harald's saga* in Snorri Sturluson's *Heimskringla*, which takes Stiklestad as the beginning of Harald's story, actually expends just a few paragraphs on his presence at the battle which had already taken up some thirty-eight chapters of *Olaf the Saint's saga* in the same collection.

From the perspective being taken here, however, Stiklestad offers a range of interest which extends beyond its selection as the starting-point of Harald's warrior's way and even beyond an attempt to deduce something more about his own part in the battle than is made explicit in the saga. Not only does the conflict provide an early opportunity to survey the arms, armour, and tactics involved in an eleventh-century Scandinavian land-battle, but in so doing might also offer some insight into the warrior culture within which Harald had been raised to the threshold of his manhood.

Of no less significance for his personal destiny, however, will be a portrait of the man who stood and fell at the centre of the blood-fray of Stiklestad, because there is every reason to recognise his half-brother Olaf as casting his long shadow across the whole subsequent course of Harald's life. While it was surely a determined loyalty to a brother and boyhood hero which brought Harald to fight his first battle under Olaf's banner at Stiklestad, something still deeper might be needed to explain why, thirty-six years later, it was to Olaf's shrine at Nidaros that Harald paid his parting homage just before he embarked upon the invasion that would lead him to his last battle at Stamford Bridge. It is almost as if the ghost of his half-brother can be sensed at Harald's shoulder on very many occasions throughout those intervening years and most especially after he himself had succeeded to the kingship of Norway. As Olaf is said to have foretold at their very first meeting, Harald was indeed to become a vengeful man: so much so that it might almost be possible to recognise his entire reign as a warrior king in terms of a twenty-year pursuit of blood-feud in vengeance for the kinsman laid low on the field of Stiklestad.

None of which is intended to suggest there was anything religious in Harald's respect for his half-brother's memory, because whatever presence might be sensed at his shoulder is assuredly the ghost of the man he remembered rather than the spirit of the martyred saint whose cult had become firmly established even within Harald's lifetime. Indeed, the alacrity with which a king slain in battle by his own people was transformed into his nation's martyred patron saint is remarkable even by medieval standards. The sagas tell of wounds healed by his blood almost before his corpse was cold and such miracle stories can be traced all the way back to the eleventh century, some of them even to men who had actually known Olaf. His body had lain buried for only a few days more than the twelvemonth when it was exhumed and found to be uncorrupted, thus enabling the bishop at Nidaros to immediately proclaim him a saint.

Recognition of his sanctity evidently spread widely and with extraordinary speed. Adam of Bremen, who was at work on his *History* scarcely forty years after Stiklestad, confirms Olaf's feast already being celebrated throughout Scandinavia, just as William of Jumièges, who was writing in Normandy at much the same time, recognised him as a martyr. One version of the *Anglo-Saxon Chronicle*, set down some twenty years earlier still, reflects the Scandinavian seam of northern English culture when it styles Olaf *halig* (or 'holy'). However, even when due allowance is made for the very different values of that world and time, what is known of the personality of the historical Olaf Haraldsson is not easily reconciled with any of the more familiar manifestations of Christian sanctity.

24

The later saga stories of his having been baptised in infancy by Olaf Tryggvason can be set aside in the light of William of Jumièges' account of the baptism at Rouen, and so it would be reasonable to assume his early life as steeped in the pagan culture of the viking warrior which, indeed, he himself was to become at the age of twelve. Having adopted the Christian faith, however, Olaf was determined to impose it upon the kingdom he was soon to claim in Norway – and, if needs be, at sword-point. Those who refused conversion, or accepted under pressure the man-god whom the northmen called the 'White Christ' and afterwards reverted to pagan practice, faced banishment, maiming, or even death at royal command.

Disloyalty to the king himself was punished with no less severity, of which the most notorious example is the saga story of five Uppland kings who first supported Olaf's bid for the kingship but shortly afterwards become so disenchanted as to conspire together for his overthrow. When word of their conspiracy was brought to Olaf, an armed force 400 strong was sent to make them captive and bring them to face his wrath. Three of the kings were despatched into exile with their families and their lands seized for the crown, a fourth had his tongue severed, while the most frightful retribution was that inflicted upon the fifth. Rorek of Hedemark had his eyes put out and, still being considered dangerously untrustworthy even thus impaired, was compelled thereafter to remain under surveillance in the king's retinue. Peremptory brutality would also appear to have characterised Olaf's foreign policy when, having seen off the jarls of Lade and knowing Cnut to be otherwise engaged in England, he still had to contend with the Swedish king Olaf Eriksson's intervention in disputed borderlands. Armed bands of Swedish officers sent to extract tribute from Norwegian bonders (*bóndi*, or yeoman farmers) provoked a stern response, and a verse set down by Olaf's skald Sigvat Thordsson tells of a full dozen Swedes hanged as a feast for the ravens when they ventured into Gaulardal and Orkadal south and east of the Trondelag.

The various saga accounts of Olaf's reign are so heavily burdened by legend as to be profoundly suspect as historical record, even though Snorri Sturluson clearly took greater pains to produce a rounded portrait of the man than did those others whose work merely offers a sanitised eulogy of the martyred saint. In so doing, he was able to place great reliance upon Sigvat Thordsson's court-poetry as a uniquely informed source of immediately contemporary evidence. Sigvat's *Vikingarvísur* (or 'viking verses'), for example, provides a catalogue of Olaf's earlier warfaring around the Baltic, in England and in Normandy which was presumably informed by the king's own reminiscences, while *Nesjavísur* ('Nesjar verses') is the poet's record of his first attendance upon his lord in battle on the occasion of the famous victory over Jarl Svein in 1016.

Indeed, and quite apart from the value of his poetry as historical record, Sigvat's relationship with his royal patron is of particular interest in that it clearly illustrates some of the paradoxes of Olaf Haraldsson's nature. Sigvat Thordsson had arrived in Norway from Iceland shortly after Olaf's return to claim the kingdom and, in the way of his trade, sought out the new king at Nidaros to offer verses composed in his honour. As a recently baptised Christian, Olaf strongly disapproved of the pagan associations of skaldic art, so his initial response to Sigvat was less than welcoming, yet the skald was able to win him over and eventually to become his most trusted friend, counsellor and emissary.

Despite that professed distaste for poetry, Olaf is known to have written verse of his own, and in the form of love-poems, a use of poetry considered beneath contempt by the high standards of the skaldic art but one which bears out his notorious susceptibility to female charms, which he himself described as his 'besetting sin' in one of the verses ascribed to him. Olaf's love-poems were addressed to the Swedish princess Ingigerd, on whom they made so favourable an impression that a betrothal was arranged through the intermediary of Rognvald Ulfsson, jarl of Gautland and himself a Swede, but closely linked to Norway by reason of his marriage to a sister of Olaf Tryggvason. In the event, however, the arrangement was to be thwarted when Ingigerd's father King Olaf of Sweden – who so despised the Norwegian Olaf that he refused even to use his name, referring to him only as 'that fat man' – insisted instead on Ingigerd's betrothal to the Russian Grand Prince Jaroslav.

Almost immediately, Olaf arranged to take another Swedish princess, Ingigerd's sister Astrid, as his bride, but only with the assistance of Sigvat who somehow circumvented her father's disapproval by travelling to Gautland and there negotiating the marriage ('among other things spoken of . . .', according to the saga) with Jarl Rognvald acting once again as intermediary and himself escorting the bride to Norway for her wedding in the first months of 1019. Rognvald thus incurred his own king's grievous displeasure and on his return Olaf of Sweden would have had him hanged for his 'treason' had it not been for Ingigerd's insistence that he escort her on her bridal journey into Russia and never again return to her father's kingdom. So it was that Rognvald Ulfsson came to settle in Russia, where he was endowed with the lordship of Staraja Ladoga on the Gulf of Finland, and it was there, some dozen years later, that his son Eilif was to be a comrade-in-arms to the Norwegian Olaf's kinsman, the young Harald Sigurdsson.

In Norway, meanwhile, marriage would appear to have placed little restraint on Olaf's 'besetting sin' when the mother of his son born around 1024 was not his queen but one Alfhild, described in the saga as 'the king's hand-maiden . . . although of good descent'. Once again Sigvat the skald was on hand, because it is he whom the saga credits with the choice of Magnus – in honour of *Karl Magnus*, the Norse name-form of the ninth-century Holy Roman Emperor Charlemagne – as the baptismal name of the new-born prince. In so doing, though, the skald might simply have been anticipating his lord's own wishes, because Olaf so greatly revered Karl Magnus that he had his portrait carved onto the figurehead of his own warship which was thus named the 'Karl's Head'.

That passing saga reference to 'other things spoken of . . .' in the course of Sigvat's negotiations with Rognvald in Gautland has already suggested a political dimension to Olaf's quest for a Swedish queen, and the marriage does appear to have eased his formerly hostile relations with Sweden through the early 1020s. The Swedish king Olaf was becoming increasingly unpopular at home, as a result of his attempts to impose Christianity on his people according to the saga, although just as possibly because of his allegiance to a Danish overlord. Olaf Eriksson is often known as *Skötkonung*, a cognomen which has been variously interpreted by historians but might well indicate that he rendered some form of tribute – or *skatt* – to Svein Forkbeard, and some similar obligation to Cnut when he succeeded Svein. Whatever the true reason, Olaf Skötkonung was eventually forced to share the kingship with his son, whom he had christened Jacob but who was to adopt the Scandinavian name of Onund before he succeeded to full sovereignty on the death of his father in 1022. Sweden's new king evidently had no inclination to accept a Danish overlord, and neither did he share his father's hostility to Olaf of Norway with whom he was soon to find himself in an aggressive alliance against Denmark.

By the mid-1020s, and thus within a decade of his return to Norway, Olaf Haraldsson had achieved the high point of his reign. He had once again restored national sovereignty, however short-lived, to Norway and effectively accomplished its conversion to Christianity. He had also affirmed his influence in the North Atlantic colonies, most importantly in the jarldom of Orkney where he apportioned disputed territories between the brothers Thorfinn and Brusi – sons of the formidable Jarl Sigurd slain at Clontarf in 1014 – and brought Brusi's son Rognvald to take up residence at his court. Friendly relations were extended still further west-over-sea to Greenland, the Faroes and especially to Iceland, whence a number of skalds and fighting-men came to the Norwegian court. Still more impressive was Olaf's achievement as a law-maker, when he revived and revised the law code of Harald Fair-hair's time with such just and equal application to all ranks of society that the skald Sigvat could claim that he had 'established the law of the nation which stands firm among all men'. In so doing, though, he constrained the lordly liberties allowed to provincial magnates when they had been subject only to the client jarls of absent overlords in other lands and thus might already be seen to have sown the seeds of his own downfall.

The saga points specifically to Olaf's prohibition of plunder-raiding within the country and his punishment of powerful chieftains' sons who had customarily engaged in viking cruises around fjord and coastland as the principal causes of discontent with his kingship, but there were other sources of resentment too, not least his draconian response to almost every instance of apostasy or disloyalty. All of these factors were to offer ample scope for the destabilisation of Olaf's sovereignty when the ambition of the mighty Cnut was eventually drawn back from his English conquest to Scandinavia. Sometime around the year 1024, he despatched emissaries to Norway with the proposal that Olaf would be allowed to govern the kingdom as his jarl if he first came to England and there paid homage to Cnut as his lord. Whether or not Olaf was reminded of that ominously prophetic warning given him by his stepfather on his return to Norway some ten years before, his response to Cnut's emissaries, as recorded in Sigvat's verse, was emphatically rendered in the negative. Cnut had thus little option but to come north in arms, which raised the prospect of his reclaiming overlordship of Norway and then turning to Sweden as the next object of his ambition, so there was every urgent reason for Olaf and Onund to form the alliance that was agreed when they met on the border at Konungahella to plan their own pre-emptive attack upon Denmark.

Olaf's fleet of sixty ships sailed south to plunder the Danish island of Zealand while Onund brought a larger force against Skaane (in what is now southern Sweden), but Cnut was soon, if not already, sailing north from England with a large fleet which he brought into Limfjord along the northern coast of Jutland where it was reinforced by Danish warships. Under the shadow of that impressive naval muster ranged out in the Kattegat, Olaf promptly withdrew his forces from Zealand to join Onund in harrying the coastland of Skaane until Cnut's fleet came in pursuit and they withdrew to take refuge in the Holy River which flows into the sea on the eastward coast of Skaane. It was there that the chase finally came to battle in circumstances left surrounded with doubt and confusion by the historical record.

Even the date of the battle of Holy River is in dispute, although the majority of modern historians assign it to the year 1026, and yet its course still remains shrouded in mystery. The saga's claim that Olaf built and then broke a dam on the river to engulf Cnut's fleet when it had been lured into the trap has been convincingly dismissed as just one of 'many tales told of Olaf's ruses at sea and this one is no more credible than the others'.[1] Although in view of the customary conduct of Scandinavian sea-fighting at the time – where vessels functioned as fighting-platforms upon which contending warriors engaged in close combat, clearing the enemy decks by the sword until victory was decided by a process of attrition – there may be an item of more convincing evidence in the next saga episode. This passage tells of Cnut's own warship beset on all sides by Norwegian and Swedish vessels, and yet built 'so high in the hull, as if it had been a fortress, with so numerous a selected crew aboard, well-armed and accomplished, that it was too difficult to assail'. Soon afterwards, Olaf and Onund 'cast their ships loose from Cnut's ship and the fleets separated'.

From this reference alone might be inferred the plausible scenario of Cnut's freshly mustered warfleet outnumbering those of Olaf and Onund, whose crews would already have been wearied by a raiding campaign, and of their suffering heavy casualties in the hail of spears and arrows which invariably opened such hostilities, leaving them with no option other than withdrawal in the face of insuperable odds. What can be said as to the outcome of the conflict is that it was not crushingly decisive, if only because none of the principals were slain, and yet the skaldic verses of Ottar the Black, a nephew of Olaf's Sigvat, have no hesitation in declaring Cnut the victor. His closely contemporary evidence must be recognised as the most convincing, especially in the light of its correspondence to the subsequent course of events.

Worthy of mention here, by way of a footnote to the conflict, is the shadowy figure of Ulf Thorgilsson, appointed by Cnut as his jarl in Denmark sometime around 1023 but who appears to have retreated to Jutland when Olaf and Onund launched their onslaught. Most of the sources ascribe a decisive role to Ulf in the battle of Holy River and yet cannot agree as to which side he was fighting for, although his murder in Roskilde church on Cnut's orders at some point after the battle must point to disloyalty, if not to outright treachery. His principal importance here, though, rests upon kinship by marriage, because both his son and his nephew will feature prominently among the enemies of Harald Hardrada. Ulf's sister Gyda became the wife of Earl Godwin in England and thus mother to the Harold Godwinson who was to triumph at Stamford Bridge, while Ulf himself was married to Cnut's sister Estrid from whom their son Svein (called 'Ulfsson' in *Heimskringla*, but usually 'Estridsson' elsewhere) inherited his claim on the kingship of Denmark, in pursuit and possession of which he was to become briefly Harald's ally and for many years afterwards his relentless foe.

Whatever really did befall at Holy River, the outcome of the engagement clearly left Cnut in the ascendant and the Norse–Swedish alliance dissolved. Onund sailed back to Sweden with as much as remained of his fleet, while Olaf – perhaps mindful of the fate suffered in just those same waters by Olaf Tryggvason at Svold – abandoned his ships to make his way home overland. In the following year of 1027, Cnut was on pilgrimage in Rome, where he is known to have attended the coronation of the Holy Roman Emperor, and would surely not have entertained the idea of such a journey had he been in any doubt as to the security of his kingdoms. Indeed, in his letter addressed to the English people in that same year, Cnut is styled 'king of all of England and of Denmark and part of *Suavorum* [by which is probably meant Skaane on the Swedish mainland]'.

Norway was to enjoy a short spell of peace in the aftermath of Holy River, but, on the evidence of English and Icelandic sources, it would not be long before Cnut's agents were active in the western and northern provinces such as the Trondelag and Halogaland where the rising tide of discontent with Olaf was to be most usefully encouraged by the gold, silver and promises they brought with them. Now returned to England from Rome, Cnut had apparently decided that Olaf's kingship was to be most effectively – and bloodlessly – undermined by bribery of Norwegian magnates greedy for wealth and esteem. 'Money will make men break their faith,' observed

Sigvat the skald, and his verses record 'enemies about with open purses; men offering heavy metal for the priceless head of the king'.

The saga tells of Olaf's commanding the execution of one young man who had accepted Cnut's bribe in the form of a golden arm-ring and thus provoking the hostility of his kinsmen. Although just one among numerous examples of draconian retribution for disloyalty, this particular instigation of blood-feud was to prove of especially ominous significance when the victim's stepfather was the powerful Kalv Arnason and his uncle Thore Hund ('the Hound'), both of whom were ultimately to confront the king in battle at Stiklestad where Kalv himself would be accused of having delivered Olaf's death-wound.

While this episode and other similar stories in the saga show how effectively Cnut's policy of destabilisation gained ground, the situation is convincingly summarised by the modern historian Gwyn Jones. He suggests that Olaf 'had more support in parts of the country, in Uppland and the Vik for example, than Snorri allows for, and that his opponents were not so much politically allied against their sovereign as disaffected for more personal reasons, including loss of land or status, change of religion, family grievances, and private quarrels with the king'.[2] The core territory of Olaf's remaining support would seem to have lain around the Vik (now Oslofjord) and, indeed, he is said by the saga to have been in that region when he heard news of Cnut's arrival in Denmark with a fleet of fifty ships from England in 1028. His immediate response was to summon a levy in defence of his kingdom and some numbers of the local people rallied to his banner, but very few came to join them from other parts of Norway and his warfleet was only such waterlogged hulks as could be salvaged from what remained of the fleet he had abandoned in Holy River two years before. Such a force hardly represented any credible resistance to the fleet of more than 1,400 ships which Cnut had assembled in Denmark and was now sailing up the west coast of Norway.

Accepting submission and taking hostages as surety wherever he touched land, Cnut sailed on until he reached the Trondelag and put in at Nidaros where a great assembly (or *thing*) of chieftains and bonders was summoned to acclaim him as king of all Norway. The great men of the north and west who swore allegiance were duly rewarded, some as his 'lendermen' (or *lendr maðr*, literally 'landed-men', effectively 'barons'), and the same Hakon Eriksson of Lade who had surrendered to Olaf on his homecoming some fourteen years before was now appointed Cnut's jarl to rule on his behalf over Olaf's kingdom.

Only when Cnut's fleet had set sail back to Denmark did Olaf bring his few ships out of the Vik, but his progress up the west coast served merely to confirm his dwindling support. The saga tells of his confrontation with Erling Skjalgsson, one of the most powerful of the chiefs who had made submission to Cnut. Defeated in battle by one of Olaf's ruses, Erling stood alone with no choice but to yield and yet was struck dead by a warrior's axe moments after he had agreed to return to Olaf's service. The saga describes that axe-blow as having struck Norway 'out of Olaf's hand', and as the royal fleet of just a dozen ships sailed north the sons of Erling were already summoning the bonders of the south-west to rise in pursuit of yet another blood-feud against the king.

Even as Olaf sailed north of Stad and learned of the great warfleet assembled against him by Jarl Hakon in the Trondelag, his desperate situation had become virtually irretrievable. The warrior who had killed Erling Skjalgsson went ashore and was slain before he could return to his vessel, while the Erlingssons had twenty-five ships in close pursuit and Jarl Hakon's great force was seen in the distance by watchers sent to look north from the hilltops. When Olaf's fleet put into Aalesund, Kalv Arnason joined with others of the few remaining lendermen and shipmasters in defecting to Hakon, leaving the king with just five ships which he drew on to the shore. Clearly, all was lost to him now and his only available course was to take flight overland, first by way of Gudbrandsdal into Hedemark where he granted his warriors leave to return home if they chose so to do.

Accompanied by his young son Magnus, his queen Astrid and their daughter Ulfhild, Olaf still had with him a loyal warrior retinue, of whom the most prominent members identified by the saga included Arne, Finn and Thorberg Arnason, brothers of the

Kalv who had defected to Jarl Hakon and was even now being promised great prospects under Cnut. One other of Olaf's loyal companions in adversity mentioned by the saga will be of further significance here, namely Rognvald Brusason who had been brought to the Norwegian court as a boy with his father, the Orkney jarl Brusi, some ten years before and stayed on, probably at first as a hostage for his father's good behaviour, but in time becoming a trusted friend to the king. Such, then, was the company that made its way through the Eida forest into Vermaland and over the border to take refuge in Sweden, where Olaf stayed until the following summer when he entrusted his daughter and his queen to the care of her brother Onund at the Swedish court before taking ship across the Baltic to Russia and the court of the Grand Prince Jaroslav at Novgorod. There he was assured of generous hospitality, not only by reason of Jaroslav's being his kinsman by marriage when both had taken daughters of the Swedish king Olaf as their brides, but because of the wider and more ancient relationship between the ruling houses of Scandinavia and Russia. Jaroslav and his background will be more fully considered later in the context of Harald Hardrada's east-faring, but it might still be useful at this point to indicate something of Russia's place within the orbit of medieval Scandinavian expansion.

The term *Rus* derives from a Finnish name applied to the Swedes who were the first of the northmen to penetrate the mainland of what later became Russia, and was taken up by the Slavonic settlers to identify Scandinavian traders who had established their bases along the northern Russian waterways long before the arrival of Rurik. The traditional forebear of medieval Russia's ruling dynasty (and thus the great-great-grandfather of Jaroslav), Rurik is said to have founded his power base at Novgorod in the year 862. As in Normandy and elsewhere throughout the Scandinavian expansion, the early settlements steadily absorbed the host culture and within less than two centuries their ruling warrior aristocracy had become thoroughly Slavonic in character, yet the traffic of Scandinavian traders and warriors along the Russian rivers still sustained close relations between the Rus and their northern cousins.

Thus Russia, or *Garðar* as it was called in Old Norse,[3] offered a convenient realm of refuge for Scandinavian kings and princes in exile, and a remarkably generous welcome to Olaf when Jaroslav offered him lordship over the Bulgars on the Volga. In the event, that proposal proved unpopular with the warriors of Olaf's retinue, who were disinclined to settle in Russia and urged him instead to return to Norway. Olaf himself, however, is said to have been considering a pilgrimage to the Holy Land when tidings came from Norway of the unexpected death of Jarl Hakon, who had been in England with Cnut that summer and was drowned on the voyage home when his ship was lost off the coast of Caithness. The news that Norway was suddenly bereft of a ruler prompted Olaf to consider attempting to reclaim his lost kingdom. While Jaroslav warned of the might of opposition he would be facing with only slender forces of his own and offered him an even more generous lordship were he to stay in Russia, the saga tells of a vision of Olaf Tryggvason in full regalia urging his return to Norway, and this supposedly divine intervention is presented as the decisive factor prompting Olaf to set out on what was to become his death-journey into martyrdom.

'Immediately after Yule', according to the saga and so presumably in the first weeks of 1030, Olaf was making ready for departure. His son Magnus was left in Jaroslav's care and stayed behind in Russia when Olaf assembled his retinue of some two hundred and forty warriors, who had been generously armed and equipped by his Russian host, and set out on horseback along the frozen rivers of northern Russia to the shore of the Baltic. When the ice broke with the approach of spring, they took ship first to the island of Gotland and then over to the Swedish mainland where Olaf was reunited with his wife and daughter and also met King Onund who, although glad to welcome his old friend, was disinclined to renew their alliance. His spies had brought back reports of the widespread hostility they had found throughout Norway and Onund feared the worst outcome for the expedition, but he was still prepared to reinforce Olaf's small company with some four hundred of his own best warriors equipped for battle,[4] granting him permission also to recruit such Swedes as were willing to join his cause on their own account.

So it was that Olaf set out for Norway with a force more than fourteen hundred strong, taking a north-westward route towards the border through Jærnberaland (the 'iron-bearing land', now the Swedish province of Dalarna) and was there joined by his half-brother Harald Sigurdsson with the seven hundred warriors whom he had raised in the Upplands on hearing the first tidings of Olaf's return. Inevitably, of course, there were others in Norway who had also had word of his movements and the saga tells of chieftains who had pledged allegiance to Cnut and his jarl Hakon having learned the news from their own spies sent into Sweden and sending out a war-summons across the land. Already in the spring, Thore Hund had crewed a warship with his housecarls and called a levy of fighting-men in his far northern province around Tromsö. So too had his neighbour, Harek of Thjotta in Halogaland, and these two most powerful chieftains of the north were now bringing their forces to join the host of Olaf's enemies gathering in the Trondelag.

Meanwhile Olaf was making his way through the woodland and moorland of the border country, offering rich rewards in lands and plunder to attract recruits from the rough folk of the forest and no small number of vagabonds besides. He had found another ally, and one of more promising military quality, in Dag Ringsson whose father is said to have been one of those Uppland kings banished for their part in the conspiracy against Olaf more than ten years before. Dag had followed his father into exile in Sweden and it was there that Olaf made contact on his own return from Russia, acknowledging him as kinsman (although, as just another of the numerous descendants of Harald Fair-hair, only a very distant one) and promising full restitution of his father's lands in Norway if he would join him with all the warriors he could muster. Dag apparently agreed with enthusiasm and is said by the saga to have brought another 'twelve hundred' men to join Olaf's forces before leading them off along his own line of march into Norway. While the Swedish contingent is said to have similarly taken its own route, the saga follows the progress of Olaf and his retinue by way of the Kjolen mountains.

When the visions and other hagiographical anecdotes encrusting these chapters of saga narrative are left aside, the plan of campaign comes quite clearly into focus as a westward advance into the Trondelag, presumably with Nidaros as the ultimate objective. The division of his forces into three contingents, each following its own route of march, can be recognised as an evasive strategy intended to outwit any watches set on the border passes, but the advance to Nidaros had evidently been anticipated by the enemy. When Olaf reached the head of Værdal a friendly bonder warned him of the great numbers of fighting-men being mustered in the Trondelag and as he moved on through the valley further intelligence confirmed that same army already on the move against him. At which point, Olaf halted his march and brought together all his forces in preparation for the conflict that would soon be upon them.

The principal concern of the saga narrative at this point appears to be the portrayal of a great Christian warrior king, even one in the mould of Charlemagne, insisting that all his warriors enter battle as Christians, chalking the symbol of a cross on their shields and advancing with the war-cry of 'Forward, forward, Christ-men, cross men, king's men!' Other evidence casts doubt on the historical accuracy of some of these claims when Sigvat the skald's verses supply a closely contemporary reference to pagans included in Olaf's forces and a very similar battle-cry is attributed to the twelfth-century Norwegian king Sverri in his own saga, a work well known to Snorri Sturluson and his contemporaries. Indeed, evidence has also been found for another war-cry of 'Press on, press on, king's warriors, hard and hard on bonder men!' used by Olaf's followers at Stiklestad.[5] Probably more reliable, and certainly more relevant here, is the saga's estimate of the numbers of Olaf's forces at something over three and a half thousand fighting-men.

Although of no very great significance, the doubts surrounding the details of that particular episode do point up the difficulties involved in filtering authentic military history from the account of Stiklestad in Snorri's *Heimskringla* version of *Olaf the Saint's saga*. Such difficulties are only to be expected when a warrior king is in the process of reinvention as a martyred saint, and are perhaps best resolved by disentangling the different sources from which the saga narrative was compiled. The more obviously hagiographical elements of Snorri's account of the battle can be traced back to the monastery of Thingeyrar where earlier *Lives* of St Olaf had been composed with the sole purpose of fostering his cult. As to sources of a more secular character and origin, the skaldic verse which usually represents the most immediately contemporary evidence preserved in the sagas is less helpful on this occasion, even though three skalds were included among Olaf's retinue at Stiklestad. The saga describes his special arrangements for their protection, in order that they should survive to record the battle for posterity, although to no avail when two of the skalds were slain in the battle and the third died very shortly afterwards of wounds he had suffered. Olaf's favourite skald Sigvat Thordsson was not present at Stiklestad, being on pilgrimage to Rome at the time, so the references to the battle in his memorial lay *Olafsdrápa*, while undeniably closely contemporary, still cannot be considered as first-hand evidence. In fact, the only skaldic verses brought back from the field appear to have been those composed as exhortations to the troops on the eve of the battle, some of whom were able to commit the verses to memory and survived to pass them into oral tradition.

Other recollections of so momentous a conflict would have been preserved in a similar way and thus, even though denied the rigour which underwrites the authority of skaldic verse, eventually found their way into the saga record. Such soldiers' stories, which almost always focus on particularly dramatic incidents, would have been brought home by the Icelandic warriors who are known to have served in Olaf's retinue at Stiklestad. Assuredly these would have been among the sources informing Snorri's account of the battle, much as his travels around Norway and Sweden would have given him access to local sources of oral tradition, while also acquainting him with the landscape which formed the setting for the events he was to describe. As to specifically military matters of arms and armour, strategy and tactics, the evidence supplied by Snorri's account is consistent with what is known of other Scandinavian land battles of the period, almost all of which follow much the same relatively unsophisticated course.

The large-scale land battle was an uncharacteristic feature of warfare in Scandinavia during the earlier medieval period principally, if not entirely, by reason of landscapes dominated by dense forest and mountain ridge. In Norway especially, mountainous areas covered with forest were virtually impenetrable and communication between settlements predominantly located along the coasts was most effectively conducted by sea. So too, of course, was warfare, even to the extent of the warship and its fighting crew representing the primary unit of Scandinavian military organisation long after the forests had begun to be cleared and overland routes made more accessible to troop movement.

Yet battles fought between fleets were not naval engagements in the more modern sense of the term, because the ships served initially as troop-transporters bringing the contending forces into contact and afterwards as floating platforms for the hand-to-hand fighting which was to decide the outcome of the engagement, usually when the principal commander of one side was slain. Battles on land were very similarly conducted, although close combat between sizeable forces long before the introduction of military uniforms posed the problem of differentiating between friend and foe, which would have been less likely to apply to a warrior crew of just a few dozen men who had shared shipboard accommodation. Thus it was important for a commander to arrange his more numerous troops into groups likely to be known to each other, and so the saga's account rings true when it tells of Olaf organising his forces into three divisions, each one assembled around a banner where its members were instructed to group themselves together with their neighbours and kinsmen.

The king's own retinue, or *hirð*, comprising his principal officers and his housecarls was to form the central division around his banner. The Upplanders were to stand with them and such local men of the Trondelag as could be rallied to the king's forces should be placed there too, along with some of the vagabonds recruited during the march through the forests. Dag Ringsson's warriors were to be deployed on the right around the second banner, while the Swedes would have a third banner and be placed on the left flank. The saga estimate of Olaf's troop numbers at 'over three thousand men' is reckoned in 'long hundreds', and so would correspond to a force well in excess of three and a half thousand, a proportion of whom – his own housecarls and those of Dag Ringsson, as well as the select Swedish troops assigned to him by Onund – can be considered 'professionals' in respect of training and equipment. Those volunteers he had been able to recruit in Sweden and along the march through the borderlands, however, were unlikely to have been of any such quality, neither in terms of arms, armour and training nor as regards battle-readiness and morale.

Having set out that deployment of troops in readiness to move on down the valley, Olaf was brought word that there would be no local recruits to his ranks. Virtually every man able to carry a weapon had joined the 'bonders' army' and those who had stayed in their homes had done so rather than join either side in the coming conflict. Finn Arnason was so angered at this news that he urged the king to plunder and burn the farms in the valley, with the intention of alarming the Trondelag men into fleeing back to their homes and thus thinning down the enemy ranks. Such would have been a tactic fully characteristic of Scandinavian warfaring, indeed one no less typical of Olaf's own domestic policy in former years, and the authenticity of Finn's proposal is reliably confirmed by the saga's quotation of lines attributed to Thormod Kolbrunarskald who was present at the time; however, the king is said to have rejected the idea as an unnecessary provocation when he yet hoped to be able to negotiate a peace with the 'bonders' army'. The only pre-emptive action he would allow was the killing of any enemy spies they might come upon, and under those orders of engagement the advance into Værdal continued, with the king taking one country road and Dag with his people another way, intending to meet in the evening for encampment overnight.

It is at this point that the saga tells of the skalds in attendance upon Olaf: the aforementioned Thormod Kolbrunarskald, Gissur Gulbraaskald and Thorfinn Mudr, all three, of course, Icelanders. When the forces were drawn up in battle array, Olaf was to have a *skjaldborg* (or 'shield-rampart') formed around him by the strongest and bravest of his housecarls. This was a familiar tactic of northern warfaring and consisted of a body of armoured warriors formed up in close order with their shields overlapping on all sides and above, thus forming a shelter to protect the commander and his chosen companions from the onslaught of missile weapons which opened hostilities between contending forces as they closed upon each other. Calling his skalds together, Olaf commanded them to go inside the shield-rampart when action was about to begin and to stay within it so as to witness at first hand the battle which they were to commemorate in poetry. At this point the skalds composed their verses to fire up the warriors for the conflict expected on the following day, although not without sarcastic exchanges bearing on the absence of the celebrated Sigvat.

By nightfall Olaf's forces were all gathered together further down the valley – where, according to the saga, a number of local men did come to join their ranks – and settled to sleep lain under their shields in the open. That particular reference in the saga draws attention to the variety of weaponry likely to have been found among so haphazard an array of fighting-men, because the one component of arms and armour which would have been carried by each and every one of them, from the fully equipped housecarl to the roughest vagabond, would most certainly have been his shield. The least expensive and yet most essential item in the armoury of the northmen, its traditional form was of a wooden disc, approximately a metre in diameter, with a metal boss at its centre covering an iron hand-grip, and such would have been the type most commonly found throughout all the forces engaged at Stiklestad. The tapered, triangular kite-shaped shield would not have reached Scandinavia as early as 1030, but heavy shields of the longer, rectangular Slav design were widely in use among the Rus and might very well have been included in the equipment supplied to Olaf's retinue before leaving Jaroslav's court.

At first light, the slumbering army was roused by Thormod the skald's singing of *Bjarkamal*, the ancient 'Lay of Bjarki' celebrating one of the legendary champions who fought for the sixth-century

Danish king Rolf Kraki. Thought to have had its origin as the work of a Danish poet in the tenth century, this song is one of the very few survivals from a great body of poetry about Rolf widely known in medieval Scandinavia. While Saxo Grammaticus supplies a Latin verse paraphrase of its content, the text of the poem is better preserved by Snorri Sturluson who quotes two strophes at this juncture in *Heimskringla* (and three more in his *Edda*), lending the authority of his own skaldic scholarship to the likelihood of a genuinely historical tradition recalling *Bjarkamal* sounding reveille for Olaf's army before Stiklestad. When Thormod had been rewarded with a gold arm-ring as his token of royal gratitude, the army moved off to resume its advance through the valley, but once again Dag Ringsson's contingent took its own separate route, although there is no explanation why it should have done so and the reference may be no more than a storytelling device to contrive his late arrival at a point of crisis in the conflict.

At which point the saga finally brings Olaf to Stiklestad, a place name which actually identified a farm in Værdal and one apparently located near the rising ground where the king chose to range his forces, and from where he now had his first sight of the bonders' host assembling below. A spurious story of an attack on an enemy troop sent to spy on the king's army and of its leader, recognised as 'Rut of Viggia', being slain by the Icelanders of Olaf's retinue is very probably one of those occasional saga anecdotes contrived to accommodate a jest based on a personal name, especially when the king offers his Icelanders 'a ram to slaughter' and *Rut* is the Icelandic term for a young ram. There might be just one nugget of historical value to be found in the tale, however, if it can be taken to confirm the likelihood of Icelanders included among Olaf's housecarls at Stiklestad. The passage immediately following in the saga narrative is another anecdote, but one of more particular significance here as the reference with which *Olaf the Saint's saga* in *Heimskringla* specifically confirms Harald Hardrada's having taken part in the battle.

The army has reached Stiklestad and been placed in battle array, although Dag Ringsson's force has yet to arrive and so the king directs the Uppland contingent to go out on to the right wing and raise their banner there, but first he advises that 'my brother Harald should not be in this battle, as he is still only a child in years'. To which Harald replies that he certainly will be in the battle 'and if I am so weak as to be unable to wield a sword, then let my hand be tied to the hilt. There is none keener than I to strike a blow against these bonders and so I shall go with my comrades.' The saga goes on to quote a verse which it attributes to Harald himself, although in a form of words which distinctly betrays Snorri's own suspicions regarding its authenticity: 'We are told that Harald made this verse on that occasion . . . .

> I shall guard the wing
> on which I stand – and
> my mother will hold worthy
> my battering reddened shields.
> Not fearful of the foemen
> bonders' spear-thrusts,
> the young warrior will wage a manly
> weapon-thing most murderous.[6]

'And Harald had his way and was given leave to be in the battle.'

There is, of course, no doubt that Harald actually did fight at Stiklestad and so the story certainly cannot be dismissed as implausible, but it still does lack the ring of authenticity, and not least because Snorri's use of the phrase 'we are told that . . .' is one of his customary forms of signalling his own doubts as to the reliability of his source material. It is very tempting to wonder whether Harald might have composed the verse some time after the battle, possibly even years later when he had succeeded his brother as king in Norway and the story elaborated as a frame in which to set it. Closer examination of the incident might even suggest as much because, while Olaf would have had a natural concern for his young kinsman's safety, it is hardly likely that he would have considered him too young to take part in the battle, especially when there is so much evidence attesting Harald's physical prowess and his quite exceptional height which would already have been apparent even in a fifteen-year-old. Neither would a prince already into his teens have been untrained in weapon-handling, especially one with a mother so ambitious for her sons to win battle-glory. This was precisely the form of induction into his warrior's way for which Harald would have been schooled since infancy and, indeed, encouraged to long for by his immersion in a culture entirely infused with the heroic warrior ethos. In fact, Olaf himself was said to have been just twelve years of age when he embarked on his first viking expedition and still only fourteen when he was fighting in England as a warrior in the army of Thorkell the Tall.

It is worth remembering, though, that the young Olaf was placed under the guardianship and guidance of his late father's principal lieutenant, Rani the Far-travelled, when he first went a-viking, and is similarly thought to have had no less a warrior than the famous Thorkell himself as his mentor in England. So it is perhaps more likely that Olaf would not have advised against his young kinsman taking part in the battle at Stiklestad, but against his being placed on the right wing with the Uppland contingent when the king would more probably have wanted to keep him closer to his own most trusted warriors, even within the shelter of his *skjaldborg* where he intended to place the skalds. There is, in fact, other evidence bearing on Harald's survival at Stiklestad – which will be considered in detail later – to suggest his having been guarded on the battlefield by one of the most trusted members of the king's personal retinue.

One other aspect of the story of timely significance here is Harald's quoted remark about wielding a sword, because this might be the most convenient point at which to expand upon the subject of weaponry at Stiklestad. While the shield, as aforementioned, was the least expensive and most essential item in the armoury of the northman, the sword was not only the most expensive but also the most prestigious, and the weapon most often celebrated by skald and saga-maker. The most famous swords were given their own names, as was Olaf's weapon, called 'Neite' (*Hneitir* in the Norse), which served him through his many battles before its gold-worked hilt fell at last from his hand at Stiklestad. Retrieved from the field by a Swedish warrior who had lost his own sword, it was kept in the man's family for some three generations until the early twelfth century when one of his descendants became a Varangian mercenary in Byzantine service and brought it with him to the east. A closely contemporary account, which was known to Snorri Sturluson, tells how its identity was revealed to the emperor John II Comnenus and how he paid a great price in gold for the sword, which was thereafter enshrined in the Varangian chapel dedicated to Saint Olaf in Constantinople.

While unlikely to have been all so richly decorated as Neite, swords of quality would usually have blades of foreign manufacture, the best of them imported from the Rhineland, double-edged, pattern-welded and more than 70 centimetres in length. Recognised as the aristocrat of the armoury in the old northern world, the sword was the weapon of the superior class of warrior, of the housecarl, the chieftain and the king, and yet it was the axe which still represents the most characteristic weapon of the northman. It was, of course, equally useful as a working tool and would have been more widely distributed, as also would the spear, especially the lighter throwing-spear as distinct from the heavier type fitted with a broader blade which was used as a thrusting weapon in hand-to-hand combat.

Thus an army as diverse as the one which Olaf brought to Stiklestad would have gone into battle bearing a disparate range of weaponry. The professional fighting-man would have his sword and shield, possibly a war-axe, probably a spear, or even a bow and arrows when no less an authority than Saxo Grammaticus acknowledged the fame of Norse archery. Those of humbler status would have been armed with the essential shield, probably with an axe and perhaps a spear – even in so basic a form as a sharpened stake – or possibly a hunting bow, while some of the very roughest recruits of the vagabond type might have wielded nothing more sophisticated than a heavy wooden club.

Social divisions would have been still more obviously apparent in respect of helmets and protective armour or, in the great majority of cases, by their absence. The saga has a lavishly detailed account of

Olaf's arms and armour comprising a gold-mounted helmet and a white shield inlaid with a golden cross, his spear (which Snorri had certainly seen beside the altar in Christ Church at Nidaros) and, of course, his keen-edged Neite. Yet the one item of his war-gear specifically confirmed by a quoted verse from Sigvat is his coat of ring-mail. This 'burnished byrnie' was probably singled out for the skald's attention by reason of its extreme rarity, because while iron was plentiful (and plate armour completely unknown) in eleventh-century Scandinavia, the laborious craftsmanship involved in the production of ring-mail made it the most prohibitively expensive item of war-gear and thus available only to the most affluent on the battlefield. It would also have been extremely hot and heavy to wear while fighting on foot, so leather may often have been preferred by those who were fortunate enough to enjoy the luxury of choice.

Helmets too, although simpler and thus less costly to produce than mail, are thought not to have been so widespread in Scandinavian warfare as is sometimes imagined. The 'winged' or 'horned' helmet of 'the Viking' has long been confidently dismissed as a fantasy, but helmets of the *spangenhelm* type – a construction of triangular iron plates held together at the base by a circular headband sometimes mounted with a nose-guard – would have represented standard equipment for the professional fighting-men in a lordly or royal retinue. Again, however, neither helmet nor mail-coat would have been likely to be found among the rougher elements in Olaf's forces, among whom a leather cap and a heavy woollen or leathern coat would have represented the most common protective clothing behind a shield.

The saga's customary reference to the enemy host as the 'bonders' army' must not be taken to indicate a seething peasant rabble, especially when the evidence for selected soldiery gifted by the Swedish king allied with vagabonds recruited from the borderland forests suggests Olaf's forces representing rather greater extremes of warrior type. The 'bonders' army' was evidently recruited across the entire social range of the free and unfree, but was led by prominent chieftains, some of them exalted to the rank of lenderman, accompanied by their own companies of housecarls, while the bonders themselves, although lower in the social order, were still free farmers recognised by a respected modern authority on the subject as 'yeomen [who] were the staple of society'.[7]

Despite there being nowhere any reference to the inclusion of any foreign element, the possibility of at least some Danish involvement cannot be discounted. When Cnut left his newly acquired Norwegian dominions under the governance of his jarl Hakon, he assigned to him a 'court-bishop' in the person of a Danish priest, Sigurd, who is said by the saga to have 'been long with Cnut', of whose cause he was assuredly an ardent advocate. This Bishop Sigurd seems to have assumed the roles of principal chaplain and political commissar to the bonders' army, inciting all possible hostility to Olaf in the speech of exhortation he is said to have delivered to the forces before the battle. It would have been quite unthinkable for any Scandinavian churchman of the time, especially one given such an assignment by the all-powerful Cnut, to have been without his own escort of housecarls. Sigurd himself is described as exceptionally haughty and hot-tempered, so there would be every reason to expect his demanding a formidable warrior retinue which would undoubtedly have been present, to whatever extent it was actively engaged, at Stiklestad.

On balance, then, there is no reason to imagine this 'bonders' army' as any the worse equipped or accomplished than Olaf's forces, and yet there is nowhere any trace of doubt as to their massive superiority in numbers. Snorri Sturluson is almost certainly drawing upon a deep and ancient well of folk-memory when he describes the muster in the Trondelag as 'a host so great that there was nobody in Norway at that time who had ever seen so large a force assembled', but as to any more precise estimate of numbers, he would seem to signal his doubts as to the accuracy of the figure he mentions in his usual form of words: 'We are told that the bonders' army was not less than a hundred times a hundred on that day'. Reckoning in 'long hundreds', that figure would represent a strength of almost fourteen and a half thousand. While not entirely beyond the bounds of credibility, even at a time when the total population of eleventh-century Norway is estimated at around two million, the phrase 'a hundred times a hundred' has a suspiciously formulaic character and so might be more cautiously read as an indication of 'a very great number, almost beyond counting'. The saga also quotes lines from Sigvat, but the obscurity of their phrasing allows for no more informative evidence than a claim for Olaf's having been defeated entirely by weight of numbers, so in the last analysis neither source can offer evidence for anything more precise than confirmation of a modest army overwhelmingly outnumbered by the enemy host.

Such was clearly Olaf's own appraisal of the situation when he addressed his troops on the morning of the battle, proposing that victory was more likely to be won by shock tactics than a long and wearying confrontation of unequal forces. His stratagem was to extend his forces thinly across a long front to prevent their being outflanked by superior numbers and then to launch a ferocious onslaught at the enemy's front line, throwing it back against the ranks behind, thus extending the impact back through the host with such resulting chaos that 'their destruction will be the greater the greater numbers there are together'.

This sort of oratory is customarily set out in the sagas at great length, and in the finest prose which is more realistically recognised as creative writing than historical record, but there is still no reason to doubt the essential accuracy of its content. The same is usually also true of negotiations between principal characters in the sagas, where the dialogue cannot be anything more than speculative reconstruction and yet the outcome corresponds well enough to the subsequent course of events, as it does in the discussion which decided the command and battle order of the bonders' army.

The first choice for its leader would have been the redoubtable Einar Eindridison, called *Tambarskelve* ('paunch-shaker'),[8] who represented the most powerful figure in the Trondelag. A long-standing enemy of Olaf and married to a sister of the jarls Erik and Svein, Einar had been promised high office by Cnut. When he learned of the death of Hakon Eriksson, Einar sailed to England in full expectation of succeeding as Cnut's jarl over Norway, thus being out of the country when Olaf returned from Russia and apparently in no hurry to return and oppose him.

In Einar's absence, the most senior of the lendermen was Harek of Thjotta and it was he whom Kalv Arnason proposed for command, but the Halogalander protested that he was too old for such a duty and suggested Thore Hund in his stead as a younger man with his own blood-feud to pursue against Olaf. Although eager for vengeance, Thore doubted whether the Trondelag men who made up the greater part of the army would take orders from someone out of the far north. At this point, Kalv Arnason introduced a note of urgency, warning that Olaf's forces might be smaller but were still fiercely loyal to a fearless leader. Assuredly well aware of the potential consequences of his own disloyalty to his king, he warned of the terrifying revenge Olaf would inflict on those he defeated, urging the bonders to attack as one united army to ensure their victory, and in response they acclaimed Kalv as their commander.

Immediately setting the forces into battle order, Kalv raised his banner and drew up his housecarls with Harek and his retinue beside them. Thore Hund and his troop were placed in front of the banner and at the head of the formation with chosen bands of the best-armed bonders on both sides. The saga describes this central formation of men of the Trondelag and Halogaland as 'long and deep', which would imply that it was formed into a column, while on its right wing was 'another formation' and on the left the men of Rogaland, Hordaland, Sogn and the Fjords stood with a third banner.

At this point the saga introduces Thorstein Knaresmed,[9] a sea-trader and master shipwright, sturdy, strong 'and a great man-slayer' who had been drawn to join the bonders' army by fierce enmity to Olaf on account of the great new merchant-ship he had built and which had been taken from him as *wergild* (the fine for man-slaughter). Now he came to join Thore Hund's company so as to be in the front line of the coming battle and the first to drive a weapon at King Olaf in repayment for his theft of the 'best ship that ever went on a trading voyage'. Quite possibly inspired by the appearance of this vengeful shipbuilder, Kalv Arnason's address to his troops before the march to battle clearly sets out to fire up their lust for vengeance, urging those with injuries to avenge upon the king to place themselves under the banner which was to advance against Olaf's own standard.

Thus the bonders' army came to the field of Stiklestad where Olaf's forces had already taken up their positions, but the plan of immediate attack intended by both sides was delayed. While the king's forces were still awaiting the arrival of Dag Ringsson's contingent, detachments of the bonders' army were lagging some way behind the front ranks and so, as Kalv and Harek were coming within closer view of their enemy, Thore and his company were assigned to marshal the laggardly rearguard and ensure that all would be present and correct when battle began.

The saga has an account – assuredly more formulaic than authentically historical, but perfectly plausible for all that – of verbal exchanges between the principals on both sides when the front ranks of the opposing forces were close enough for individuals to recognise each other. Olaf upbraided Kalv for disloyalty to his king, and to his kin when he had brothers standing with the forces he was about to attack. The tone of Kalv's reply might have been thought to hint at reconciliation, but Finn warned the king of his brother's habit of speaking fairly when he meant ill and then Thorgeir of Quiststad, who had formerly been one of Olaf's lendermen, shouted to the king that he should have such peace as many had earlier suffered at his hands, 'and which you shall now pay for!' The saga endows Olaf's response with the tenor of a prophecy when he shouted a warning back to Thorgeir that fate had not decreed him a victory this day. At this point Thore Hund moved forward with his warriors shouting the battle-cry of 'Forward, forward, bonder men!' and the battle of Stiklestad began.

Olaf's forces countered with their 'Forward, forward, Christ-men! cross-men! king's men!' and the saga interpolates an anecdote, and one not entirely implausible, of confusion caused in the more distant ranks of the bonders' army where some took up their enemy's war-cry and warriors turned on each other imagining that the king's forces were among them. As Dag Ringsson's company was now coming into view, Olaf launched into his battle plan and commanded the opening assault from his position on the higher ground. The sun shone in a clear sky as the headlong charge rolled downhill and drove into the enemy lines with such impact that the bonders' array bent before it. While many in the farther ranks of the bonders were already turning to flee, the lendermen and their housecarls stood firm against an onslaught described by Sigvat as the 'steel-storm raging at Stiklar Stad'. Their stand stemmed the flight of their own reluctant rearguard, who were forced to re-form into a counter-attack which was soon pushing on from all sides, its front line slashing with swords, while those behind them thrust with spears and all the ranks in the rear shot arrows, cast throwing-spears and hand-axes, or let fly with stones and sharpened stakes.

This was the murderous hand-to-hand combat which marked the crucial phase of battle. Many were falling now on both sides and the lines in front of Olaf's shield-rampart were steadily growing thin when the king commanded his banner to be brought forward. Thord Folason the standard-bearer advanced and Olaf himself followed, emerging from the shield-rampart and leading those warriors he had chosen as the best-armed and most accomplished to stand with him in battle. Sigvat's verses tell of bonders rearing back in awe at the sight of the king's entry into the fray, although one who remained undeterred was the aforementioned Thorgeir of Quiststad, at least until Olaf's sword slashed across his face, cutting the nose-piece of his helmet and cleaving his head down below the eyes. 'Did I not speak true, Thorgeir, when I warned that you would not be the victor at our meeting?'

Thord the standard-bearer drove his banner-pole so deep into the earth that it remained standing there even when he himself had been dealt his death-wound and fell beneath it. There also fell two of Olaf's skalds, first Thorfinn Mudr and after him Gissur Gulbraaskald who was attacked by two warriors, one of whom he slew and the other wounded before he himself was slain. At around this same time Dag Ringsson arrived on the field, raising his banner and setting his troops into array, yet finding the light becoming so poor that he could hardly make out the men of Hordaland and Rogaland who were facing him on the left wing of the bonders' army.

The cause of this sudden darkening of what had been a bright summer sky only shortly before was an eclipse of the sun which is reliably recorded for the summer of 1030, but which raises its own point of difficulty as to the precise date of the battle. Snorri Sturluson firmly assigns the death of Olaf to the 'fourth kalends of August' or 29 July in modern reckoning, and so too does Theodoric the Monk in his *Historia*. The Feast of St Olaf in commemoration of the day of his martyrdom is entered in the church calendars at that same date, and yet the total eclipse – which would certainly have been visible from Stiklestad in the year 1030 – actually occurred on 31 August.

There are really only two possible explanations, of which the first is that the battle was fought in July and the eclipse merely a fictional accretion inspired by the actual phenomenon which occurred a month later. Yet the tradition of the eclipse taking place while the battle was in progress must be almost immediately contemporary when it is described in Sigvat's verses on the battle composed within very recent memory of the event. No less significant is the impressive correspondence between the timings recorded in the saga – which record the armies meeting near midday, the battle beginning in early afternoon and the king slain at three o'clock – and those calculated for the historical eclipse of August which would have begun at 1.40 p.m., become total at 2.53, and was over by four in the afternoon.

All of which might suggest the alternative explanation – which proposes 31 August as the true date of the battle and construes 29 July as a misreckoning – being the more likely; and that same likelihood is convincingly developed by the editor of a long-respected English translation of *Olaf the Saint's saga*,[10] who suggests the discrepancy may have derived from misinterpretation of an original text which would probably have given the date in a customary medieval form as '1029 years and two hundred and nine days since Christ's birth'. Reckoning in 'long hundreds' (as 249 days) from 25 December would actually give a date of 31 August, while reckoning in 'continental' hundreds (or 209 days) from 1 January would give the date of 29 July which is found in Theodoric's *Historia* and Snorri's *Heimskringla*. The prime significance of the eclipse in the saga, as it is also in Sigvat's verse referring to the same phenomenon, is its ominous portent, perhaps even making an implied allusion to Christ's crucifixion, because it is at just this point that Olaf is about to meet his martyrdom.

In fact, the saga narrative itself reads as if abruptly distracted from Dag's entry into the battle when it suddenly turns to identify the warriors who were at that moment closing with the king on the field. Kalv Arnason stood with two of his kinsmen, one of them also called Kalv (yet more precisely identified as Kalv Arnfinsson, and thus as Kalv Arnason's cousin), while on his other side stood Thore Hund, clad in a reindeer-skin coat he had brought back from a trading voyage to Lapland and believed to have been rendered as weapon-proof as ring-mail by the witchcraft of the Lapps. This is clearly a reference to legend, and yet to one of closely contemporary provenance when Sigvat's verses on the battle tell how 'the mighty magic of the Finns sheltered Thore from maim'.[11]

It was Thore with whom Olaf first engaged when he hewed at shoulders protected by reindeer skin and found that his famously sharp sword had no effect. Turning to Bjorn his marshal, Olaf commanded him to 'strike the dog whom steel will not bite', but a great blow from Bjorn's axe similarly bounced off the magic hide and allowed Thore to retaliate with a spear-thrust which killed the marshal outright, proclaiming that 'this is how we hunt the bear'. It is, of course, quite characteristic of the Norse heroic tradition to engage in such name-play at the very edge of a death-dealing combat, and just such is reflected in Snorri's narrative before it moves on to the specific detail of Olaf's martyrdom.

Having slain one of Kalv Arnason's kinsmen, Olaf next found himself facing Thorstein Knaresmed who struck with his axe to wound the king in the left thigh. Finn Arnason retaliated by slaying the shipwright, as Olaf staggered to support himself against a rock, dropping his sword as Thore Hund made another spear-thrust beneath the king's mail-coat to wound him in the stomach and Kalv inflicted a third wound, this to the left side of his neck. While Snorri's narrative confirms that 'those three wounds were King Olaf's death', he goes on to say that not all are agreed as to which of the two Kalvs delivered the wound to the neck. Theodoric the Monk's *Historia*, set down a century and a half after the event, tells of men still disagreed as to the number of wounds suffered by Olaf as well as the identity of those who dealt them, but there is evidence found in the saga record to confirm both Olaf's son Magnus and half-brother Harald having reason to believe Kalv Arnason guilty. Perhaps most convincing of all is a story stamped with impressive authority – although preserved only in *Orkneyinga saga* – which tells of Kalv himself having 'repented of his crime of killing King Olaf the Saint' when confronted by Rognvald Brusason in Russia five years after the battle.

Meanwhile, there is more to be told of events on the field of Stiklestad in the immediate aftermath of the king's death because, while the greater part of the force which had advanced with him fell with him also, Dag Ringsson is said to have kept up the battle with a fierce assault in which many bonders and lendermen fell and from which many others fled. This onset was apparently well remembered in tradition as 'Dag's Storm', a byname which was to have the strangest echo in another battle fought thirty-six years later. Eventually, though, Dag Ringsson's force was confronted by the greater strength of the bonders' army with Kalv Arnason, Harek of Thjotta and Thore Hund in the forefront, and was so hopelessly overwhelmed by superior numbers that he and his surviving warriors were left with no course other than flight.

It may have been at this point – or, perhaps more probably, somewhat earlier – that the young Harald Sigurdsson escaped what must by now have been a scene of fearsome carnage. Whether he had been with the Upplanders or within the king's *skjaldborg*, he would almost certainly have been drawn into the forces gathered around Olaf's entry into the blood-fray. When Olaf's sword is said to have been retrieved by a Swede who had lost his own weapon, it would appear that all three divisions of the initial battle order had come together around the king's retinue when he emerged from his shield-rampart.

One who would assuredly have been found among the select company who formed Olaf's bodyguard was the Orkneyman Rognvald Brusason. Through the years since his first arrival as a ten-year-old boy at the Norwegian court, he had grown into a formidable warrior who had demonstrated unswerving loyalty to the king, travelling with him to Russia and back to Scandinavia on the grim progress which led to Stiklestad.

The most comprehensive account of Rognvald's life and career is preserved in the work now known as *Orkneyinga saga* and subtitled as 'a history of the jarls of Orkney'. Completed in Iceland in 1234/5, it is effectively the updated version of an earlier text, usually referred to by the title *Jarls' saga*, also the work of an Icelander and set down in the last years of the twelfth century. It was this *Jarls' saga* which was known to Snorri Sturluson, providing his chief source of information on Rognvald Brusason (who was himself to become one of the most celebrated Orkney jarls after 1037), and thus representing one of the two principal sources for the opening chapter of his *Harald's saga* in *Heimskringla*, which begins with Rognvald's rescue of the young Harald from the carnage of Stiklestad. The other, and elder, of those sources was a strophe quoted by Snorri in the saga where it is attributed to Thjodolf Arnorsson, the skald authoritatively recognised as Harald's 'favourite poet . . . who spent many years in his company'.[12]

Thus when Thjodolf's verse bearing on Stiklestad opens with the line 'I have heard how the shield-storm raged near to Haug [a farm in Værdal]', the likelihood is of his having heard all of this from Harald himself and so, even though the verses were composed at least sixteen years after the event, they can be considered to represent the most reliably informed evidence. In fact, it would seem to have been from Thjodolf's reference in that same verse to 'fifteen years a youth then' that the saga (and the subsequent historical record) came to know of Harald's precise age in the year 1030.

It was not from Thjodolf, however, but from *Jarls' saga* that Snorri appears to have learned of Harald's being 'severely wounded' in the battle and, although no source confides any such detail, he most probably suffered his injury in the maelstrom which would have undoubtedly followed the death of Olaf. As in many similar conflicts of that world and time, the death of a principal warlord was of decisive bearing on the outcome as the signal of defeat for his forces, and so it would have been at Stiklestad when such as remained of Olaf's battle array crumbled and the survivors who were able to do so took flight from the field. Among those fugitives was Rognvald Brusason and with him the wounded Harald Sigurdsson whom 'he had rescued from the battle' (and who may well not otherwise have survived the fray).

Apparently so badly injured as to be unable to travel any greater distance, Harald was led by Rognvald to the steading of a farmer who lived in a remote part of the forest. On this particular point of detail, the evidence of *Jarls' saga* is confirmed by Thjodolf's reference to Harald as 'fifteen years a youth then . . . hiding beyond the woods'. There he could be cared for in safety until his wounds were healed and he was sufficiently recovered to cross the Kjolen mountains into Jamtaland and on into Sweden where Rognvald was awaiting him. When the time came to set out on that journey, Harald avoided more usually travelled paths and made his way along forest trails guided by the farmer's son who (according to Snorri's account and, apparently, no other) was unaware of the identity of his charge.

It was while they were riding through the wild woodland that Harald is said to have spoken the verse attributed to him by Snorri and by *Orkneyinga saga*:

> Through endless woods I crawl
> on my way now, with little honour.
> Who knows but that my name may
> yet be far and wide renowned.

II

Varangian

Russia, 1031–1034

The Baltic was known as *Bahr Varank*, or the 'Varangian Sea', to the authors of the tenth-century Arab writings which preserve some of the most colourful accounts of early medieval Russia. These sources were informed by traders and travellers among the Rus on the Volga and so their use of an Arabic form of 'Varangian' (which occurs as *Væringjar* in Old Norse and *Varjazi* in Slavonic) supplies its own testimony for the term having emerged in Russia, yet the word itself is of Scandinavian derivation and believed to stem from the Old Norse terms *vár* ('oath') or *várar* ('trust'). The original meaning of 'Varangians', then, could be proposed as 'men who pledge each other loyalty', probably a group bound together by some form of oath along the lines of 'all for one, one for all'.

Used in that sense, it is a name which would certainly have befitted the Scandinavian venturers – travelling in companies on the principle of 'safety in numbers' and sworn to mutual defence and protection of their selves, their craft and their cargoes – who had been crossing the Baltic since at least as early as the eighth century to penetrate the Russian river system along which furs from northern forests were to be traded for silver from the east. Before the mid-point of the following century, the kith and kin of these warrior-traders were recognised as the *Rus* and as men of power in the north of the land later to be named for them.

By the tenth century, and alike to their compatriots elsewhere in the Scandinavian expansion from the Hebrides to Normandy, these Rus had absorbed much of the culture and custom of neighbouring peoples whom they encountered along the east-way, and most evidently in their adoption of the Slavonic tongue. It may well be this new cultural identity which is reflected in a new application of the term 'Varangian' as a generic name for northmen (similar to the modern usage of the term 'Viking'), in which sense it probably served to distinguish themselves from their Scandinavian cousins. At the same time, however, the occurrence of the term in the documentary record is almost invariably associated with warfare, and it is this usage which points to the later – and ultimately enduring – definition of Varangian as 'mercenary warrior of Scandinavian origin'.

The history of the first centuries of the Rus, as recorded in the annals begun in the eleventh century and most usually known in English as the *Russian Primary Chronicle*,[1] represents a catalogue of almost incessant warfare, in establishment of lordship over subject peoples, contention with predatory neighbours or internecine conflict between rival siblings of the ruling Rurikid kindred. For reasons which will bear further consideration here, Rus princes of the tenth and eleventh centuries were greatly dependent upon the services of mercenary fighting-men, of whom the most renowned were Scandinavians brought across the 'Varangian Sea'. Just such were the fugitive survivors from the Norwegian king Olaf's forces at the battle of Stiklestad who crossed the Baltic to Russia from Sweden in the summer of 1031, led by the Orkneyman Rognvald Brusason and including in their company Olaf's half-brother, Harald Sigurdsson.

Having begun *Harald's saga* in *Heimskringla* with Rognvald Brusason's rescue of the young warrior from the field of Stiklestad, Snorri Sturluson goes on to tell how Harald crossed over into Sweden – possibly later in 1030, but more probably in the following spring – to join Rognvald and other survivors of Olaf's defeated army on their passage across the Baltic. It must be said, though, that Snorri's scant account of Harald's warrior's way through Russia does not represent the most convincing example of saga as historical record. Indeed, its value as a source of history rests almost entirely upon its quotation of two strophes from Harald's court-poets, so it is fortunate that Snorri's evidence can be supplemented by reference to other sources in order to attempt a reconstruction of three or four years which were to prove of key significance in the military education of a future warrior king.

Snorri's account simply tells of Harald's finding his way to meet Rognvald and others of Olaf's warriors in Sweden and of their having assembled ships in the spring before sailing east to Russia in the summer. There he and Rognvald were welcomed by the Grand Prince Jaroslav who appointed Harald to share command of his 'forces for defence of the country' with Eilif, son of Rognvald Ulfsson, the former jarl of Gautland in Sweden who had been endowed with lordship of Staraja Ladoga after escorting Jaroslav's Swedish bride to Russia. The suggestion that a Rus grand prince would delegate even joint command of his military to a Norwegian princeling scarcely sixteen years of age and on such brief acquaintance is itself unconvincing, but set into the military and political context of Jaroslav's Russia in the early 1030s it lies entirely beyond the bounds of plausibility.

First of all, there was no national military force in early medieval Russia where the only semblance of a standing army was the *druzhina*, effectively the military retinue of a prince or lordly magnate and originally intended as his military escort for protection and enforcement on tribute-gathering expeditions. Although references in the *Primary Chronicle* most often indicate its strength at around the hundred mark, the size of a *druzhina* varied according to the wealth and status of its lord and ranged between a quarter and twice that number. However impressively armed and equipped, such a force could not have amounted to a realistic field army for a major campaign without substantial reinforcement and it was always preferable to expend the lives of lesser troops in action than to place the *druzhina* at unnecessary risk.

While there is one example of a Rus prince supplementing his forces with those of a foreign ally in the early eleventh century, other sources of auxiliary manpower are more frequently indicated by the historical record. Such were to be found in tribal levies, known as *voi*, which were being superseded by militias raised in urban centres that had grown up in size and importance from the fortified trading-posts established by the earlier warrior-traders along Russian river routes. The origin of these urban militias lay in the need for defence of towns while the lord's *druzhina* was away, sometimes for months at a time, on expeditions conducted over the vast distances which posed the major logistical problem of warfaring among the Rus. It could often also present difficulties in recruiting militias for longer range campaigning when their principal concern was always for the security of their own territory, but so too could other factors. Urban militias were able to draw upon surrounding rural areas for additional manpower and thus field a force numbering in the few thousands, but their co-operation still depended upon the loyalty owed to their lord by independent-minded townsfolk who still expected payment (even, if needs be, in the form of plunder) for their services.

Of perhaps more crucial bearing is the fact that neither urban militias nor tribal levies were possessed of the same mettle and morale as was the truly professional fighting-man. For military of that quality, the Rus warlord would invariably turn to the mercenary forces who represented his other source of reinforcement – and for Jaroslav, as for his father Vladimir before him, mercenaries invariably meant Varangians. There is little doubt that Vladimir, returning to Russia from exile in Scandinavia in the 970s, owed his initial seizure of power from his brothers to the mercenary fighting-men he had brought with him, but his greatest contribution to the history of the Varangians rests on the sturdy shoulders of the six thousand warriors he sent to the aid of the Byzantine emperor Basil II, for whom they were to form the nucleus of the famous Varangian Guard of Byzantium. The same enthusiasm was evidently shared by Vladimir's son and eventual successor Jaroslav, whose deployment of Varangians is noticed on no less than six significant occasions by the *Primary Chronicle* and whose reign is said by a highly respected history of the period to have seen 'both a flowering and a fading, though not a complete withering of the special relationship between the Varangians and the Rus princes'.[2] Nonetheless, both Vladimir and Jaroslav are more often remembered in the sagas for their tardiness, and even parsimony, when payment was due. The Varangians were of undoubted, even incomparable, value in the heat of the action and would always be the first choice of their Russian employers (as also of the Byzantines) for the most unsavoury duties, but in the last analysis the mercenary was only the hired hand of warfaring, never held in the same regard as the *druzhina* and all too often a problem when the wineskins were opened after the fighting was done.

When the great Vladimir – revered for his conversion of the Rus to Christianity and creation of the Russian Orthodox Church – died at Kiev in the summer of 1015, Jaroslav was away in the north at Novgorod, which would seem always to have been his preferred power base. He had been endowed with the lordship of Novgorod by his father, but relations between the two had soured and Jaroslav felt himself so greatly under threat from Vladimir that he is said by the *Primary Chronicle* to have 'sent across the sea and brought Varangians' to bolster his forces early in 1015. In the event, he would have need of those Varangians, but against a sinister sibling instead of an angry father because his ambitious half-brother Sviatopolk had moved with speed to seize Kiev as soon as Vladimir was dead. Known in Russian tradition as 'the Accursed', not least because his Byzantine mother had formerly been a nun and even his true paternity was in doubt, Sviatopolk is said to have bribed the people of Kiev to accept his succession and thereafter arranged the assassination of two of Vladimir's other sons, Boris and Gleb, who were soon to follow their father into the growing Russian calendar of saints.

Another son was killed while attempting to flee into Hungary, but the approach of autumn presented Sviatopolk with his most formidable rival in the form of Jaroslav advancing south towards the Dnieper with his Novgorod militia and a thousand Varangian mercenaries. Meanwhile, Sviatopolk had recruited his own mercenary auxiliaries from the Pechenegs, a Turkic people who represented a fearsome military presence, alternately as mercenaries for hire or as predatory raiders, in the steppe country extending into southern Russia from the north shores of the Black Sea. When Jaroslav's forces reached Liubech on the west bank of the Dnieper some 90 miles north of Kiev, Sviatopolk's host was ranged along the eastern bank. For three months the opposing armies faced each other across the river, until Jaroslav contrived to isolate Sviatopolk's *druzhina* from their Pechenegs and trap them on a thinly frozen lake where the breaking ice ensured their destruction.

Jaroslav entered Kiev in triumph and Sviatopolk fled west into Poland to find refuge with his wife's father, the Polish king Boleslaw. He returned to Russia in 1018, bringing with him a Polish army led by his father-in-law and reinforced with German, Hungarian and Pecheneg mercenary contingents which met and defeated Jaroslav's force of Varangians and militias of Kiev and Novgorod in the contested border zone along the western Bug river. Now it was Sviatopolk who advanced on Kiev while Jaroslav took flight north to Novgorod. But the real victor was almost certainly Boleslaw who paid off his mercenary forces with the plundering of Kiev before making his own departure back to Poland, and taking possession of the Cherven border towns en route.

Meanwhile, Jaroslav was back in Novgorod and levying new taxation to pay for more Varangians to renew his offensive. Left vulnerable without his Polish allies, Sviatopolk was likewise engaged in the south and still trying to recruit fresh forces of Pecheneg mercenaries even while Jaroslav was advancing again on Kiev in the spring of 1019. The last battle between the two was fought beside the River Alta not far from Kiev where Jaroslav won a great victory and Sviatopolk again took flight, although he is said to have fallen ill and died before reaching Poland. Having regained the ascendancy, Jaroslav was still not yet secure because another of the numerous sons of Vladimir was about to mount his own challenge.

This was Mstislav whose power base lay at Tmutorokan where he had carved out his own impressive dominion in the south-east around the Sea of Azov. Perhaps tempted towards the Dnieper by Jaroslav's evident preference for Novgorod, Mstislav moved north of the steppe sometime around 1024 and based himself at Chernigov within striking distance of Kiev. Once again, according to the *Primary Chronicle*, Jaroslav 'sent across the sea for Varangians' to face Mstislav's 'Kasogians and Khazars' recruited from his subject peoples around the Sea of Azov and supplemented with Severians

(Slav auxiliaries, presumably from Chernigov). These Severians would seem to have played the greater part in defeating Jaroslav's northmen in an extraordinary battle fought at night in a thunderstorm at Listven, and Mstislav's exclamation in his hour of victory is a remark of telling military significance: 'Who does not rejoice at this? Here lies slain a Severian and here a Varangian, and yet the *druzhina* is unharmed!'

After the defeat at Listven, Jaroslav withdrew back to the north and yet, for whatever reason, Mstislav did not pursue his flight from the battlefield, but instead conceded Kiev (whose people had earlier refused him entry) to his brother while retaining Chernigov as his own power base. Relations remained cautious and Jaroslav continued to build up his forces at Novgorod until 1026 when the two met again near Kiev and formally agreed to a division of the lands of the Rus along the line of the Dnieper, those to the east for Mstislav and those to the west for Jaroslav. 'Thus they began to live in peace and brotherhood', according to the *Primary Chronicle*. 'Conflict and tumult ceased and there was tranquillity in the land.' Under that arrangement each brother would have been responsible for defence of his own dominions, although the two did join forces in common cause on at least one occasion, until Mstislav died of sickness sometime around the year 1036 and with no surviving son, leaving Jaroslav as *samovlastets* ('sole ruler') – and 'Grand Prince' in the full sense, although the Turkic style of *khagan* (or 'khan') was still in use until the twelfth century – over all the lands of the Rus.

All of which is intended to provide some outline of the Russian political and military context into which Harald Sigurdsson made entry – although assuredly not as commander of defence forces – on his arrival from Scandinavia in the summer of 1031. Dispensing with the account offered at this point in Snorri's *Harald's saga*, the greater detail found in *Orkneyinga saga* will provide the more useful starting-point for any attempt at a realistic reconstruction of this particular passage of his warrior's way.

By way of example, one such detail of which Snorri makes no mention is the reference in *Orkneyinga saga* to Rognvald Brusason and his fellow survivors of Stiklestad making their way to the court of King Onund (presumably at Sigtuna south of Uppsala) on arrival in Sweden and thus it would be reasonable to assume that Harald also made his way to Onund's court, probably by prior arrangement to join them there, when he followed them into Sweden. Having crossed the Baltic to Russia, probably aboard ships provided and provisioned by Onund, *Orkneyinga saga* describes their going directly to Novgorod where 'King Jaroslav [or *Jarisleif* in the Norse name-form used in the sagas] welcomed them kindly out of respect for the holy king Olaf'.

It is at this point that the saga introduces the 'Varangian dimension' of Jaroslav's welcome when it specifies that 'all of the Norwegians' joined Jarl Eilif to 'take over the defences of Gardariki'. The interest of *Orkneyinga saga* in these events centres upon Rognvald Brusason, who was later to succeed his father as jarl of Orkney, and an account of his having remained in Russia while Harald went on to Byzantium. Lines from the skald Arnor Thordsson (usually called *Arnor jarlaskald* by reason of his service as court-poet to the Orkney jarls) are quoted in support of the saga's claim for Rognvald's fighting ten battles in Russia where he was held in the highest regard by Jaroslav and in whose service he 'defended the country in the summers, but stayed in Novgorod over the winter'.

With the benefit of just those few more precise details, it already becomes possible to elaborate upon Snorri's account of Harald's entry into his career as a Varangian. There is, first of all, a useful geographical indication in the saga reference to Rognvald's company going directly to Novgorod because it points to their ships' having passed through the Gulf of Finland and continued along the waterway to Lake Ladoga where Staraja Ladoga (or *Aldeigjuborg* in the Norse) represented the most usual port of entry for Scandinavian arrivals in Russia.

Staraja Ladoga had long been a centre of great importance on Russia's Baltic coast, and not least by reason of its proximity to the Finno-Ugrian peoples of the northern forests from whom the Rus obtained the furs they needed for trading along the east-way, initially by way of the Volga to Bulghar, and later down the Dnieper to the lucrative market of Byzantium. Archaeological evidence has identified Staraja Ladoga as the site of the earliest settled Scandinavian presence in Russia, so it must have been one of the very first fortified trading-posts known as *goroda* (from which term, of course, is derived the Norse name of *Garðar*) and, assuredly also by the eleventh century, one of the wealthiest. Indeed, lordship of Ladoga had been the bride-price asked of Jaroslav by Ingigerd when she arrived in Russia for their wedding and, once granted, she immediately conferred it upon Rognvald Ulfsson who had been her escort on the journey from Sweden. Formerly jarl of Gautland, Rognvald thus became 'jarl' (according to the saga, but perhaps more properly styled *boyar* in this Russian context) of Staraja Ladoga. Rognvald Ulfsson had died at some point during the decade before Harald reached Russia, however, and been succeeded in the lordship by his son Eilif who is already styled *jarl* in *Orkneyinga saga*, so when Rognvald Brusason's company sailed on from Ladoga to follow the River Volkhov down to Novgorod (called by its Norse name of *Holmgarð* in the sagas), Eilif Rognvaldsson probably travelled with them to provide an escort for distinguished visitors to Jaroslav's court.

It is at this point that a cautious reading between the lines of *Orkneyinga saga* would indicate Harald and Rognvald Brusason having been differently assigned in Russian service. Rognvald, first of all, would already have been known to Jaroslav as a prominent member of King Olaf's retinue in Novgorod just two years earlier and the clear inference from the saga is of his having been recruited to Jaroslav's own *druzhina*, and not only 'out of respect for the holy king' when he himself was held in high regard on his own account and was to offer such sterling service through the ten 'teeming arrow-storms' recalled by Arnor's verses. Interestingly, Arnor's use of the term 'arrow-storm' might be read in this instance as a more specific reference than a stock skaldic kenning, because Jaroslav's pressing military concern in the mid-1030s was the defence of Kiev and the middle Dnieper against the Pechenegs of the steppe whose characteristic and most feared warrior-type was the mounted archer.

To which should be added a reminder that Rognvald was an Orkneyman, which would have neatly excepted him (but not Harald) from 'all the Norwegians' who were assigned to Eilif 'to take over the defences of Gardariki'. In fact, there is good reason to believe that Eilif would have been in need of Varangian reinforcements in the summer of 1031 because an entry in the *Primary Chronicle* under the previous year records that 'Jaroslav attacked the Chuds and conquered them'. The Chuds, whose territory lay in what is now Estonia, were one of the numerous Finno-Ugrian tribes of importance to the Rus as the source, either by way of trade or tribute, of the greatly prized furs, so Jaroslav's 'conquest' of the Chuds would have been a campaign to impose or to enforce the rendering of just such tribute.

Presumably by reason of their strange tongue and shamanic culture, these Finno-Ugrian denizens of the northern forests and sub-Arctic tundra were believed by the northmen to be possessed of sinister occult powers, as was evidenced by the weapon-proof reindeer coats Thore Hund acquired from the Lapps to armour himself and his housecarls at Stiklestad. Similar beliefs were apparently shared by the Rus and yet, while these peoples must have first appeared as shadowy hunter-gatherers magically materialising out of the dark forests, some of their kind nonetheless represented a formidable military presence and one which reflected the influence of warrior cultures from the steppes. Indeed, some Finno-Ugrian tribes boasted their own warrior elites, not least among these the Chuds who are known to have been recruited as mercenary auxiliaries by the Rus in Vladimir's time.

There is every likelihood, then, that Jaroslav's campaign of 1030 – whether of initial conquest or in retribution for refusal of tribute already imposed – would have been hard fought against fierce resistance. If only by reason of the proximity of Staraja Ladoga, Eilif's forces would have formed a part of Jaroslav's host, but the further implication of the saga evidence is of Eilif Rognvaldsson as Jaroslav's *voevoda* in the north, effectively commander-in-chief of all the forces of the principalities of Novgorod and Staraja Ladoga and thus most prominently involved in the campaign against the Chuds.

In which case, his Varangians, who invariably bore the heat and burden of such warfaring, may have sustained heavy losses and so Eilif would have welcomed a newly arrived phalanx of battle-hardened Norwegian housecarls to replenish his mercenary forces – and all the more so when Jaroslav would already have been mustering a great army for another war of conquest.

This campaign, entered in the *Primary Chronicle* under the year 1031, is of key importance here because it represents the one Russian military operation for which there appears to be quite specific evidence of Harald's personal involvement. This evidence is found in lines attributed to Harald's skald Thjodolf and quoted by Snorri which tell of Harald's fighting beside 'Rognvald's son' as they drove hard against the *Læsir* 'to whom harsh terms were given'. *Læsir* is the Norse form of *Liasi* (or *Lyakh* in the Slavonic) by which is meant the Poles, and so Thjodolf's reference is generally accepted as closely contemporary evidence for the involvement of Harald and Eilif in the invasion of Poland by Jaroslav and Mstislav with a large army which 'ravaged the Polish countryside', according to the *Primary Chronicle*, and successfully recaptured the Cherven towns seized by Boleslaw in 1018.

Thjodolf's strophe also makes a more puzzling reference to 'both chieftains' (meaning Harald and Eilif) fighting against an enemy it calls the *Austr-Vinðum*, a people unknown (at least by that name) to any other source and whose identity poses a problem for translators of the saga. The most convincing attempt at translation of *Austr-Vinðum* is probably as 'East Wends', because the Wends (or *Winida* in Old High German, which would reasonably correspond to the Norse *Vinðum*) were a Slavic people settled in north Germany and familiar to the skalds and saga-makers as an enemy of more than one Scandinavian king of the time, so it is not entirely implausible to imagine that an easterly extension of their eleventh-century settlement could have fallen victim to the ravaging Rus in 1031.

What can be said of the Russian invasion is that it was surely prompted by the anarchy (also noticed in some detail by the *Primary Chronicle*) which had convulsed Poland after the death of Boleslaw in the previous year and so offered Jaroslav an ideal opportunity to reclaim the towns which had been a focal point of Russo-Polish contention since their seizure by Vladimir during his westward expansion of the 980s. Indeed, Jaroslav was to take further advantage of Poland's disordered state when he relocated some numbers of Polish prisoners to his own new settlements along the Ros river which formed an extension of Russia's lines of defence against the mounting tide of Pecheneg hostilities – and there is reason to believe that it was in this more southerly theatre of operations that Harald was to spend the later period of his Russian service.

While the date of Harald's arrival in Russia can be securely placed in the summer of 1031 and the date of 1034 is generally accepted by historians for his arrival in Constantinople, the saga record supplies scarcely any indication, and still less detail, of his activities during the intervening three years. Indeed, were it not for the reference to *Læsir* made by the skald Thjodolf history would have no evidence for his involvement in the Polish campaign of 1031. The other skaldic strophe quoted by Snorri provides even less helpful detail in its fairly formulaic paean of praise for Harald's military accomplishment in Russia and, indeed, would seem to add to the uncertainty with its couplet bearing on the duration of Harald's stay in Russia: 'You were the next, and the next after year, O warlike one, in Gardar.'

In fact, there is a question mark over authorship of this strophe when Snorri ascribes it to Bolverk Arnorsson and the same lines quoted in *Fagrskinna* are attributed to Valgard of Voll. Less is known of Valgard than of Bolverk, who is thought to have been a brother of the more famous Thjodolf, but both are reliably included in the list of Harald's court-poets and so the historical authority of the lines in no way depends on the precise identity of their author. Their implication for the duration of Harald's stay in Russia would seem to pose a problem, though, because, as Sigfús Blöndal observed in his study of the Varangians, the reference could be taken to mean that Harald spent no more than the two years after Stiklestad in Russia, although neither Snorri nor the *Fagrskinna* author reads it that way. Indeed, Snorri claims that Harald spent 'several years in Gardariki and made expeditions east of the Baltic', a statement convincingly interpreted by Blöndal as evidence for his being 'employed on the arduous *pólútasvarf*'.[3] By this term *pólútasvarf* (which will occur again at a crucial point in Harald's Varangian service) is meant the winter round of tribute-gathering from subject peoples conducted by the *druzhina*, which would have been accompanied by Varangian mercenaries. These expeditions, conducted on horseback and by sled along frozen rivers in the depth of the northern winter, would have been an arduous duty indeed and probably a dangerous one too, when the least welcome could be expected from hosts confronted with the demands of heavily armed representatives of a distant overlord.

As to the dating problem implied by 'the next, and the next after year . . . in Gardar', Blöndal's suggestion that the reference may have applied only to the period of Harald's stay with Eilif in Novgorod would seem to provide the most plausible explanation – and one with further bearing on Harald's Russian service when it makes all the more apparent the liberties taken by Snorri Sturluson with the source material he had drawn from the Orkney *Jarls' saga*. Assuming, of course, that the *Jarls' saga* account has been accurately preserved in *Orkneyinga saga* (and there is no reason to think otherwise), then Snorri stands accused of gross exaggeration in his claim for Harald having shared command of Russian forces with Eilif Rognvaldsson. What *Orkneyinga saga* actually says is that all the Norwegians who had come to Novgorod with Rognvald Brusason joined Eilif's forces, and presumably in the capacity of Varangian mercenaries. Thus their taking over the 'defences of Gardariki' only makes sense if 'Gardariki' is understood to mean Jaroslav's northern dominions centred upon Novgorod, which would also correspond to Eilif's sphere of command as Jaroslav's *voevoda* but still falls a long way short of responsibility for defence of all the lands of the Rus.

So too, the skaldic reference to Harald fighting beside Eilif – 'in phalanx tight with Rognvald's son' being the literal translation – need mean nothing more than his having been in action with Eilif's forces, even though his personal qualities and royal kinship would have very probably have afforded him a status beyond that of a rank-and-file warrior, even placing him in some capacity of command, if only over the new Norwegian Varangian recruits to whom he would already have been a familiar comrade-in–arms. While Rognvald Brusason was almost certainly admitted to Jaroslav's *druzhina*, there cannot be said to be any real evidence for Harald's serving in Russia in any other capacity than that of a Varangian mercenary, albeit one recognised for his remarkable qualities even by the Grand Prince Jaroslav himself. A couplet attributed to the skald Thjodolf, although preserved only in *Flateyjarbók* and not quoted by Snorri, would seem to allude to just this point in Harald's career when it tells how 'Jarisleif saw the way in which the king [Harald] was developing; the fame grew of the holy king's [Olaf's] brother'.

The relationship between Harald and Jaroslav, founded on genuine mutual respect and sustained over more than a decade, was certainly formed before Harald left for Byzantium. His military qualities might even have come to Jaroslav's notice during the Polish campaign, but the skald's reference to his growing fame would seem to suggest a later date for Jaroslav's recognition of the true potential of this unusually ambitious seventeen-year-old Varangian. At some point between his service with Eilif and his departure for Byzantium, Harald had evidently gravitated southward from Novgorod to Kiev which served as the focal point of assembly for Russian trading fleets bound down the Dnieper route to the Black Sea and the beckoning marketplaces of *Grikaland* (literally the 'land of the Greeks'), as the empire of the Byzantines was known to the northmen.

Kiev's key location along the east-way to Byzantium was the reason for its displacement of Novgorod as the new capital centre of the Rus towards the end of the ninth century. The earlier prominence of Novgorod derived from its proximity to the northern source of furs and its access to the Volga route along which they could be traded for silver from the east. But the progress of the Rus in that direction was so constrained by the might of the Bulgars on the middle Volga and the power of the Khazars (a highly sophisticated people of Turkic origin) along its lower reaches that they were rarely able to venture further south than the great marketplace of Bulghar. So it was that their trade with the Arabs was largely conducted through powerful 'middle men' in an arrangement demanding great outlay of effort in return for suspiciously chiselled profits, whereas the Dnieper route to Constantinople promised direct dealing with the famously wealthy Greeks in a market ever eager for the most exotic and luxurious of merchandise.

The Rus were still northmen in character and culture throughout the ninth century, and so it was only to be expected that their first contact with Byzantium – launched from Novgorod in 860 – was as viking raiders, but the mighty walls of Constantinople (or *Miklagarð* as it was called in the Norse) and the fire-breathing warships of the imperial fleet had driven off the raid of 860 as they were to do again on occasions through the following two centuries. Trading, rather than raiding, was clearly going to be the safer and more profitable approach to the Greeks, as would be confirmed by the generous trade treaties (of which the texts, terms and names of signatories still survive) made by the Byzantines with the Rus in 907 and 911.

Hence the new importance of Kiev, standing high above the point where the northern riverways flow into the broad stream of the Dnieper and already established not only as a Slav settlement but apparently also as a tribute-collection point for officials of the Khazar khans. The *Primary Chronicle* tells of the Rus seizure of Kiev during the infancy of Rurik's son Igor – the first reliably historical prince of the Rus and great-grandfather of Jaroslav – but only in the form of folk-tales which would be of little value were it not for the apparent authenticity of its claim that the Slavs, who themselves had only been on the Dnieper since the seventh century, were happy to welcome the Rus as their overlords instead of the displaced Khazars. Indeed, the Slavs were to have a key role in the annual supply of the vessels – called *monoxyla* and of typically Slav design as a single hollowed-out tree trunk, much like a giant dug-out canoe before it was built up and widened with planking – which formed the merchant fleets for the voyage from Kiev down the Dnieper to the Black Sea and Constantinople. It is unlikely, however, that Harald would have gone directly from Novgorod to Byzantium by way of Kiev in 1034 and much more probable that he had been earlier drawn south by the demand for mercenary forces in the region of the middle Dnieper.

There is evidence in the saga record for the custom of the Rus in Jaroslav's time having been to hire their Varangians on a contractual basis, providing their maintenance over a twelve month period and, upon its completion, rewarding their services either in coin or in kind, usually in the form of furs which had been rendered as tribute or taken as plunder. If such had been the case with Harald and the other Norwegians recruited by Eilif in the summer of 1031, a twelve months' contract would not only have covered their service on the Polish campaign and the winter round of *pólútasvarf*, but possibly also on the expedition of 1032 from Novgorod to the 'Iron Gates', by which is meant the domain of the Ob-Ugrian tribes in the far north-eastern region of the Pechora river under the Urals. The most remote of all the Finno-Ugrian peoples, these were considered so terrifying that Russian tradition believed them to have been locked behind iron (or copper) gates until the Day of Judgement and, indeed, a similar expedition to the Ob river beyond the Urals disappeared entirely without trace in 1079.

Whether or not Harald and his Varangians were engaged on so daunting an enterprise before their contract expired, they evidently survived the experience to be rewarded with their payment due from the proceeds of tribute collected through the winter. By the later summer of 1032, then, they would have been free to enter mercenary service elsewhere and the most promising opportunity is indicated by the entry under that year in the *Primary Chronicle* which notices that 'Jaroslav began to found towns along the Ros'. Jaroslav's intended policy of re-settlement of his Polish captives along the Ros river had already been mentioned in the chronicle entry under the previous year and this new entry confirms its implementation.

Something more needs to be said about this, however, because the foundation of townships along the Ros was just one component of a wider policy for defence of the middle Dnieper which had come under increasing pressure from incursions by Pecheneg raiders. These Pechenegs were just one of a long sequence of Turkic-speaking nomad warrior tribes, which had begun with the Huns and was to culminate in the Mongol invasion, who swept westward across the vast swathe of grassland known as the steppe which extended over some five thousand miles of Eurasia from Manchuria in the east to the Hungarian plain.

This steppe provided the natural domain of a people who were constantly on the move, settling only in tent encampments, and whose livelihood depended upon their livestock, cattle and sheep bred for meat, fleece and hide, and most importantly upon the hardy ponies which served as well for following flocks and herds across great distances as for lightning raids upon the more sedentary peoples whose lands were overrun by the nomad warriors. 'We cannot fight them,' replied the Magyars of Hungary to a Byzantine suggestion that they should rise against the Pechenegs, 'because their land is vast, their people are numerous, and they are the devil's brats!' Such, then, was the new presence faced by the Rus in the last decades of the ninth century when, having only recently broken the power of the Khazars to gain control over the trade route to Byzantium, the Pechenegs irrupted on to the steppe north of the Black Sea in their drive towards the fertile plains of Hungary.

Ferocious raiders who fought with lance and spear, sabre and hand-axe, their most characteristic weapon was the composite bow formed of a light wood (or, better still, bamboo) core strengthened with horn and bound with sinew, painstakingly bonded with glues and skilfully shaped into a curved weapon, much smaller than the northern self-bow (such as the traditional English longbow) and yet of equal power, more efficient and perfectly designed to fill every requirement of the mounted archer. Whether as friend, at least of a sort, or more often as foe, the influence of the Pecheneg steppe warrior had a dramatic impact on the character of the Rus, and not exclusively in terms of military practice, although it was probably first apparent in the urgent adoption of cavalry warfare by a people whose ancestors had always fought on foot.

While the first Scandinavian venturers into Russia, who would have crossed the Baltic after the spring thaw, found their ships perfectly suited to a system of rivers up to half a mile wide and linked by overland portages across which clinker-built craft were easily carried or rolled on logs by their crews, they would soon have discovered that the same routes, when hard-frozen through the winter, could serve equally well as thoroughfares between impenetrable forest for warriors travelling on horseback or by horse-drawn sled. Horse travel is one thing, of course, and cavalry warfare quite another, so the Rus on the Dnieper must have lost no time in adapting to the new presence of fighting-men who spent virtually their entire lives, whether at work or at war, in the saddle. The influence of the steppe warrior culture on the Rus becomes most vividly apparent in the second half of the tenth century and in the person of Jaroslav's grandfather, the warlike Sviatoslav of Kiev who inflicted a number of defeats on the Pechenegs and yet is known – most graphically from a first-hand Byzantine account – to have adopted the style and appearance of a steppe khan. Ironically enough, when he had included a Pecheneg contingent (as allies or as mercenaries) in the host he led on his last campaign to the lower Danube, Sviatoslav was making his desolate homeward retreat, following his surrender to the Byzantines, when he was slain by Pechenegs as he passed up the same Dnieper rapids where Rus convoys heavy-laden with goods for Constantinople faced the choice of paying off a Pecheneg ambush or hiring a Varangian escort to fight it off.

By contrast to the devastating sweep of later Mongol hordes, the effectiveness of the Pecheneg incursions lay in repeated raiding until the social order of the afflicted territory collapsed under the unrelenting strain. Such was the character of their campaign against the middle Dnieper where it made agricultural settlement almost impossibly difficult, and to oppose it Sviatoslav's son and eventual successor Vladimir devised a system of earthworks some 3 or 4 metres in height, their interiors reinforced by logs laid parallel to the rampart which was fronted by ditches up to three times as wide.

During the last twenty-five years of his reign, Vladimir erected some 300 miles of these defences, known as the Snake Ramparts, which were raised just too high for a steppe pony to clear at its full speed and so intended to slow down the nomad horsemen, denying them the advantage of a surprise attack and obstructing their line of retreat while Rus warriors came in pursuit. Fortified strongpoints were added to this defensive network, similarly constructed as earthwork with timber reinforcement and built at points along the line of ramparts, some of which were large enough to accommodate a cavalry squadron, which itself attests the new accomplishment of the Rus in mounted warfare. Within this defended region of the middle Dnieper, Vladimir established a number of fortified towns as well as unfortified settlements, all of them peopled with thousands of settlers brought in from subject and conquered tribes such as the Slovenes and the Chuds.

Impressively reassuring as they must have been to the Rus and their settlers, the Snake Ramparts would seem to have offered as much a provocation as a deterrent to the Pechenegs, who considered the Dnieper valley their own summer grazings, so their incursions continued and with a renewed vigour during the wars of succession which followed Vladimir's death. In consequence, and despite his preference for Novgorod and the north, Jaroslav's attention was drawn down to his southern frontier along the Dnieper where he followed his father's example in extending the Snake Ramparts and establishing new townships, such as those along the Ros where he settled prisoners from his Polish conquest. Relocation of prisoners of war, and presumably in some numbers, was a military operation requiring larger forces than the *druzhina*, who would probably have considered it a duty beneath their dignity anyway. Neither was it a short-term operation, because the newly settled communities would probably need some measure of supervision and no less a measure of armed protection should Pechenegs make an appearance. The solution, as always for Jaroslav, would have been to recruit Varangians and so Harald and his company, not only veterans of the Polish campaign but also experienced in dealing with subject peoples, would have been the ideal choice. To which can be added just one key fragment of evidence and it is supplied by Adam of Bremen, probably Harald's most hostile historian but who can still offer occasional items of information preserved in no other source, such as his reference to Harald having 'fought many battles with the Saracens by sea [in Byzantine service] and the Scythians by land'.

The Scythians were one of the very earliest steppe warrior peoples, although of Iranian rather than Turkic origin, and first recorded north of the Black Sea in the seventh century BC, flourishing thereafter until they were displaced by the Sarmatians three hundred years later. Although there had been no Scythians around for fourteen centuries by the time Adam was writing, the name was still retained in literary currency as a generic term for 'barbarians'. Byzantine writings, for example, are known to refer to Varangians as 'Tauro-Scythians', meaning 'northern barbarians', but in its eleventh-century usage the term 'Scythian' almost invariably meant Pechenegs. Even though it is not entirely beyond possibility that Harald could have encountered Pechenegs during the earlier years of his Byzantine service, he was very much more likely to have done so in Russia on the Dnieper and there, while he would certainly have run the risk of ambush on the way to Byzantium, his greatest likelihood of meeting them in 'many battles' was while engaged on the Ros and the Snake Ramparts.

For all Jaroslav's efforts, the Pecheneg menace remained undiminished through the mid-1030s, coming to its point of crisis in 1036 when the death of Mstislav left something of a hiatus on the middle Dnieper. Jaroslav was in the north and more immediately engaged with the installation of his eldest surviving son, Vladimir, as prince of Novgorod, when a Pecheneg host seized the opportunity to besiege Kiev. In response, 'Jaroslav gathered a large army of Varangians and Slovenes' (according to the *Primary Chronicle*) and came south to lift the siege. In a ferocious battle fought into the evening on the fields outside the city he inflicted a crushing defeat which effectively marked the end of the Pecheneg ascendancy because within twenty years they had been driven from the Russian steppe by the next wave of Turkic warrior nomads, a people known to the Rus as Polovtsy and to the Byzantines as Cumans, although they called themselves the Kipchaks.

This triumph over the Pechenegs would have served as a fitting climax to the ten 'arrow-storms' in which Rognvald Brusason is said to have fought so valiantly for Jaroslav, had not the Orkneyman returned with the young prince Magnus who had been invited back to Norway as his father's successor the year before. Neither could the saga-makers include the victory at Kiev among Harald Sigurdsson's Russian battle-honours because by 1036 he had already been some two years in Byzantine service.

It was love for a woman which prompted Harald's departure for Constantinople, at least according to the 'Separate' version of his saga in *Flateyjarbók* which tells how he was refused the hand in marriage of Jaroslav's daughter Elizaveta until he had won greater wealth and glory. More recent historical opinion casts doubt upon the dating of the *Flateyjarbók* story, because Elizaveta – who is known in the sagas by her Norse name-form of *Ellisif* and called 'the bracelet-goddess in Gardar' in Harald's own poetry – was scarcely ten years old in 1034. Nonetheless, the couple were eventually to be married, although not until Harald had returned from Constantinople a full decade later, so there may indeed have been some sort of prior arrangement because Jaroslav evidently made a habit of marrying his daughters to foreign magnates and Harald was, by that time, preparing his return to claim kingship in Norway.

Whatever promises might have been made to him in 1034, the more immediate motive behind Harald's further venture along the east-way was assuredly his great desire (a greed freely admitted in his sagas) for fame and riches which, as he would have heard from others returned from Varangian service in the east, were generously available to a warrior such as he in the land of the Greeks. The promise of such wealth would likewise have been the lure for his comrades-in-arms, because Snorri's *Harald's saga* tells of his arrival in Constantinople 'with a large following' of fighting-men, which would have comprised his Varangian troop in Russia, probably still including those of Olaf's housecarls who had come to Russia with Rognvald and been recruited alongside Harald into Eilif's forces.

For these men, Harald Sigurdsson would surely have also offered a natural leader and not only by reason of his kinship to Olaf and descent from Harald Fair-hair, because he would by now have been a truly formidable fighting-man in his own right. Harald is well known to have been exceptionally tall (even allowing for exaggeration in the saga estimate of his height at 'five ells' or seven feet six inches). Although he was scarcely nineteen years of age when he left Russia, it is salutary to remember that Cnut had been much the same age when he fought his way to kingship of England in 1015 and, in strictly military terms, Harald was the more widely experienced of the two. He had been just fifteen when he fought at Stiklestad and there is nowhere any indication of his being discouraged by what he had seen there of the realities of warfare, although there can be little doubt that the death of Olaf – which Harald himself may well have witnessed at first-hand – assuredly cut a long, deep scar in his psyche. Both mentally and physically then, he was ideally equipped by nature for the profession of arms and, while his first experience of battle would have corresponded to the expectations instilled by the heroic culture in which he had been raised, a more expansive education – and not only in the way of the warrior – awaited him in Russia.

While the distinctly Scandinavian atmosphere in Novgorod and Ladoga – where, for example, the Norse tongue was to be heard spoken – would not have been so very unfamiliar, he would have been increasingly aware of the advance of Slavic influence on the Rus, and not least in the orbit of Jaroslav's court. Not so much farther afield, he would have encountered the Balt and Finno-Ugrian peoples, while further south – as, for example, on the Polish campaign – Harald was to become much more widely acquainted with the variety of cultures which had already exerted their influence on the Rus, and not least in the military sphere. There is, of course, no way of knowing the extent to which Harald himself was similarly influenced, in particular as regards his weaponry and war-gear, although it was usually characteristic of the mercenary employed abroad to bring his own style of arms and armour with him and afterwards to return home with those of the warriors with whom he had fought. Harald may very well have brought a sword to Russia, but probably little else unless he had been supplied with a helmet and mail-coat at the Swedish court. It is more than likely, of course, that he would have equipped himself with new war-gear among the Rus, where the more fashionable members of a *druzhina* displayed the influence of both Byzantium and the steppe in their adoption of *lamellar* armour (formed of upward-overlapping metal, horn or leather plates laced together with leather thongs), in the decorated metalwork of their helmets, or even in their use of the typically Turkic single-edged curved sabre.

Interestingly though, Varangian warriors would seem to have stayed loyal to the ring-mail, the double-edged straight-bladed sword and, most especially, the characteristic battle-axe they had known and used in the northland, so it can be fairly safely assumed that Harald and his troop would have been similarly armed when they left for Byzantine service. The most likely Russian influence would probably have been on their more basic clothing, where straight-legged Scandinavian trousers would long since have been replaced with the baggy Slav style adopted by the Rus, while fur cloaks which had proved their worth in sub-Arctic winters would soon realise a new value in the marketplaces of Grikaland.

As to Harald's choice of route to Byzantium, the version of his saga in *Morkinskinna* supplies its own unfortunate illustration of the hazards awaiting a saga-maker who misunderstands the evidence he finds in skaldic poetry. Having read Thjodolf's description of Harald's march through 'the land of the *Langbards*' and Illugi Bryndælskald's mention of his combat with Franks, the author of the *Morkinskinna* saga picked up other skaldic references to construct a route which took Harald from Russia, through Wendland in northern Germany, to France and on to Lombardy in the north of Italy before he reached Constantinople. Thjodolf's apparent reference to Wends has already been considered here, but his reference to *Langbardaland* actually meant the Byzantine province of *Longobardia* in southern Italy and not Lombardy in the north. Similarly, by *Frakkar*, or 'Franks', Illugi was referring to the

French Norman mercenaries who mutinied from Byzantine forces in Sicily to join a revolt raised against imperial lordship in the south of Italy. Thus neither skald was referring to the route of Harald's journey to Constantinople in 1034, but both were actually celebrating his service with the Varangians of Byzantium in the southern Italian campaign of 1040.

Although no saga source specifically says as much (perhaps because the voyage to Byzantium was considered insufficiently remarkable for the skalds to notice in such detail), it is virtually certain that Harald's way to Constantinople followed the same Dnieper route taken by the Rus merchant fleets which he would have seen being assembled when he looked down from the Snake Ramparts raised to protect the fortified marshalling yard at Vitichev some 28 miles downriver from Kiev. The most thorough description of this Dnieper route is that contained in *De Administrando Imperio*, a treatise written for the education of his son by the Byzantine emperor Constantine VII in the mid-tenth century, which tells how tribute-collection began in the November of each year and how the furs and slaves thus acquired were brought down the various rivers flowing into the Dnieper around Kiev. There the tribute became the cargo loaded aboard the *monoxyla*, similarly brought to Kiev where they were sold to the Rus by Slav boat-makers, which formed the merchant fleet setting out downriver in June and bound for the Black Sea.

The one item of closely contemporary evidence for Harald's arrival at Constantinople is found in a strophe by the skald Bolverk which would fully correspond to his having followed the Dnieper route, and yet unmistakably indicates his ships having been of Scandinavian type, possibly including *knorr* if they were also shipping any quantity of goods for trade, but with warrior crews and rather more dignity than would have attended the barge-like *monoxyla*. Even so, their own craft would still need skill and care in the handling, especially when they reached the notorious stretch of rapids along the lower Dnieper, some of which required crews to climb overboard so as to manhandle their vessels between rocks and others where the cargo had to be unloaded and the boat carried along the bank by its crew while guards kept careful watch for a Pecheneg ambush.

Steppe raiders were still a hazard on the passage through the last of the rapids, fast flowing but also fordable and vulnerable to attack from archers on the overlooking cliffs. Beyond this point and out of danger from predators, the craft could be brought to shore and their crews rested on St Gregory's Island before continuing out into the Black Sea where the course held close to the shoreline until it reached the Danube estuary and there turned southward across open sea to the Bosporus – and it would seem to be this passage which is described by Bolverk in his strophe celebrating Harald's first sight of the Byzantine capital:

> Bleak gales lashed prows
> hard along the shoreline.
> Iron-shielded, our ships
> rode proud to harbour.
> Of Miklagard, our famous prince
> first saw the golden gables.
> Many a sea-ship, fine arrayed,
> swept toward the high-walled city.

Byzantine Empire, 1034–1041

'At that time, the empire of the Greeks was ruled by Queen Zoe the Great with Michael Katalakos.' Thus Snorri Sturluson begins his account of Harald in Byzantium, and with a sentence which supplies a key item of evidence for the date of his arrival in Constantinople while also introducing two personalities who are attributed particular significance for his subsequent career in imperial service.

The extraordinary Zoe – more properly, of course, styled Empress than 'Queen' – would seem to have figured no less prominently in Varangian tradition than in the formal history of Byzantium. As one of the three daughters of the dissolute emperor Constantine VIII, Zoe was *porphyrogenita* ('born into the [imperial] purple') and thus empress in her own right, as well as conferring the imperial title upon no fewer than three husbands and ruling jointly, albeit briefly, with her younger sister Theodora.[4] In 1002, and while still an attractive young princess, Zoe had been promised in marriage to the Holy Roman Emperor Otto III, but he died before the ceremony could be solemnised and more than a quarter of a century was to pass before the imminent demise of her ailing father made it imperative that a husband be found for her so as to ensure the succession. Consequently, she was almost fifty at the time of her first marriage, in the year 1028, to the elderly Byzantine aristocrat Romanus Argyrus who relinquished his own wife to accept the union only under extreme duress and just in time to become the new emperor Romanus III following the death of his father-in-law on the very day after the wedding. Hardly surprisingly, and despite application of all available medical alchemy, the marriage bed proved barren and was soon deserted by Romanus for that of a mistress. Already humiliated, Zoe was further enraged by being deprived access to the imperial treasury and first vented at least some of her fury on her sister Theodora, whom she despatched to a nunnery in 1031 before she herself fell prey to the sinister ambitions of John the Orphanotrophus.

A eunuch who had risen from modest origins in Paphlagonia on the southern shore of the Black Sea to the prestigious office of director of the capital's principal orphanage, John presented his youngest brother Michael to the embittered empress, who found the handsome teenager so irresistibly attractive that she took him as her lover and the city buzzed with rumours of poisoning when her estranged husband soon afterwards succumbed to an inexplicable illness. Romanus had been found dead in his bath-house only hours before the Patriarch of Constantinople was summoned to the palace at dawn on Good Friday, 12 April in the year 1034, to join the newly widowed empress in marriage to a man almost forty years her junior and to consecrate him as the Emperor Michael IV.

By virtue of that precise record of the date of consecration of a new Byzantine emperor, Snorri's statement that the empire was 'ruled by Zoe the Great and Michael Katalakos' at the time of Harald's arrival in Constantinople firmly places it after the Easter of that year. Incidentally, Snorri's use of the cognomen 'Katalakos' indicates Varangian tradition as his source of information, because Michael IV was formally known as 'the Paphlagonian' and *Katalak* represents the Norse form of his popular nickname *Parapinakes*, meaning 'clipper of the coinage' and deriving from his family's trade of silversmith while also making allusion to his own alleged practice of devaluing the currency.

A more specific timing for Harald's appearance in the Byzantine capital might be deduced from what is known of the seasonal organisation of traffic along the Dnieper route. The Rus trading fleets customarily set out from Kiev in June to allow their return from Constantinople before the rivers froze up again in the autumn and also because the water level reached the point best suited for negotiation of the rapids at that time of year. For that reason alone, Harald would quite certainly have chosen the month of June for his own departure. The duration of the voyage from Kiev to Constantinople has been estimated at some ten weeks and so – even allowing for his sea-ships having made a better time on the Black Sea crossing than the more cumbersome *monoxyla* – Harald would have been unlikely to have reached his destination before August.

In fact, that estimate of his time of arrival would correspond perfectly well to Snorri's placing Harald's first assignment as a Varangian mercenary in Byzantine service in 'that same autumn', but perhaps less convincing is the saga-maker's claim for Harald's presenting himself to Zoe immediately upon his arrival in Constantinople. While it is scarcely likely that a *porphyrogenita* empress would have made herself available for duty as a receptionist for mercenary recruits, it is perhaps just possible that she might have granted an audience to a warrior prince of distinguished Norse descent and held in high esteem by the Grand Prince of Kiev.

Such would seem to be the only plausible explanation of Snorri's account – and yet the other saga sources suggest a quite different situation when they tell of Harald's attempt to conceal his true identity in Constantinople on account of the Byzantine policy of discouraging high-born recruits in their mercenary forces. For that reason, he is said by *Morkinskinna* and *Flateyjarbók* to have entered imperial service under the pseudonym *Nordbrikt*, which aroused the suspicions of an Icelander in command of a detachment of the Varangian Guard to the point where he tried, albeit unsuccessfully, to discover Harald's real name from Halldor Snorrason. That reference alone would point to Halldor as the original source of the story and might be thought to endorse its authenticity, were it not for a closely contemporary document – known as the *Book of Advice to an Emperor* and dated to the 1070s – which has no hesitation in confirming Harald's true identity and distinguished kinship having been known to the Byzantines, while also confirming Michael IV as the reigning emperor who received Harald 'with a proper courtesy' upon his arrival in Constantinople.

This account of *Araltes* (calling him, of course, by his Greek name-form) is considered the most authoritative record of his Byzantine service, and not least because its anonymous author mentions having served alongside Harald in the Bulgarian campaign of 1041, yet it appears to make no reference to his military activities prior to the invasion of Sicily which was launched in 1038. What is known of the earlier years of his Byzantine career, during which he appears to have served as a Varangian mercenary before his promotion to the Varangian Guard proper, derives from the skalds and the saga-makers, whose evidence requires some measure of corroboration by the more formal historical record.

As before in Russia, Snorri is equally impatient in Byzantium to promote Harald to the highest possible level of command, even to that of the 'acknowledged leader of all the Varangians', a statement which closer examination places under some measure of doubt. Whether or not Harald really was welcomed to Constantinople by the emperor or empress, there appears to have been nothing at all unusual about his entry into their service as a Varangian mercenary or in command of the warriors he had brought with him from Russia, who would have formed a unit typical of foreign contingents in the Byzantine armed forces.

The use of foreign fighting-men, under various forms of arrangement, had always been the practice of the Byzantine military and can be recognised as a legacy from the old Roman Empire, of which the new imperium founded upon the ancient Greek city of Byzantium by Constantine the Great in the early fourth century considered itself to be the true successor. This eastern empire, which has long been called 'Byzantine' by historians, was known to the Rus and to the northmen as that of 'the Greeks' (and reasonably so when Greek had replaced Latin as its official language in the early seventh century), yet the Byzantines themselves, almost all of whom were of Greek and Slav ethnicity, still considered themselves 'Romans' (in the Greek form of *Rhomaioi*) in Harald's time. Indeed, the *Advice* tells of 'Araltes, the son of an emperor of Varangia . . . [having] determined to go and pay homage to the most blessed Emperor Michael the Paphlagonian, and to see for himself the ways of the Romans'.

Just as there had been few, if any, Italians in the 'Roman Army' of the western empire through most of its last four hundred years when the greater part of its military comprised fighting-men recruited from the free peoples east of the Rhine, foreign contingents were to make up more than half of the strength of Byzantine forces by the later eleventh century. Even before then, the 'thematic' structure of imperial military organisation, which had first appeared in Asia Minor during the seventh century, had already entered into serious decline. Since the ninth century, the eastern empire had been organised into *themata* (or 'themes') under military governors usually known as *strategoi*, each of whom raised his own army corps on the basis of land held in return for military service. Much like the later western European feudal system, this land-holding was passed from father to son and with it the obligation to provide a soldier, either a family member or a proxy, equipped with arms and armour, as well as his own mount when cavalry represented the principal component of Byzantine land forces.

By the eleventh century, these themes had become the increasingly independent provinces of a land-owning aristocracy, where smaller holdings were absorbed into larger estates supplying a diminishing flow of manpower to the thematic armies. In consequence, the *strategoi* became ever more dependent upon the hire of mercenaries and thus drew in more and more foreign fighting-men to maintain the strength of the forces of the empire: Normans and Italians, Germans and Magyars, Pechenegs and Khazars, Arabs and Slavs, and – most importantly here, of course – Scandinavians who had come from the northlands by way of Russia, thus being known first to the Byzantines as *Tauro-Skuthai* ('Northern-Scythians') and afterwards as *Rhos* (the Greek form of Rus) before they acquired their more celebrated name of *Varangoi* or 'Varangians'. Such mercenaries are on record as early as the reign of Michael III in the 840s and further notices of *Rhos* serving with imperial forces punctuate the chronicles of the following century, especially after the Russo-Byzantine trade agreements of 907 and 911 which actually include provision for a military levy. A reference to two Rus ships with the imperial fleet sent to Italy in 968 represents an early, if not the earliest, item of evidence for the deployment of Varangians in Byzantine naval operations, and is of particular interest here because

Snorri makes specific mention of Harald's first assignment in imperial service having been with the 'fleet in the Greek sea' in the autumn of 1034.

Before investigating that particular passage of his warrior's way in further detail, however, it should be emphasised that all these Varangians – by whatever name they might be called in the Greek sources – represented effectively auxiliary contingents within a larger imperial force and so, while each unit was probably led by one of its own kind, all would have served under the supreme command of a Byzantine general. Indeed, Snorri himself indicates as much when he tells of Harald having 'kept his men together as a separate company' before adding that 'the commander-in-chief of the fleet was a man called *Gyrgir*'. The same *Gyrgir* is mentioned in *Fagrskinna*, where it is explained that this was the Norse name-form of Georgios Maniakes, the outstanding Byzantine general of his time and a figure to whom the sagas attribute a key significance in the course of Harald's Varangian career.

It should be explained that the Varangian mercenaries mentioned thus far were distinct from the 'Varangian Guard' proper, known to the Byzantines as the 'Varangians of the City' and including the emperor's personal bodyguard, which formed its own regiment of the imperial forces based at Constantinople. The longest-standing division of these forces was the *Tagmata*, which comprised four elite regiments of horse, each under its own commander who was usually styled *domestikos*. Not unlike the Household Cavalry of the British army in more recent centuries, the Tagmata's first duty was to serve the emperor as his lifeguard, whether on campaign or in the capital itself where it also performed a range of ceremonial duties, while an associated infantry regiment known as the *Numeri* provided a garrison for defence of the city. Naturally enough, the professional soldiery making up these regiments was largely drawn from the Byzantine Greek aristocracy, yet it was just that characteristic of the Tagmata which brought it under suspicion, and not at all unreasonably in the intrigue-ridden climate of Constantinople where its regiments were openly associated with rival political factions. Consequently, the loyalty of the Tagmata was never considered entirely reliable during times of internal political crisis, and a source of more trustworthy lifeguards was offered by the emperor's own foreign mercenary troops, whose loyalty depended upon nothing more complex than the generosity of their paymaster. Some divisions of these forces were assigned duties in the capital much like those of the Tagmata and thus formed a part of the emperor's lifeguard which became known as the *Hetairia*, of which the best-known component was the Varangian Guard established as a regiment in its own right by Basil II, elder brother of Zoe's father, Constantine VIII.

The eleventh-century Byzantine chronicler Michael Psellus remembers Basil as having been 'well aware of the disloyalty of the Romans' and understandably so because he was just eighteen when he became emperor in 976 and the first dozen years of his reign were plagued by contention with two rival claimants to his imperial crown. That distraction encouraged the ambitious Bulgarian tsar Samuel to extend his dominions at the expense of the Empire and when Basil led an army into Thessaly against him it suffered devastating defeat in a Bulgar ambush at the pass called Trajan's Gate. While Basil would eventually take the ferocious revenge which was to earn him the soubriquet of *Bulgaroctonos* ('Bulgar-slayer'), he was more immediately concerned with the most dangerous of his rivals, Bardas Phocas, whose forces were already converging on Constantinople in 988. With his own military still crippled by the losses inflicted at Trajan's Gate, Basil turned for assistance to Vladimir of Kiev, who supplied him with the force of 6,000 axe-wielding Scandinavian fighting-men which threw back Bardas and his army in the early weeks of 989 and went on to achieve their total destruction at Abydos on the coast of the Dardanelles some three months later.

By way of return for his generosity, Vladimir requested for himself a Byzantine bride – in the person of Basil's sister, the *porphyrogenita* Anna – and even agreed to facilitate the union by accepting conversion of himself and his people to the Orthodox faith. Although Basil was in no hurry to arrange the marriage, which was not solemnised until the summer of 989 and only then after Vladimir had increased the pressure by occupying the Byzantine outpost of Cherson on the Black Sea, he was so greatly impressed by the performance of these *Varangoi* that he formed them into an elite regiment of the Hetairia and the one which was also to provide his own personal bodyguard. So it was that Basil created the celebrated Varangian Guard which was to serve his successor emperors for more than two hundred years until the fall of Constantinople to the Fourth Crusade in 1204.

It is often assumed – sometimes, indeed, actually asserted – that it was this Varangian Guard of which Harald was later to take supreme command. An unsuspecting reading of Snorri's saga might give no less an impression, but it is one emphatically denied by the *Book of Advice to an Emperor* when it supplies precise detail of the ranks which Harald held as an illustration of how it was both unnecessary and undesirable to promote foreigners, however able they might be, to positions of the highest rank. By way of reward for his service in the Sicilian and Italian campaigns, Harald was first appointed to the rank of *manglavites* (which reliably confirms his entry into the 'Varangians of the City') and later promoted to that of *spatharokandidatos* on his return with the emperor from the suppression of the Bulgarian revolt in 1041. While there are references in Byzantine sources to commanders of the Varangian Guard with the title of *Akoluthos* (or 'Acolyte' in the sense of 'follower', presumably of the emperor himself), the officer in command of the *manglavites* held the rank of *protospatharios*, but neither of the two ranks held by Harald approached such seniority. Indeed, their comparatively modest status is unmistakably acknowledged by the author of the *Advice* when he observes with approval that *Araltes* 'did not grumble about the titles of *manglavites* and *spatharokandidatos* with which he had been honoured'.

In fact, no less an authority than Sigfús Blöndal is of the opinion that 'if he held no higher rank in imperial service, then he is unlikely to have ever held independent command of an army larger than the small force needed to reduce a small fortress or minor township'.[5] Just such a 'small force' need not have been so very much larger than the 'five hundred men' said by the *Advice* to have accompanied

Harald on his arrival in Constantinople, although there is no reason to doubt Snorri's claim for new recruits having been attracted to his troop by the growing reputation of its commander, and especially by his well-documented accomplishment in garnering profit by plunder. A mercenary warrior, by definition, fought for financial gain, and there can be little doubt that it was the prospect of great wealth which had brought Harald to the land of the Greeks in the first place – a factor which must never be overlooked in any realistic reconstruction of his military career in Byzantine service.

Having described Harald's arrival in Constantinople, Snorri goes straight on to tell how in the 'same autumn he sailed with some galleys together with the fleet into the Greek sea'. This would seem to have been a customary form of introduction into Varangian service and especially in the early years of the reign of Michael IV when Arab pirates or corsairs (*kussurum* in the Norse of the sagas) represented a persistent menace to ship and to shore throughout the eastern orbit of the Mediterranean.

Byzantine annals for the 1030s record a great fleet from Arab-held Sicily and north Africa raiding the islands of the Aegean, the Greek mainland and the shores of Thrace, even taking the town of Myra in Asia Minor before it was overtaken by a naval force, commanded by the *strategos* of the Cibarrote, which destroyed most of its ships and either butchered or enslaved their crews. The Cibarrote, on the southern coast of Asia Minor, was one of the maritime themes responsible for the upkeep of the 'Fleet of the Themes', which bore much of the responsibility for defence of the Aegean and its surrounding waters against Arab piracy. A similar policing duty was borne by one of the two divisions of the imperial fleet, which was also regularly assigned to naval support of military expeditions (the other division being responsible for transport of the imperial family and defence of the capital).

Foreign mercenaries were often recruited to man the ships of these fleets, many of them being Varangians chosen to begin their service to the Empire in its navy on account of the seafaring and sea-fighting expertise for which the northmen were traditionally renowned. While the capital ships of the fleet (larger vessels known as *dromoi*) were manned by a complement more than two hundred strong and equipped with siphons to unleash the devastating incendiary flare known as 'Greek Fire', the Varangians were more usually deployed to crew the lighter, faster and more manoeuvrable craft called *ousiai* and considered especially effective in pursuit of the similarly speedy lateen-sailed Arab *dhows*. So when Snorri writes of Harald having 'sailed widely around the Greek islands and inflicted heavy damage there upon the corsairs', it would seem virtually certain that he and his company were serving aboard these *ousiai*, each of which carried a crew of about 110 including 50 or more soldiers. Snorri's reference would also indicate his theatre of operations as the Aegean Sea, although there is a further possibility, which may be implied by the *Advice* and is certainly suggested by a reference in one of Harald's own verses to sailing 'on the sea of Sicily . . . with a warrior crew'. Unless this refers to his later involvement with Maniakes' invasion in 1038, it could be taken as evidence for Harald's earlier naval service having included an assignment to the auxiliary fleet stationed off the Sicilian coast by Michael IV to safeguard the seaway between Sicily and North Africa.

For all the efforts of his skalds to portray Harald at sea as a free-spirited viking, he and his men would have been subject to the same command structure as other foreign mercenaries engaged on naval service, taking their orders from officers of the Hetairia who reported in their turn to the *strategos* in command of the Fleet of the Themes or to the admiral directing the operations of an imperial fleet. Nonetheless, the claim made by the skald Bolverk for Harald 'having begun a fight where he wanted to have one' during these early years in Byzantine service might not be entirely without foundation if a superior officer had been sufficiently impressed by Harald's undoubted abilities and rapidly acquired experience to encourage his initiative by allowing him more than usual licence in pursuit of the enemy.

There is also every reason to expect that Harald would have had his own keen financial interest in seeking out and overhauling a well-laden Arab pirate craft, because his saga in *Flateyjarbók* has a precise note of the profit thereby accrued. Just 100 marks was due to the emperor's coffers for every corsair taken, and once that had been rendered any surplus plunder was kept by Harald and his men. Varangians in naval service were paid less generously than those in the Hetairia, so the entitlement to a share of captured booty must have represented a lucrative source of performance-related pay and one of which Harald would certainly have taken full advantage. Although Snorri has nothing to say about this remunerative aspect of Harald's sea-service, he soon has occasion to tell of the 'hoard of money and gold and treasure of every kind' acquired on the subsequent land campaign in 'the parts of *Affrika* which the Varangians call *Serkland*'.

Snorri's source for these references would appear to have been surviving verses by the skald Thjodolf, one of which is actually quoted in the saga, but doubt is cast upon his interpretation of that source material by the absence of any record of a Byzantine expedition to Africa during the reign of Michael IV. When the poetry of the skald represents the most closely contemporary evidence, the disparity between saga account and historical record must be attributed, once again, to a misinterpretation on the part of the saga-maker, which can only derive from the use of the Norse word *Serkir* (often translated as 'Saracen') as a generic term for Arabs and Arabic-speaking peoples, and likewise to the use of *Serkland* for any region of the Islamic conquest wherein they might have been encountered.

Snorri had already mentioned the Byzantine general Georgios Maniakes, even implying his involvement with Harald in the action against Arab corsairs in the Greek islands, and yet, while Maniakes was effectively commander-in-chief of Byzantine forces at that time, he was unlikely to have been in immediate command of naval operations. So when Snorri places an anecdote (which will be considered in more detail later) concerning Harald and Maniakes immediately before the chapter bearing on Serkland, it would suggest that Harald and his troop had been brought ashore when the campaign against the corsairs was extended inland to strike at their support bases in Asia Minor, where there was conflict with the Arabs during the early years of Michael's reign and where Georgios Maniakes and the emperor's brother Constantine, *strategos* of Antioch, were in command of the Byzantine forces.

Having driven the Saracens out of Asia Minor by the end of 1035, the Byzantine campaign pressed on through Armenia and Syria towards the Euphrates and it may well have been that theatre of operations to which Thjodolf referred in his strophe telling of Harald's capture of 'twice-forty towns in Serkland' before he 'bore his war-making to smooth Sicily'. Although the total of 'twice-forty towns' is realistically read only as an approximation – the figure 'eighty' being thought to represent a traditional indication of 'very many' – there is no reason to doubt the placing of these conquests prior to Harald's known involvement in the Sicilian invasion some two years later. Other lines from Thjodolf, preserved in *Flateyjarbók* and probably known to Snorri, although not quoted in the saga, refer to the 'king of Africa' finding it difficult to guard his people against Harald and these may also allude to the campaign in Serkland or, perhaps more probably, to the Caliph of Tunis whose son commanded the Arab forces encountered in the invasion of Sicily. Another half-strophe of skaldic verse, also preserved in *Flateyjarbók* and in *Morkinskinna*, clearly does recall the fighting in Serkland and is worthy of quotation here because it is attributed to Harald himself, although composed in Norway many years after his return from Byzantium.

> One other time there was, when I
> reddened blades from my homeland;
> the sword singing in the Arab town
> – and yet that was long ago.

It has thus far been possible to follow the chronology of Snorri Sturluson's *Harald's saga* in *Heimskringla* quite closely – as, indeed, was my original intention – but his sequence of events through the next five or six years of Harald's Byzantine career diverges so far from that suggested by more reliable historical record as to require some rearrangement here. Snorri may well have already entangled anecdotes refering to the Sicilian invasion of 1038 with others, similarly derived from Varangian tradition, relating to Harald's earlier activities located by the skalds in the regions they know only as 'Serkland'.

At this point in the saga, however, its narrative enters upon a further series of anecdotal accounts concerning four sieges (only one of which is specifically placed in Sicily) preceded by two episodes refering to Harald's contentious relationship with Georgios Maniakes, which might be assigned either to the Sicilian invasion or the earlier campaigning in Asia Minor. The historicity of almost all these stories is dubious at best, especially when none has the support of any skaldic verses, while some of them can be safely dismissed as apocryphal. There is another chapter, however, which quite clearly derives from court-poetry – two strophes quoted in the saga and both attributed to the sightless skald Stúf Kattason – describing Harald in the Holy Land and thus representing reliable evidence for a genuinely historical Varangian assignment, even though its true character is largely disguised by the aggrandising enthusiasm of the skald and the saga-maker.

The initial difficulty with the saga account is Snorri's placing of Harald's journey to the Holy Land after his return from the Sicilian campaign (which had taken him on into southern Italy in its later phase) and thus in the year 1041, when the more reliable evidence of the *Advice* places him in Bulgaria with a contingent of the Varangian Guard accompanying the emperor in suppression of the rebellion. The historical record of the turbulent events crammed into these few months would allow only just enough time for Harald's withdrawal from the Sicilio-Italian theatre, his promotion to the rank of *manglavites*, and his participation in the Bulgarian campaign (all reliably recorded by the author of the *Advice*) and would thus entirely exclude the many weeks required for an expedition as far as Jerusalem.

The first of the strophes accredited to Stúf tells of the 'weapon-bold warrior' having journeyed from Grikaland 'Jerusalem-wards' and of Palestine being rendered 'unburned in submission to his hand', while the second tells of his enforcing justice on both sides of the Jordan, having 'made an end of men's treacheries, inflicting sure trouble for proven crime'. Although evidently derived from these verses, Snorri's account is clearly intended to portray Harald in the guise of a pilgrim making generous offerings at the holy places and enshrined relics, its underlying motive probably being to ensure that its hero was not to be outdone by other northern magnates such as Cnut of Denmark and Jarl Thorfinn of Orkney, both of whom made pilgrimages to Jerusalem in the eleventh century. While the skaldic verses can be taken as authoritative evidence for Harald's journey to the Holy Land, it is their reference to his punishment of criminal elements which might be said to supply the vital clue to what really brought him there.

There is, first of all, no question of his having 'conquered' Palestine for the empire, when relations between Constantinople and the Caliphs of Egypt had been remarkably harmonious since 1027, in which year it had been agreed that the emperor Constantine VIII should be allowed to rebuild the church of the Holy Sepulchre. There had been no further progress in that direction through the last year of the ailing Constantine's reign, nor through that of his immediate successor, Romanus Argyrus, until the succession of Moustansir-Billah to the Caliphate in 1035. Perhaps because he was the son of a Byzantine mother, this new caliph was generously tolerant of other faiths and strongly opposed to religious persecution, having already freed many thousands of Christian captives before he signed a thirty-year peace treaty with Michael IV in the following year. Included in this treaty was a renewal of the agreement to permit restoration of the Holy Sepulchre and so architects, masons and other Byzantine craftsmen were immediately despatched to Jerusalem, escorted on their journey by a troop of Varangians entrusted with their protection from attack by desert bandits. While there is every reason for confidence in the ability of formidable Varangian fighting-men to deal with such predators, their deployment on this escort duty is of particular significance because the choice of such elite soldiery would indicate the working party having been accompanied by very high-ranking pilgrims, probably even members of the imperial family, taking advantage of a rare opportunity to visit the holy places.

The most likely imperial personages to undertake such a pilgrimage were the empress Zoe's sisters Eudocia and Theodora, both of whom were nuns at that time, and their eminence alone would have ensured that all the travellers would have been welcomed with open gates at every point along the journey, a reception naturally interpreted by the skald as the willing 'submission' to Harald as he progressed along the same route. All of which corresponds so well to much of the detail encoded in Stúf's verses as to propose the Varangian escort having been none other than Harald and his troop, a possibility – even if no more than that – which would provide the most plausible basis for Snorri's saga account, and might also have some further bearing on Harald's involvement in events in Constantinople some eight years later.

Allowing for Snorri having misplaced the date of Harald's expedition to Jerusalem, his account may still be correct in its claim for Harald having afterwards returned to the capital, particularly if he had made the journey in the capacity of military escort for *porphyrogenita* pilgrims. All of which might even point to the likelihood of Harald and his troop having already been admitted to the Varangian Guard proper by 1036, quite possibly as a result of their qualities demonstrated on active service in Asia Minor having attracted the attention of the emperor's brother Constantine. In which case, Harald would surely have established himself as a formidable presence in the Varangian ranks by the following year when he and his men were assigned to Georgios Maniakes' forces for the invasion of Sicily – and it is that campaign which offers the most likely setting for the saga accounts of personal contention between two of the most extraordinary soldiers of their time.

Crete had been lost to the Empire two centuries before, following the appearance in the Mediterranean of a fleet carrying 10,000 Muslim warriors who had been first expelled from Andalusia and some years later from Alexandria which they had captured in 818. Once more on the loose in the Middle Sea, they seized Crete, compelling the conversion of its inhabitants to Islam before enslaving them and turning their island into a pirate base for the corsairs who became the terror of the eastern Mediterranean. Within just a couple of years, Saracens had claimed Sicily too, although in this case at the invitation of a Byzantine renegade, a former admiral who rose in revolt after being dismissed from imperial service and sought the support of a North African emir. Thus in 827 a hundred Arab ships were brought to Sicily, the ex-admiral was slain and the island transformed into another, still more vexatious, stronghold of corsairs and forward base for Saracen incursions across the Strait of Messina even to the Dalmatian coast.

The Empire had eventually managed to reclaim Crete in 961, but Sicily remained in Saracen hands. Basil II had been planning its recapture and may well have achieved it had he not died in the year before his fleet was due to sail, so the island remained a threat to the security of Byzantine southern Italy, a plague upon ship-borne trade so important to the imperial economy, and an affront to an empire which still considered itself 'Roman'. Through the decade after Basil's death, however, Saracen Sicily became the battleground for a struggle between its two Arab chieftains, one of whom sought imperial assistance against his brother and rival. In response, the *catepan* (the local equivalent to the title of *strategos* elsewhere in the empire) of Italy was sent to Sicily in 1037, but meanwhile the other brother had appealed for help from the Caliph of Tunis who similarly despatched forces under the able command of his son Abdallah-ibn-Muizz, who attracted increasing support and so well outfought the *catepan* as to force his withdrawal (although in apparently good order) to the Italian mainland. The emperor Michael resolved to try again, and this time with his finest available forces – including 300 Norman mercenaries from Salerno as well as an elite company of Varangians from Constantinople – under the command of his finest general, who was, of course, the afore-mentioned Maniakes.

Said to have been Turkish-born and evidently of lowly origins, Georgios Maniakes was possessed of the physique of a giant and naturally endowed with 'all the attributes of a man born to command . . . a voice of thunder, hands strong enough to shake gates of brass and the scowl upon his face terrible to behold', as recalled by the chronicler Michael Psellus, who knew him personally. For all these qualities, Georgios had climbed only slowly to the peak of command, having started out on his military career as a menial servant – 'among the baggage-men', according to Psellus – but steadily rising through the ranks until he 'attained the highest position open to a soldier'. First emerging as a commander – in the post of *strategos* of the lesser theme of the Euphrates Cities – during the reign of Romanus Argyrus, he rose to real prominence with his capture of the great city of Edessa on the mid-Euphrates in 1032, and so when the emperor Michael appointed him *strategos* of Longobardia he would have had every reason to believe Maniakes capable of achieving no less a triumph in Sicily.

This, then, was the *Gyrgir* who is said by Snorri to have come up against Harald while both were marching overland (although neither the campaign nor its location is specified). The Varangians were the first troops to arrive in the place where it was planned to set up camp for the night and so Harald was able to choose the higher ground, rather than the lower lying marshy land, on which to have his men pitch their tents. When Gyrgir arrived, he immediately ordered their tents taken down so as to make his own camp on the better ground, but Harald refused to comply, insisting on the Varangians' independence of any command other than that of the emperor and empress to whom they had sworn allegiance (a privilege, incidentally, of which there is no known record). An argument between the two was approaching the point of drawn weapons when it was agreed to resolve the matter by the drawing of lots, in which Harald outwitted his superior officer by sleight of hand. Anecdotes based around the same 'triumph by trickery' formula are found so often in Snorri's storytelling – and, indeed, throughout the whole saga literature – that this tale would be considered of dubious authenticity, even if a strikingly similar battle of wills were not to occur in a later passage of this same saga where Harald scores over his nephew Magnus in a dispute over precedence in ship-berthing.

All that is known of the mighty Maniakes, and especially of his merciless mode of military discipline, would put the story itself almost entirely beyond the bounds of credibility, and yet it might still have some genuine basis if it reflects the inevitability of contention between two men possessed of such powerful personalities formed by such dramatically contrasting backgrounds. In the event of such a confrontation, and when Maniakes is said by Psellus to have been so tall that 'men who saw him had to look up as if at the summit of a mountain', it is scarcely likely that any concession would have been made to a young prince, however physically impressive, still in his early twenties and recently arrived out of the north. Indeed, there is much to be said for the trenchant analysis made by Benedikt Benedikz when he suggests that Harald 'as a somewhat undisciplined junior, was rather frequently carpeted by the Chief, and that the smart repartee and spectacular action contained in [the "Separate"] *Harald's saga* and *Heimskringla* alike are much-expanded self-justifications, originally told by Harald and blown up by his flatterers'.[6]

Curiously enough, and especially in view of the prominence accorded him in Snorri's saga, there is no mention of Georgios Maniakes in any surviving skaldic verse, yet the skalds do supply their own further confirmation of Harald's involvement in the invasion of Sicily. Indeed, Valgard of Voll would seem to have been in Harald's company during the later years of his Byzantine service and makes specific reference to the Sicilian campaign when he writes of Harald taking 'a great force south of the broad lands . . . eventually Sicily was depopulated'. So too does Bolverk who would seem to be describing Harald's courageous part in seizing a beach-head for the landing of Maniakes' forces when he tells how 'ships ran to shore and the lord [Harald] fought nobly, winning sand beneath him for a great army in the south of Sicily'.

Just such would have been a fully plausible deployment of Varangians, in view of the renowned Scandinavian accomplishment in seaborne warfare. It is also probable that a troop such as that under Harald's command might have been deployed in the capture of smaller towns or coastal forts (of the type called *ribāt*, many of which were raised in Arab-held Sicily), although the northmen are not known to have used siege engines on their own account and the earlier record of viking sieges invariably attributes their success to guile. Snorri does not put a name to any of the fortified towns which he claims to have fallen to Harald's Varangians, and neither does he indicate even the approximate whereabouts of three of them, specifically locating only one of the sieges in Sicily, and that the most glaring example of what has been called an 'itinerant folk-tale' (meaning a story long current in various different traditions before its attachment to whichever current hero).

In fact, three of his four siege stories might be recognised as tales of that kind, the first of them telling of a Sicilian town which falls to Harald's forces by means of a firestorm contrived by capturing birds who have flown out of the town's buildings, fixing kindling, wax and sulphur to their tails and setting it alight, so as to return the poor creatures to their roosts as flying firebombs. Not only utterly implausible, the story is also notoriously unoriginal when it was also told of Harald's contemporary, the Norman Robert Guiscard in Sicily, of the Russian princess Olga taking revenge upon a Slav town a hundred years earlier, and of the Danish viking Guthrum at the siege of Cirencester in the century before that.

Indeed, similar stories have been attached to Alexander the Great and Genghis Khan, but Snorri's version probably originated in Armenia where the legend was associated with an emir of Baghdad before finding its way into the currency of Varangian tradition, which has been described by the modern authority Omeljan Pritsak as 'a kind of "hatchery" for old Icelandic storytelling'. Pritsak's essay goes on to explain how 'Constantinople was the meeting place for peoples of different cultures, and the higher milieu of the imperial capital stimulated the soldiers to tell stories in which truth and fantasy could be easily combined'.[7]

A great many tales from those same wellsprings were brought back to Iceland by returning Varangians and thus passed down to the saga-makers, by which time some number of them had become attached to the heroic legendry accumulating around Harald. Such was assuredly the source of Snorri's tale of the incendiary birds, as it must likewise have been for the story of Harald's faking his own illness and death so as to enable his Varangians to gain entry into another besieged town with his 'funeral' cortege before casting aside the charade and seizing the victory. It is thought likely that Snorri's version of this tale originated in southern Italy, where it was associated with Robert Guiscard's capture of a monastery, before being picked up by Varangian tradition, yet a similar episode is attached to a more ancient hero by Saxo Grammaticus and other examples are found elsewhere in medieval sources, although usually those informed by Norman tradition.

Snorri's third variation on this same theme tells of Harald having a tunnel dug beneath the town under siege, while maintaining an attack on its walls so as to distract the attention of the defending garrison. This ruse is perhaps more plausible than the first two, but the story is scarcely original when it had been widely current since classical times – and if Harald had been engaged in such a tactic, it would surely have involved Byzantine military engineers and been under the direction of a superior officer. Even so, it is perhaps worth noticing that Snorri once again mentions the 'vast hoard of booty' won by Harald's troops after they had burst out of the tunnel to seize the town.

The fourth anecdote making up this quartet of siege stories in the saga is the one taken most seriously by historians and by reason of its involving Harald's companion-in-arms, Halldor Snorrason, who was one of Snorri's own ancestors and thus quite certainly the original source for a tale included in *Heimskringla* but in no other version of Harald's saga. The story itself is simple enough, telling how Harald's Varangian troop laid siege to the 'largest and strongest, wealthiest and most populous' of the towns they captured and one well defended against assault by a moat surrounding its walls. Harald's ruse in this instance was to send some of his men, apparently unarmed and unconcerned, to engage in games within view of the town walls but beyond the range of the defenders' weapons. This activity continued for some days while the townsfolk mocked them with taunts, eventually becoming so confident as to leave their gates open and thus providing the opportunity for

Harald's men to draw the weapons hidden in their cloaks and make a charge into the town. Harald let them lead the assault and yet he himself took longer than expected to follow up with the rest of his force, thus exposing the vanguard – including Halldor and his fellow-Icelander, Ulf Ospaksson, both described by Snorri as 'outstanding warriors and very dear to Harald's heart' – to bear the brunt of fierce fighting. Some Varangians had been killed and many wounded before Harald reached the gates and even as he did so his own standard-bearer was slain. At which point he called upon Halldor to take up the standard, a command which the Icelander refused, accusing Harald of timidity in holding back from the fray. While Snorri offers swift assurance that 'these words were spoken in anger rather than truth', other evidence preserved in the Icelandic sources indicates Halldor's loyalty to his future king having been tempered with a critical cutting-edge and, indeed, other versions of Harald's saga include the same acrimonious exchange with Halldor, but which they otherwise append to the tale of the 'fake funeral' ruse. 'Let the trolls carry the standard for you, you coward' is perhaps the most convincingly idiomatic of these alternative renderings, all of which might be taken to suggest Halldor's response to Harald having been a favourite feature of the storytelling for which he became renowned in Iceland in the years after his return home from the Norwegian court.

Snorri's version of the story tells how Halldor himself was wounded in the fighting, suffering a deep gash to his face which left him marked with 'an ugly scar for the rest of his life' and it seems very likely that his scar might have prompted a variety of tales explaining how it came to be inflicted, each one including his sharp retort to the king as its punch-line. None of which lends especial credibility to Snorri's story of the 'Varangian games', which may even have been contrived for inclusion in the saga as a convenient opportunity to introduce the genuinely historical characters of Halldor and Ulf, both of them reliably identified as sons of prominent Icelandic families, into the narrative of his *Harald's saga*.

There is nowhere any indication of when these two remarkable men first joined Harald's retinue, although it is not impossible that they might have been among those Icelanders who fought in Olaf's army at Stiklestad and afterwards followed Harald to Russia and Byzantium. It is just as likely, though, that they were already employed in Byzantine mercenary service (possibly in company with their fellow-Icelander, Bolli Bollason, whose Varangian career is well-known from *Laxdæla saga*) when they joined Harald's troop, perhaps attracted by its reputation for profitable plundering or accepting personal invitations which might well have been offered to fighting-men of the outstanding quality described by Snorri. However and whenever they were first recruited into Harald's company, Halldor and Ulf evidently rose swiftly to become his principal lieutenants by the time of the Sicilian campaign, afterwards accompanying the rise and fall of his career in the Varangians of the City before returning with him to Scandinavia.

While Ulf spent the rest of his life in Norway where he was made a lenderman, and in Harald's service where he held the premier military post of king's marshal (or *stallari*), Halldor would seem to have settled uneasily into life at court and chose to go home to Iceland sometime around 1051, bearing with him all the tales of Varangian adventure which were to establish his reputation as a storyteller of outstanding authority. As the favourite son of a famous chieftain of Helgafell, Halldor makes appearances in a number of Icelandic sources, but the most impressive testimonial to his renown as a teller of tales is found in *Morkinskinna*, where the *Tale of the Story-wise Icelander* tells of a young man who came to King Harald in Norway where his storytelling kept the court enthralled through all twelve days of Yule. Harald himself was particularly impressed by the performance and so asked the young Icelander where he had learned the story he told. 'It was my custom in Iceland to journey each summer to the *Althing* and it was there that I learned the story, piece by piece each year, from the telling of Halldor Snorrason.' 'In that case,' said Harald, 'it is little wonder that your knowledge is so excellent, and good fortune will attend you now.'

It should be said, of course, that Halldor's reminiscences are unlikely to have been preserved intact and uncorrupted through almost two hundred years of oral transmission, and even then that they represented only a small proportion of the Varangian lore – assuredly including many even taller tales – which found its way into Icelandic tradition and thus provided Snorri with his reservoir of source material. Consequently, Halldor is not necessarily to be blamed for those occasions when the saga's chronology becomes unhelpfully confused or when its aggrandising enthusiasm bursts the bounds of historical credibility. Nonetheless, such passages from the saga are still of interest when they might reflect something of the feelings of Varangians about their commanders, as appears to be the case in Snorri's chapter which contrasts Harald with Georgios Maniakes in the context of a campaign only loosely identified and yet bearing unmistakable resemblance to aspects of the Sicilian invasion.

Snorri claims that Harald tried always to keep his own men out of the heat of battle when the forces were in action together and yet drove them fiercely against the enemy whenever they were engaged as a separate unit. Thus victories were won when Harald was in sole command and the troops acclaimed him as a better commander than Maniakes, who countered that the Varangians were not giving him their full support and responded to the criticism by ordering Harald to take his men off on their own while he himself remained in command of the rest of the army. When Harald did so, Snorri tells of his taking not only his Varangians, but also a contingent of 'Latin-men', by which must be meant Norman mercenaries, and this reference alone would associate the story with the Sicilian campaign where Byzantine forces did include a Norman contingent, although Snorri's narrative places it earlier, presumably in Asia Minor, and probably conflates tales told of more than one theatre of operations.

Of key significance in Snorri's account is the passage telling of ambitious young soldiers leaving the main army to join Harald's troop when they learned of the greater booty being shared by the men under his command, because the most usual source of contention between Maniakes and his mercenaries in Sicily is known to have been the sharing of plunder. When disputes of this sort are set beside Maniakes' code of iron discipline, it is not difficult to imagine the sort of problems which would have been presented by a contingent of northmen under their own young officer, brimming over with self-confidence and mercenary avarice.

So too, the Normans – who had proudly aristocratic commanders of their own – are known to have clashed with the heavy-handed Georgios over battle-booty in the Sicilian campaign, but one thing of which Maniakes cannot be accused is failure in pursuit of victory. Within two years of campaigning in Sicily, he had reclaimed virtually all the island from a Saracen enemy possessed of superior numbers. The Byzantine army certainly included first-class fighting-men in its Norman and Varangian mercenaries – and likewise in the force of sturdy Armenians led by Katalokon Cecaumenus (who has been suggested as one possible candidate for authorship of the account of Harald in the *Advice*) – but others, such as the reluctant Longobard recruits from Apulia, were of lesser quality and so the elite units must have borne the heat and burden of the day in the fiercely fought battles which led to the defeat of the Saracen commander Abdallah at Traina in 1040.

The immediate aftermath of Traina heralded Maniakes' dramatic fall from imperial favour – and entirely as a consequence of his own fearsome temper. He was never going to be well-disposed towards the naval commander assigned to the Sicilian invasion, because the admiral Stephen had been a caulker in the shipyards of Constantinople until his brother-in-law the emperor Michael appointed him to the rank of *patricius* and to command of the fleet which brought Maniakes' army to the shores of Sicily. Having accomplished that duty, presumably to the best of his modest abilities, Stephen was later held personally responsible for allowing Abdallah to escape by ship to Tunis in the wake of the defeat at Traina. So explosive was Maniakes' rage at this oversight that he actually took a whip to the unfortunate admiral, provoking Stephen's bitter complaint to the emperor accompanied by allegations of treason on the part of the general, charges sufficiently serious to prompt the recall of Maniakes to the capital where he was to spend most of the next two years in prison.

Before his loss of command, Maniakes was to assert his arrogance of power over his subordinates with disastrous consequences, first causing affront by seizing a fine warhorse which had been chosen as his own prize by Arduin, commander of the Longobard contingent, and then by denying the Normans the full share of booty which they believed to be their due. As a result, the Norman mercenaries defected to join the latest rebellion brewing up among imperial subjects in the south of Italy, thus depriving the Byzantine forces of their best mercenary cavalry just as Maniakes was replaced in command by the scarcely comparable admiral Stephen. In the event, Stephen was dead within the year and replaced in his turn by an obscure eunuch known only as Basil who soon managed to lose almost all that had been won in Sicily, leaving Messina as the one remaining imperial possession on the island.

It does seem very likely that the defection of Norman mercenaries who felt themselves to have been short-changed by the overbearing Maniakes might have formed the subject of a story brought back to Iceland – quite possibly by Halldor – and thus found its way into Snorri's saga in the form of his reference to 'Latin-men'. While there is good reason to believe the Varangians having similarly resented Maniakes, there is no question of Harald and his troop having followed the Normans, either in their defection or in their alliance with the Italian rebellion, because it is perfectly clear from the evidence of the skalds alone that when Harald and his troop were despatched to Italy they were fighting against the same Normans who had earlier been their comrades-in-arms in Sicily.

There had been trouble already in Byzantine Italy, where rebels had seized the town of Bari in 1038, and there was still greater trouble ahead through the three decades which it took the Normans to break the last imperial hold on the Italian mainland in 1071. In 1040, however, the empire was still prepared to put down any insurgency in its Italian provinces. Indeed, Bari was retaken in that same year just before a new rebellion broke out in Mottola where it claimed the lives of the catepan and other imperial officials before the rebel leader made his peace and submitted to the emperor. A newly appointed catepan arrived towards the end of the year with the support of a force of Varangians, some of whom must have been assigned to him from the army in Sicily because they included the troop commanded by Harald, who 'led the march in the land of the Longobards' – according to the skald Thjodolf – when a separatist revolt in Apulia had Norman cavalry as its cutting-edge.

Norman mercenaries had first emerged in Italy in 1015, when a band of young pilgrims had been recruited to fight for the Longobards against imperial forces. When word of this new source of demand for fighting-men got back to Normandy, other young warriors looking for action and profit made their way south until a steady tide of Normans was flowing down into Italy. Eventually Norman mercenaries were also to be found in Byzantine forces – being available, as was ever the way of the professional, to fight for whichever paymaster might be recruiting – engaged against the Saracens in Sicily and Pechenegs in the Balkans.

Already in the later 1030s, the sons of Tancred de Hauteville, who himself had been just another knight in the service of the dukes of Normandy, can be recognised as the first representatives of a formidable Italo-Norman dynasty. William (called 'Iron-arm') and his brother Drogo led the Norman contingent with Maniakes in Sicily in 1038, while their more famous brother – the afore-mentioned Robert called *Guiscard*, or 'the crafty' – was to be appointed by the Pope to new dukedoms of Apulia and Calabria in 1059, as also of Sicily which he first invaded with his younger brother Roger in 1061 and which was finally wrested from the Saracens in 1072.

Only recently mercenaries in imperial service, these Normans now presented the most serious opposition facing Byzantine forces in Italy. It has been suggested that it was their highly effective development of the close-formation cavalry charge which gave the Normans the edge over the Byzantines, 'who hated the solid lines of horsemen with levelled lances',[8] and this may well have brought them the victory over superior numbers of imperial troops in the two major battles fought in southern Italy in the spring of 1041. Varangians served with the Byzantine forces in both of these conflicts and are said by the Greek annalists to have suffered heavy losses first at Olivento in April and again in the second battle fought early in the following month at Montemaggiore, where a great part of the catepan's army was drowned in the full flood of the Ofanto river.

The skald Illugi tells of Harald's going early 'to disturb the peace of the Frakkar', by whom can only be meant the Normans, and so it would seem likely that he and his troop would have been engaged in the fighting on at least one of these occasions. Nothing more is known of Harald's part in this Italian campaign, other than that he clearly came out of it alive and with full honour on the evidence of his subsequent promotion to the rank of *manglavites*. His was not the only contingent of Varangians serving in Italy, because others are mentioned by the annals when Harald is known to have been already on campaign with the emperor against the Bulgars, so it is not impossible that he and his troop may have been withdrawn to the capital before the more serious of the defeats inflicted on Byzantine forces in that spring.

Snorri himself has nothing to say of Harald in Bulgaria, because the solitary reference to that campaign found in his saga is a single phrase in a strophe from the skald Thjodolf quoted at the foot of its opening paragraph. Thjodolf's verse is principally concerned with the battle of Stiklestad, although set down many years after the event, and yet refers to Harald as *Bolgara brennir* or 'burner of the Bulgars', thus supplying the only fragment of skaldic testimony to corroborate the eminently authoritative evidence of the *Advice* for his part in the emperor Michael's final suppression of the Bulgar rebellion in 1041.

An outline of the background might be helpful at this point, because there has been little reference to Bulgaro–Byzantine relations here since the Bulgarian tsar Samuel destroyed the emperor Basil's army at Trajan's Gate in the year before the foundation of the Varangian Guard. Basil had sworn to take his revenge on the Bulgars for that devastating defeat and, although it took him a full twenty-five years to do so, that vengeance was terrible indeed. Having rebuilt the Byzantine military into a war-machine capable of outfighting the Bulgars in their own rough Balkan terrain, Basil had already reclaimed most of the eastern extent of the peninsula for the empire by 1004. Ten years later, he defeated a Bulgar host in the narrow pass of Cimbalongus north of Serrae and earned himself enduring infamy after the battle when he put out the eyes of 15,000 prisoners, leaving one out of every hundred with the sight of a single eye so as to be able to lead their comrades home. When the tsar Samuel, already a sick man by that time, beheld the return of so many grievously mutilated warriors, he is said to have suffered an apoplexy and died a few days later, yet his people fought on for four more years until finally surrendering to Basil the Bulgar-slayer in 1018.

The name 'Bulgar' derives from the Old Turkic *bulgha*, meaning 'to mix', and the earliest ancestors of the people who were known by that name in the tenth and eleventh centuries would have been a Turkic steppe tribe akin to the Huns and Pechenegs – as also, indeed, to the later Mongols. That original stock of nomadic warrior-herdsmen had long since been diffused by its passage through the various gene pools of the Balkans, and most influentially those of the Slav pastoralists, by the time of the creation of the 'First Bulgarian Empire' under its tsar Samuel, who was himself of largely Armenian descent. There were, of course, other branches of the same original stock – principally the Volga Bulgars, who adopted the Islamic faith from their Arab trading contacts – but the Bulgar subjects of the Byzantine empire were those settled around Macedonia.

As frighteningly vindictive as he had been after his victory over the Bulgars in battle, Basil was to show a remarkable generosity towards them once they had become imperial subjects, and most particularly in allowing them to pay their taxes in kind rather than in cash, but the same generosity was soon to be discontinued during the reign of Michael IV, especially when the emperor's health had entered into its terminal decline and responsibility for imperial finances had passed to John the Orphanotrophus. Now the great power at the Byzantine court, he was soon to demand taxation rendered in hard currency, thus provoking a tide of hostility among the Bulgars, which only awaited the emergence of some sort of leader before it erupted into full-scale revolt.

Just such a figurehead appeared in 1040 when one Peter Deljan declared himself tsar in Belgrade. This 'Tsar Peter' is sometimes identified as an escaped slave and sometimes as a grandson of the great Samuel, yet he could well have been both because he was possibly a son of Samuel's son and short-lived successor, Gabriel Radomir. His claim would seem to have had some measure of legitimacy, because he was joined in early autumn by an ally in the person of Alusian – presumably Peter's cousin, because he was not only a grandson of Samuel but also a son and younger brother of the last two Bulgarian tsars – who had escaped from house arrest in Constantinople (where he had been held by order of the Orphanotrophus but on an unknown charge) to take his place beside Peter Deljan at the head of the rebellion.

With its joint lords of revolt in place, the Bulgar rising was unleashed against an imperial authority already under pressure from Saracens in Sicily and Normans in southern Italy, so the rebels would seem to have had a head-start for their surge through Macedonia and into northern Greece, where they inflicted a heavy defeat on the garrison at Thebes. The emperor Michael was in his palace at Thessalonika when the rebellion broke out and lost no time in hurrying back to Constantinople to organise his military response – which may well have included the recall of Harald and his troop from Italy and, if so, then in all likelihood on the recommendation of Michael's brother, the general Constantine.

Constantine remained in Thessalonika and held the city when the Bulgars arrived to lay it siege. He was supported by forces apparently drawn from a regiment of the Tagmata, but identified only as the 'Tagma of the Great-hearted', who made a magnificent sortie in the last week of October to win an impressive victory in throwing back the besieging Bulgars, who suffered casualties in the thousands and the rest of their forces put to flight. Nonetheless, the rebels were evidently able to recover and to fight on, because they had driven westward to storm Dyrrachium on the Adriatic coast before the end of the year. In the spring of 1041, however, their prospects were beginning to darken when an impressive imperial army – assuredly now including Harald and his Varangians – was in

Thessalonika with the emperor who declared his intention of leading his forces in person.

This was, indeed, an extraordinary announcement because, although still only in his twenties, Michael the Paphlagonian was a chronic invalid obviously nearing the end of his life. He had long suffered from epilepsy, but what Psellus calls his 'internal trouble' had caused him to become bloated to the point of semi-paralysis, his legs hideously swollen and afflicted by gangrene so that every movement must have been a torment. Yet Michael was determined to lead his army on a carefully planned operation, which would have been confident of victory even if the rebel leaders had not fallen out with each other and thus ensured its absolute certainty.

When he was accused of treachery by Deljan, Alusian had struck back with a cook's knife (at least according to Psellus, who describes the whole grisly exchange enacted at a banquet) to put out both of his cousin's eyes and then to slice off his nose. Now in full command of the rebels, Alusian led them against the Byzantine army but with so little success that he had to flee into hiding when their onset was thrown back. Presumably recognising the inevitability of total defeat, Alusian entered into his own secret negotiations with the emperor, offering surrender in exchange for restoration of such honours as were due to him and to his family. When these conditions were accepted, Alusian proceeded with a pre-agreed charade of advancing his horsemen once more towards the enemy before suddenly abandoning them in a theatrical rush to throw himself upon the emperor's mercy. While he was granted a full pardon and returned to Constantinople, the Bulgar host persisted in its dogged resistance, now with the mutilated Deljan at its head and refusing to surrender until it was finally crushed by the emperor's army at the battle of Prilep.

When the skald Thjodolf makes mention of Harald having fought 'eighteen fierce battles' before his return to Norway, it is reasonable to assume that these would have been the major engagements in which he saw action as a Varangian mercenary in the service of Michael IV. So too, when Thjodolf's description of his king as

113

'burner of the Bulgars' is set beside the reference made by the author of the *Advice* to 'the revolt of Delianos in Bulgaria [where] Araltes went on campaign with the emperor, with his own troops, and demonstrated deeds against the foe worthy of his birth and nobility', Harald was quite certainly involved in this later phase of the Bulgarian war and (if Thjodolf's words might be taken literally) possibly deployed on a firebrand-wielding intimidation of the rebel heartland.

What can also be said with certainty is that this campaign was to be his last in imperial service – leading on to the probability of the battle at Prilep having been the last that he fought as a Varangian mercenary. Once again though, Harald clearly served the emperor with sufficient distinction to merit promotion, and this time to the rank of *spatharokandidatos* when he accompanied Michael's triumphal return to the capital.

PLATE 1: This eleventh-century elk horn carving found at Sigtuna in Sweden provides an immediately contemporary representation of a Scandinavian warrior – or even a warrior king – of Harald Hardrada's time. *(© 2000 Topham Picturepoint)*

PLATE 2: The three death-wounds inflicted on King Olaf the saint at the climax of the battle of Stiklestad, as illustrated in the *Flateyjarbók* manuscript of his saga. (© *Werner Forman/ Corbis*)

PLATE 3: A coat of ring mail found in Værdal, thought to be of a somewhat later date than the battle of Stiklestad but still identical in every respect to the byrnie worn by Scandinavian fighting-men in the eleventh century and earlier. (© *Museum of Cultural History – University of Oslo, Norway/Louis Smestad*)

PLATE 4: Elizaveta, the Russian princess who became Harald's queen Ellisif, is portrayed (probably second from the right) with her mother, Ingigerd, and her two sisters in this closely contemporary wall-painting from the Hagia Sophia church, Kiev. (© Ted Spiegel/Corbis)

PLATE 5: Contemporary portraits of the empress Zoe and her third husband, the emperor Constantine IX Monomachus, flanking the figure of Christ on a mosaic panel in the Hagia Sophia, Constantinople. *(© Private Collection/Bridgeman Art Library)*

PLATE 6: The great iron chain slung across the Golden Horn for the defence of Constantinople from attack by sea – and over which Harald is said to have manoeuvred his galley in the course of his defiant departure from imperial service. (© *The original one is in the Military Museum (Harbiye-Istanbul)*)

PLATE 7: Stamford Bridge is now effectively a suburb of the city of York and the precise site of its battlefield unmarked, but this rugged memorial stone and its accompanying plaque serve to commemorate Harald's death in the blood-fray fought nearby. *(Photo © Geoff Green)*

PLATE 8: The famous 'Fairy Flag' of the Clan Macleod, now preserved in Dunvegan Castle on the Isle of Skye, may well be Harald's war-banner 'Land-ravager' rescued from the field of Stamford Bridge by Godred Crovan, founding dynast of the Norse kingdom of Man and the Isles and ultimate ancestor of the Macleods. *(© 2003 Charles Walker/Topfoto)*

Constantinople, 1041–1042

Probably the most extraordinary aspect of the Varangian Guard is the fact of the personal protection of the *Basileus* (as the Byzantine emperor was formally styled in Greek), who was 'held to be the sole legitimate sovereign of the Christian world' and represented as 'the earthly counterpart and vice-regent of the Christ Pantokrator',[9] having been entrusted to fighting-men out of the remote northland whose two best-known characteristics were their mighty battle-axes and notorious appetite for alcohol. Customarily referred to in the Greek annals as 'the axe-bearing Guard' – and on one occasion by a contemporary observer as the 'Emperor's wine-bags' – at least there is some reflection of ceremonial dignity encoded in the Greek titles bestowed on the various ranks of the Varangians of the City.

The title of *manglavites*, for example, had its origin in *manglavion*, the name given to a short whip borne by officers of the Hetairia preceding the emperor in procession and used by them to clear the way for the progress of the imperial party. Although thought to be largely honorary in Harald's time, the rank of *manglavites* still carried with it the privilege of wearing a gold-hilted sword, such as that described in *Laxdæla saga* when Bolli Bollason returns home from his service in the palace guard with his sword 'now inlaid with gold at the top and shank and with gold bands wound around the hilt'. This reference is of particular interest because it confirms an officer of the Varangian Guard having used gold decoration on his own sword (in some cases a valued heirloom and given its own name, as in the case of Bolli's 'Leg-Biter'), while Michael Psellus describes a quite different weapon, 'a single-edged sword of heavy iron' known as the *rhomphaia*, which was 'slung from the right shoulder' of every palace guardsman. This must have been a dress sword and thus quite distinct from the double-edged blade of the traditional northern type which accompanied the spear (of a heavier type than that found in the Byzantine armoury) and, of course, the famous two-handed axe to make up the more typical complement of Varangian battle-weaponry.

Nonetheless, a ceremonial association with sword-bearing is clearly indicated by the *spatharo-* prefix found in the titles applied to ranks such as that of *spatharokandidatos*, to which Harald was promoted on his return from Bulgaria, and likewise that of the superior *protospatharios*, both of these having their origin in an earlier Hetairia lifeguard called the *basilikoi anthropoi* (literally the 'emperor's men') which pre-dated the formation of the Varangian Guard. The *Laxdæla saga* account of Bolli Bollason's return from Constantinople also supplies some evidence for the dress uniform of the palace guard when it describes the eleven men of his retinue 'dressed in clothes of scarlet' and Bolli himself wearing 'a cloak of red scarlet given him by the emperor of Byzantium'. This has been taken to indicate 'red scarlet' as the uniform colour of the *manglavites*, while that worn by officers of the Hetairia holding the honorary rank of *spatharokandidatos* had traditionally been white (with the distinguishing badge of a golden torque) and may still have been so in the eleventh century. Again, it must be stressed that these were items of ceremonial garb as distinct from war-gear, which would have been essentially a helmet, shield and coat of ring-mail for a Varangian on campaign or even garrison duty in the capital.

The conical helmet might well have been of 'spangenhelm' construction, although some would have reflected Slavic or Turkic influence and, in the case of the more affluent warrior, may even have been decorated with precious metals. The longer a man remained in mercenary service, of course, the more likely he was to adopt items of foreign arms and armour, but Scandinavian military taste was invariably conservative in character and the mail-coat would seem to have been at least as characteristic of Varangian war-gear as was the axe. So it was in Harald's case, although his mail-coat is said by Snorri to have been unusually long and so would have been similar in style to those worn by the mailed Norman knights with whom he served in Sicily. The shield most often used by Varangians of Harald's time would have been of the traditional Scandinavian circular design, and thus much larger than the disc-shaped shields carried by Byzantine cavalry, although the long, tapered 'kite' shields favoured by the Normans were finding their way into Russian and Byzantine armouries through the eleventh and twelfth centuries when fragments of saga evidence also suggest shields of that type brought back to Iceland, presumably by returning Varangians.

One further item of military equipment particularly associated with Harald is his banner, known as *Landeyðuna* ('Land-ravager') and noticed on more than one occasion in Snorri's saga where it is said to have been his most highly prized possession. The name alone bears testimony to the banner's long active service before it was raised on his last campaign of 1066 and if this was the same banner which featured in Halldor's anecdote connected with the siege story then it must have come into Harald's possession while he was in Byzantine service, and perhaps in emulation of those carried by the standard-bearers of the Tagmata regiments. These regimental standards were highly honoured, in much the same way as the eagles carried by the old Roman legions, and yet smaller units within a regiment (companies or cavalry squadrons known as *banda*) also had their own banners, known as *bandophorai*, one of which might have found its way into Harald's hands – but the story of Land-ravager is a long one indeed, and worthy of its own appointed place later in these pages.

What can be said of Land-ravager at this point – and especially if Thjodolf's phrase 'burner of the Bulgars' can be taken at face value – is that it would have fluttered proudly over Harald's troop on the march into Constantinople with the imperial forces returning victorious from the Bulgarian campaign in 1041. Michael Psellus – reporting, as usual, at first-hand – describes the entry of the emperor's army into the city as 'a brilliant occasion', with the whole populace thronging to greet their emperor as he 'returned in glory to his palace, bringing with him a host of captives, among whom were the most notable men of the Bulgars, including their leader, the pretender [Peter Deljan] himself, minus his nose and deprived of his eyes'.

The whole performance was a typically Byzantine blend of splendour and savagery, reaching its climax when the Bulgar prisoners were force-marched through the stadium of the Hippodrome in which the high and low usually gathered to watch horse-races, and yet for Psellus the really tragic figure was that of the emperor Michael himself: 'I saw him on this occasion . . . swaying in the saddle of his horse. The fingers gripping his bridle were as if those of a giant, each of them as thick and as large as a man's arm, the result of his internal trouble, while his features preserved not a trace of their former likeness.' This was to be the last public appearance of an unlikely and yet remarkable *Basileus* whose personal tragedy has been justly recognised by one of the outstanding modern English historians of Byzantium: 'Few emperors had risen from more lowly origins, or by more questionable methods; none suffered a more agonising end. He possessed wisdom, vision and courage . . . and in the reigns that followed, there would be many who regretted his loss'.[10]

One who certainly would have had his own reason to do so was the newly promoted *spatharokandidatos* of the Varangian Guard, because the passing of Michael the Paphlagonian – who had himself carried to a monastery of his own foundation on 10 December 1041 and there took the monk's habit and tonsure before he died on the same evening – was to mark the decisive point of downturn in Harald's fortunes in imperial service.

The fast-failing health of the emperor had been apparent in court circles for more than a year – and not least to his brother, John the Orphanotrophus, who was thus in need of a successor who could secure the avaricious interest of himself and his kin. His one remaining brother with manhood left intact was Constantine, but he was now as widely disliked as John himself. Stephen, the lowly shipyard worker promoted to admiral of the imperial fleet by reason of his marriage to Michael's sister Maria, had been dead for over a year but had left a son – also named Michael – and it was he who offered the family its last potential candidate for the succession if he were to be accepted as an adopted son by the ailing emperor and an empress now in her sixties.

All of which had been neatly accomplished by the scheming Orphanotrophus before the emperor went away to war and so his favoured successor was already on hand when the death of Michael IV was announced. All that was needed was his endorsement by the *porphyrogenita* Zoe, now utterly alone and as gullible as ever, who could hardly refuse the proclamation of her adopted son as the emperor Michael V – although he was to be more popularly known as Michael *Calaphates* ('the Caulker') in satirical reference to his father's erstwhile employment with the tar-brush. In the event, John's manipulation proved disastrous for his family and, indeed, most immediately for himself because the uncle preferred by the new emperor was Constantine whom he raised to the eminence of *nobilissimus* and appointed to command of the forces as 'Grand *Domestikos*', while the Orphanotrophus was shortly to find himself aboard a galley carrying him into the exile from which he was never to return.

Not the least astonishing move in this reshuffling of imperial favourites was the restoration of the man only recently disgraced for taking a whip to the emperor's late father, because Georgios Maniakes was released from imprisonment and offered the ships and men he needed to reclaim Italy from the new Norman ascendancy (where just four towns remained in imperial control) and to make yet another attempt to win back Sicily from Saracen control. The return of the formidable Maniakes was never going to bode well for Harald, especially when the young emperor apparently shared a similar ill-disposition towards Varangians, replacing them as his bodyguard with 'young Scythians' (almost certainly Pechenegs) said by Psellus to have been eunuchs 'who knew his [Michael's] temper and were well suited to the services he required of them'. The Varangian regiment itself was not disbanded and those of its members who had formerly served as the imperial lifeguard were simply reassigned to garrison duty in the capital. While these ominous developments cannot be placed into precise sequence, they must have been implemented within the first few months of 1042 and so might seem to form a prelude to the more dramatic events which were to bring the short reign of Michael V to its gruesome conclusion in the third week of April.

One of the first of these is of particular importance here by reason of its involving the imprisonment of three officers of the Varangian Guard – namely, Harald Sigurdsson, Halldor Snorrason and Ulf Ospaksson. It should be said, first of all, that there is no reference to Harald's arrest and confinement in the most closely contemporary evidence of skaldic verse or Byzantine records, so all that is known of this episode derives from later northern sources and principally from accounts included in the different versions of Harald's saga, of which that set down by Snorri Sturluson must have its own claim to be the best informed. The original sources informing all these saga accounts can only have been stories brought back to the northlands by returning Varangians, as Snorri himself effectively admits in the saga, and so his family connection with Halldor Snorrason must lend at least some measure of first-hand authority to his version of events.

Nonetheless, Snorri's account is grossly distorted by misin-terpretation and confusion, and most unhelpfully in his sequence of events, as in his opening passage which links Harald's imprison-ment (from which he had evidently escaped by 21 April) with his decision to leave Constantinople, being eager to return to his homeland again 'having heard' that his nephew Magnus had become king of both Norway and Denmark (which indeed he did, but not until after the death of Hardacnut early in June of the same year). Snorri goes on to tell how Harald's intention to depart so enraged the empress Zoe that she accused him of defrauding the imperial treasury of plunder won on expeditions under his command – even though the true reason for her anger was of a more personal nature.

Harald is said to have asked for the hand in marriage of 'Maria, the beautiful maiden daughter of Queen Zoe's brother' and to have been refused, although 'some Varangians who had served in *Miklagarð* and returned to Iceland' claimed the empress herself wanted to marry Harald and that this had been the true objection to his request to depart the capital, 'although a quite different story was given to the public'. Having thus confirmed Varangian tradition as his source of information for this passage of his narrative, Snorri immediately demonstrates how such source material can so easily and often fall short as reliable historical record. The only Maria known in the court circle of the time was the emperor's sister and the admiral Stephen's widow who would scarcely correspond to Snorri's description, so if this 'Maria' existed at all she could not possibly have been a niece of the empress when Zoe had no brother and neither of her two sisters had ever married.

It is, of course, not at all unlikely that a young officer might have enjoyed some sort of liaison with a Byzantine noblewoman and yet no Varangian, however well born, would have been considered a proper choice of husband for such a lady when Greek society took so dim a view of the regiment's character. Neither would an empress in her sixties have considered – or been allowed to consider – a marriage so far beneath her imperial dignity, even though another anecdote, which is found in *Morkinskinna* where it tells of Harald's utterly ungracious response to Zoe's request for a lock of his hair, would suggest that the two names were linked by salacious gossip (unfounded or otherwise) apparently current in mercenary barracks at the time and assuredly providing the source of both saga references.

The allegation of Harald's defrauding the emperor (also attributed to Zoe in *Fagrskinna*) is quite another matter, however, and especially in view of so much evidence preserved elsewhere in the sagas, not least in that set down by Snorri himself which makes frequent mention of the wealth accumulated by Harald in Byzantine service. When first on campaign in Serkland, Harald was already gathering a 'hoard of money and gold and treasure of every kind' which he sent 'in the care of trusted men to *Holmgarð*' for Jaroslav's safe-keeping, while two of Snorri's four siege stories conclude with similar notes of the 'immense booty' collected when the towns had fallen to Harald's guile. Presumably most of this plunder also found its way to Novgorod because, when Harald eventually reached Russia on his return from Constantinople, he is said to have spent the winter gathering together 'all the gold he had taken from *Miklagarð*, together with other valuable treasure of all kinds' into a hoard 'greater than had ever been seen in the north in one man's possession'.

At which point, Snorri comes up with the dubious explanation that much of this wealth had been acquired by means of Harald's having thrice taken part in *pólútasvarf*, a term which he interprets as 'palace plunder' and a Byzantine custom whereby Varangians were allowed to ransack all the imperial palaces on the death of an emperor and to take as much of his treasure as they could carry away. There has been evidence found for a similar custom of 'palace plunder' known in Rome after the passing of a pope or his bishops (until abolished in 904) and likewise in Baghdad on the death of the caliph, but no such practice was known in Constantinople and Blöndal dismisses any such idea as 'inconceivable' in a Byzantine context (although he admits it is not impossible that guards on duty at the time of an emperor's passing might have been allowed to take certain precious objects as personal mementoes).

Having said that, Blöndal does subject the whole question to a meticulous examination leading to his suggestion that the key may well lie in Snorri's use of the term *pólútasvarf*. Russian in origin, of course, it was applied there to a tax-collecting expedition accompanied by a military escort, not infrequently comprised of Varangian mercenaries who were remunerated with a share of the tribute collected. Mention has already been made here of the probability that the young Harald would have been engaged on just such duties with Eilif Rognvaldsson in Novgorod, but he spent no more than two winters in the north of Russia and so would have had no time to amass any very great wealth before he left for Byzantium. Neither, indeed, would Snorri's explanation suggest as much, because he specifically applies *pólútasvarf* to Harald's Byzantine service, and thus leads Blöndal to his proposal of the term 'having become Varangian slang for tax-gathering expeditions in Imperial service'.[11] If so, then the inference must be of Harald's extortion of unlawful revenue for himself and his men while engaged on tax-collection in imperial service, although the substance of the allegations brought against him in Constantinople bears only upon his holding back more than the legitimate share of battle-booty.

While the saga leaves no doubt of Harald's Varangian career having been 'mercenary' in every sense of the term, it is still impossible to know whether or not he was justly accused, especially when there is the further possibility that Georgios Maniakes might have had some part to play in putting Harald and his lieutenants in prison. Released from his own imprisonment and restored to imperial favour, he was in a position to take revenge on those who had been his enemies just two years before, including Harald and his troop who may even have taken Stephen's side in the acrimony which was to deprive Maniakes of command. If the general did have any knowledge, or even suspicion, of wrong-doing on Harald's part, he would have been well placed to set retribution in process, a possibility further supported by stories in the *Morkinskinna* and *Flateyjarbók* versions of the saga which tell of at least one earlier occasion when *Gyrgir* had complained to the Emperor of Harald wanting to keep all the booty that he took for himself.

On this occasion, however, Snorri himself makes no attempt to implicate Maniakes (who, by this time, would already have left for Italy and Sicily) and lays the blame for Harald's arraignment squarely upon the empress Zoe while thrusting the responsibility for his arrest and imprisonment upon Constantine Monomachus, 'who at that time ruled as king of the Greeks'. At this point it is clear that Snorri's chronology has gone completely awry and so much so as to make a nonsense of the conclusion to the next passage of his narrative, which tells of Harald having seen a vision of St Olaf promising to come to his aid, just before he, Halldor and Ulf were thrust through a door on the street and into their cell inside a tall, roofless tower. As fully expected, the saint was as good as his promise and made yet another appearance in Constantinople, this time to 'a lady of high birth' he had once healed of some ill whose aid he now sought in the rescue of his brother. Following Olaf's supernatural guidance, the noblewoman came to the prison on the following night, bringing with her two servants who set ladders against the wall and scaled the tower so as to lower down a rope and haul the three prisoners up out of their cell to freedom.

The more expansive variation on the same theme in *Morkinskinna* also has a vision of Olaf appearing to Harald as he approaches his prison, but in this version to advise him as to the whereabouts of a hidden knife. With this weapon and the assistance of his two loyal lieutenants, Harald is able to slay the fearsome serpent lurking in the dark cell before the three make their escape. Curiously, it is this story which is taken up by Saxo Grammaticus in his history, having learned it from the Danish king Valdemar who claimed to have the very same knife in his own possession. Snorri must have known of this story which would seem to have formed part of Halldor's repertoire – one of the tales told of Halldor refers to a mocking rhyme claiming he had only sat upon the *wurm* and left the knife-work to Harald and Ulf – yet he would seem to have given it so little credence that it was omitted from his own saga. In fact, it might be thought rather more credible than any supernatural intervention by Olaf, because a snake or similar reptile would have been a very likely resident in a Byzantine dungeon and one easily re-cast by a saga-maker into some more alarming form of monster, especially in view of a number of similar 'prisoner in snake-tower' tales of south-east European origin current during the twelfth century.

They were evidently of no interest whatsoever to Snorri, however, because his account of the rescue by way of the roofless tower moves swiftly on with Harald's urgent quest for revenge. Having been brought to freedom, he went directly to his Varangians who took up their weapons and followed him to find the emperor asleep in his bedchamber, from which he was seized to suffer the putting out of his eyes. At this point in the narrative, Snorri summons up the support of his most authoritative source of evidence in the form of two passages of skaldic verse by Harald's court-poets, the first attributed to Thorarin Skeggjason, the second to the oft-quoted Thjodolf, and both informed by Harald himself for their description of his blinding of a Byzantine emperor – although one whom neither skald identifies by name.

The timely introduction of this impressively contemporary evidence from the skalds at last enables the alignment of Snorri's narrative with the more reliable historical record of events in Constantinople in the spring of 1042 when an emperor was blinded and deposed on 21 April after one of the bloodiest days in the capital's history. That emperor could not have been the Constantine Monomachus named by Snorri, however, and neither could it have been he who committed Harald to prison because some seven more weeks were to pass before he made his formal entry into Byzantine history as the emperor Constantine IX when he became Zoe's third husband in the second week of June. The emperor who suffered the mutilation described by the skalds can only have been Michael V Calaphates.

Having disposed of his uncle the Orphanotrophus and cowed the courtier aristocracy – even emasculating dissenting members of his own family – Michael now believed himself sufficiently beloved of the people to proceed with the removal of his co-empress Zoe. Probably inspired to action by the sight of the cheering crowds lining his processional route to the great church of the Hagia Sophia on the first Sunday after Easter (18 April in 1042), Michael had Zoe arrested, arraigned in front of witnesses he had prepared earlier, and forcibly transported through the night – garbed in a nun's habit and shorn of her hair – to a convent on the island of Prinkipo in the Sea of Marmara. It is, perhaps, tempting to wonder whether rumours associating Zoe with a Varangian *spatharokandidatos* might have prompted Harald's arrest around this time, possibly to neutralise any potential military challenge before Michael addressed the Senate on the following morning to announce Zoe's punishment for allegedly attempting to poison her co-emperor. While the senators had no realistic alternative to approval of the emperor's action, a very different response greeted the proclamation made to the crowd on the street outside, where voices were immediately heard denouncing the caulker's son as a blasphemer and demanding the return of the *porphyrogenita*.

Those isolated calls soon swelled to the point where the *sebastokrator* (or 'city prefect') who had made the proclamation only just escaped with his life from an angry mob grown so huge that it seemed as if the whole city had risen in open revolt, especially when the Patriarch of Constantinople ordered all the bells to be rung calling the people to arms. A number of Varangians had apparently responded to the summoning bells, because Psellus makes mention of many axes wielded among the crowds surging to besiege the imperial palace and attack the mansions of the emperor's family, with particular attention directed towards the palace of the *nobilissimus* Constantine. Some of those Varangians must have been those formerly in service with the imperial lifeguard – on the evidence of Psellus' reference to discontented *Tauro-Skuthai* who departed the palace – but others of their kind, who had probably been long in Constantine's service, remained loyal to the Grand Domestic as he fought his way through a mile and a half of crowded city streets before coming to the aid of his nephew under siege in the imperial palace.

A man of genuine military experience and evident personal courage, Constantine first deployed his bowmen and *ballistae* on the high towers to drive the mob back from the gates with a hail of arrows and bolts, before despatching a boat across the Marmara to bring Zoe back from the island of Prinkipo with all possible speed. In the desperate hope that a personal appearance by his co-empress might just save Michael and his faction from their encircling doom, the old lady was brought ashore and hastily robed in the imperial purple before being taken through the palace to stand with her adopted son in the imperial box of the Hippodrome. It was now afternoon and the mob had been too angry for too long to be persuaded by any such charade. They saw Zoe still held in thrall by the son of a shipyard caulker and renewed their demand, now not only for the removal of Michael but for his replacement with the only other surviving *porphyrogenita*. Thus emissaries were sent forth to bring a reluctant Theodora out of the convent where she had spent the last fifteen years and bear her by force to the Hagia Sophia where she too was garbed in the purple before accepting the imperial crown.

It must have been very late in the evening before a proclamation in the name of the two sister empresses declared the emperor deposed and the congregation moved out of the cathedral to join the crowd still besieging the palace where Michael and his uncle had now received reinforcements – probably including more Varangian mercenaries – brought back from a recent victory in Sicily. Crack front-line troops fresh from active service would have been gratefully welcomed by the beleaguered Grand Domestic and were to be desperately needed early in the following morning when the palace was attacked from three sides. One of the routes chosen for this three-pronged onslaught was by way of the great bronze gate known as the *Chalke* – and it may well have been some of the insurgents following this line of approach who paused to break Harald and his companions out of their dungeon.

There has been more than one suggestion as to the prison in which Harald was held. The version of his saga in the *Flateyjarbók* places it on the same street as the 'church of the Varangians', of which the oldest is thought to have been that dedicated to St Mary near the Hagia Sophia, but the other and, perhaps, greater likelihood is of his being imprisoned in the *Numera* (its cells having been used at one time by the *Numeri* garrison) which lay in close proximity to the Varangian barracks and would have been most easily reached from the Chalke. The Patriarch had already directed the mob to break open the city's prisons and release their inmates on the Monday, but the Numera would have been under military control and so was more likely to have been breached during the dark hours of Tuesday morning. Indeed, Snorri's saga account indicates the rescue having been accomplished in the night-time and, unlikely as his story of the noblewoman may seem, Psellus remarks on the numbers of women and girls included in the mob so it is fully possible that one of these may have taken some part in releasing the three Varangians from their cell. It is still more likely that some prisoners of particular importance would have been located for urgent rescue by those directing the insurgency and Harald would surely have been one of these, and not only because his release would have encouraged the support of most of the Varangians. There were now those in high places who may already have known of him and, perhaps, even foreseen a particular role for his services.

Whichever was the prison that held him, Harald would have been free of its confines in time for him and his men to take some part in the fighting which engulfed Constantinople throughout that Tuesday – because 20 April in the year 1042 was to go down in the annals with singular notoriety as the bloodiest day in the long history of the Byzantine capital. More than three thousand are said to have been slain before the palace finally fell in the early hours of the following morning when the forces around the emperor either surrendered or escaped, allowing the mob to overrun the whole vast complex, pillaging its treasures and paying especial attention to the imperial treasury, where the archives of the tax-collectors were destroyed. At least one Varangian might have had reason to see some treasury documents in shreds or aflame and he would not have been alone in so doing, although the more pressing concern of the mob was to find and kill the ex-emperor.

For the moment, though, it was to be frustrated because Michael and his uncle Constantine had gone from the palace before the first light of dawn when they took a boat along the coast to seek sanctuary in the monastery of St John of the Studion. There they had taken the tonsure and been admitted as monks while Zoe, left alone in the palace, was raised up on the shoulders of the insurgents who bore her aloft and placed her on the imperial throne. If her delight and relief were soon to be tempered when she learned of the return and coronation of the sister she had hated for so long, the sound of cheering crowds around the Hagia Sophia left Zoe no other option than to acknowledge the decision of the people and accept Theodora as her co-empress. Meanwhile, the whereabouts of Michael and Constantine had been discovered and the mob was gathering outside the church of the Studion monastery, still bent upon their destruction but not yet prepared to violate the sanctuary.

Evening was approaching by the time one of the newly appointed officials arrived from the city with orders from Theodora to bring the ex-emperor and his uncle out of the church, but talk of public execution was already to be heard and the two fugitives clung ever more desperately to the altar. Despite assurances of their safe-conduct back to the city, the pair still refused to relinquish their sanctuary and so the official abandoned persuasion for violence, commanding some of the mob to drag them from the church and compel their progress back to the palace. All of this is described in detail by Michael Psellus, who had already reached the Studion before the arrival of the official party and was thus enabled to provide a first-hand account of the fearful course of subsequent events.

Outside the monastery now, Michael and Constantine had been brought only a short distance along their route before they were confronted by a detachment of guards, apparently recognised by Psellus who describes them as 'brave men who shrank from nothing'. These new arrivals bore with them further orders, officially authorised by the new *sebastokrator* of Constantinople and yet thought to have originally issued from the empress Theodora herself: the deposed emperor and his uncle the *nobilissimus* were to be blinded forthwith. Psellus tells how the captives were taken on to the Sigma, an open space outside the Studion, but pauses to pay genuine tribute to Constantine's extraordinary bravery in offering himself as the first to suffer mutilation and lying down, unrestrained, as it was administered. His nephew was possessed of no such courage, howling with terror at the fate awaiting him and having to be held down by the guards before their orders could be carried out. Thereafter Michael was taken to a monastery to live out the rest of his days, as also was his uncle – although the *nobilissimus* Constantine was later brought out of his cell for interrogation as to the whereabouts of funds misappropriated during his nephew's reign.

When Psellus' account is set beside the similarly contemporary evidence preserved by the skalds, there can be no doubt that the detachment of guards charged with the grim duty carried out on Wednesday 21 April 1042, was Harald and his troop of Varangians. Thjodolf's lines bear their own clear testimony: 'On both eyes blinded was then . . . Grikaland's great lord by the destroyer of the wolf's grief [meaning a renowned warrior, presumably Harald himself].' Likewise, 'Norway's ruler [certainly meaning Harald] placed the grim mark on the brave man [apparently meaning Constantine]'. It is important to point out that neither skald suggests this as an act of personal revenge on Harald's part, and indeed Thorarin provides the clearest description of a mercenary warrior paid for services rendered: 'Our valiant chieftain gained still more of the glow-red gold; Grikaland's king was made stone-blind as his chief suffering'.

It is clear now that Snorri's saga bears scarcely any correspondence to the most likely historical context of Harald's escape from imprisonment and his mutilation of the emperor. There is no reason to believe that Harald acted other than as a mercenary officer under orders, although the source of those orders and the choice of Harald and his troop to carry them out prompt further consideration here. Psellus' account of the background to what befell at the Studion and on the Sigma points directly to the newly consecrated empress who was well aware of Zoe's hostility and feared she might yet prefer to restore Michael than share the imperium with her sister. Thus determined to extinguish any possibility of political recovery on the part or in the name of the deposed emperor and yet unwilling to have him slain, Theodora and her advisers apparently decided to command the traditional form of mutilation as the most effective means to that end. Duties of that type were customarily and conveniently assigned to Varangians, who were still known to the Greeks as 'Tauro-Scythians' and recognised as barbarians from the remote northlands for whom naked brutality was stock-in-trade.

It is true, of course, that Harald and his troop were just one of many such mercenary units available in the ferment consuming Constantinople in those April days of 1042 and so it is fully possible that their selection for this task was either purely arbitrary or entirely accidental. Yet the empress Theodora – who had been a nun just days before she had been dragged out by the mob to share the imperial throne with the hostile sister who had once already incarcerated her in a convent – had urgent need of someone whom she knew to be not only utterly trustworthy but fully capable of the task assigned him. In such anxiety and so precarious a situation, she might very well have had some recollection of the name of the officer commanding the escort which brought her in safety through the dangerous deserts of the Holy Land on the pilgrimage to Jerusalem just six years before.

None of which is more than speculation, of course, but Harald's assignment to the gruesome duty outside the Studion must have greatly enhanced his prominence and authority in the Varangian

Guard of the new regime. So much so that he might very well have been appointed judge and executioner in a purge of those who had found themselves on the losing side in the fighting which brought about the palace revolution. Varangians in Byzantine service had evidently long held the privilege of dealing with those within their own ranks accused of a crime or misdemeanour. That custom was very probably rooted in the rough justice meted out to those who had infringed the oaths sworn by members of the original Varangian companies. Some very similar discipline would have prevailed among Russo-Scandinavian mercenaries in imperial service prior to the establishment of the Varangian regiment by Basil II and continued thereafter as a special regimental privilege with particular application within the Varangian Guard. There would be good reason, then, to see this practice reflected in the half-strophe preserved in *Fagrskinna* and attributed to Valgard of Voll which tells of Harald having 'commanded the half of them to hang then and there; so you have done and there are fewer *Væringjar* remaining'. Although this fragment has been variously interpreted, Valgard himself is thought to have served with Harald during this later period of his imperial service and there is no doubt that Varangians fighting for Michael and Constantine could have been justly accused of treason when they had broken a solemn oath to defend the legitimate *porphyrogenita* empresses. Judged guilty by their commander – in the person of Harald – they would quite certainly have been condemned to death by hanging.

While the *Advice* denies Harald's promotion above the rank of *spatharokandidatos*, it fully confirms the high personal esteem in which he was held by the new imperial regime – in which the sister empresses were shortly to be joined by a co-emperor when Zoe took Constantine Monomachus as her new husband. This must have been a quite unexpected development and not only because both sisters were now in their sixties. The tall, thin Theodora was unlikely to abandon the chaste habit of a lifetime and while the same could never be said of her shorter, chubbier elder sister, Zoe had already had two husbands and third marriages were viewed with the sternest disapproval by the Orthodox Church. Nonetheless, the reputedly lascivious Zoe is said by Psellus to have wanted another husband if only to help guard against any reversal of her restored fortunes and her choice fell upon the charming and aristocratic Constantine Monomachus. Even while her second husband was still alive, Zoe had developed a close friendship with this Constantine, thus arousing the suspicion of the ever-watchful Orphanotrophus who ordered him into exile on the island of Lesbos and it was from there that he was summoned back to Constantinople in the early summer of 1042.

The Patriarch apparently found a way around his Church's disapproval so as to conduct their wedding on 11 June and afterwards to consecrate the empress's new husband as her co-emperor Constantine IX who was to reign for thirteen years until his death in 1055. In fact, the term 'co-emperor' was soon to become no more than a formality, because within three months Zoe and Theodora had retired from public life leaving Constantine as the sole effective imperial figure and it must have been around this time that the emperor known in the saga as 'Konstantinus Monomakus' made his genuinely historical entry into Harald's story.

Snorri Sturluson's confused account indicating Constantine Monomachus as the emperor mutilated by Harald has led at least one historian to discount the whole episode, and yet quite unjustly so in view of the impressively convincing and closely contemporary evidence provided by the two skalds. The emperor in question can only have been Michael Calaphates and so Snorri's unfortunate error is perhaps best explained as a confusion of two Constantines having led him to the assumption that the *nobilissimus* Constantine who suffered blinding on the same occasion as his nephew was the same Constantine who refused Harald permission to leave Constantinople. At least there can be no doubt as to the accuracy of Snorri's identification of the Constantine in that latter instance because it is fully confirmed by the reliable evidence of the *Advice* when it states that 'Araltes wished in the reign of the emperor Monomachus to be given permission to return to his own land, but it was not forthcoming. Indeed, his way was obstructed and yet he slipped away by stealth . . .'

Unfortunately, the *Advice* supplies no further detail of just how Harald 'slipped away by stealth' from Constantinople and so the saga preserves the only full account of the adventure which forms a characteristically bold finale to his career as a Varangian mercenary in Byzantine service. Yet the saga fails to offer any very convincing explanation as to the reason for his sudden and urgent departure. The simple desire to see his homeland once again cannot really be accepted as sufficient explanation and so there must have been a more pressing reason – and indeed there was, but it is one which will become more clearly apparent from the viewpoint of Kiev than from that of Constantinople. The tidings which did prompt Harald's request for leave to resign from imperial service assuredly reached him from Russia – possibly even under diplomatic cover if they came from the Grand Prince Jaroslav himself – and at some time in August when the annual trading fleet from Kiev came to harbour after its passage across the Black Sea.

That particular estimate of timing is fortuitous here, because it would also have been in August when imperial authority passed to the new emperor Constantine Monomachus and so it would have been to him that Harald brought his request for leave of departure. In the event, of course, it was refused – and for good reason in the light of subsequent developments – but Harald's own reason for departure was of the greatest urgency. Even in August, there was little enough time left to prepare for the crossing of the Black Sea and long journey up the Dnieper back to Kiev, which was indeed Harald's intended destination.

Snorri tells how Harald and a select company of his comrades took two of the Varangian galleys and rowed them out until they came to the iron chains slung across the entrance to the harbour. On approaching this obstacle, the oarsmen were commanded to pull with all strength while others of the crew, heavy-laden with their gear, were ordered to the stern of the ships as they ran up to the chains. At which point, as the craft lost momentum to hang over the chain barrier, the crewmen were ordered back to the bows, their weight tilting Harald's galley forward into a slide down from the chain and into open water. The same tactic was followed by those aboard the other galley, but without the same success because their keel stuck fast on the chain and the ship broke its back, allowing only some of its crew to be pulled to safety aboard Harald's galley while others were lost beneath the waves.

Thus Snorri tells of Harald's escape from Constantinople with no lesser authorities than Blöndal and Benedikz pronouncing the story 'in all probability . . . correct in its essentials'. That credibility is only fractionally defrayed by the inclusion of 'a silly, romantic fable' dragging the aforementioned 'Maria' into the story when she is forcibly abducted, taken aboard one of the galleys and rowed out into the Black Sea before being set ashore with a retinue who were to escort her back to Zoe as proof of Harald's ability to do just as he chose.[12] When that unlikely element is set aside, the technical detail is certainly unusually convincing when compared with that found in many of the anecdotes included in Snorri's saga, as also is the specific reference to Harald's galley sailing 'north to *Ellipalt*' (identified as a lagoon in the mouth of the Dnieper) and on from there 'through the eastern realm' (meaning Russia). There certainly was a great iron chain supported on rafts across the Golden Horn (and another across the Bosporus, but that is not known to have been in use until a century after Harald's departure) floated out through the hours of darkness to provide a defence for the Harbour of Neorion where the imperial fleet was berthed beside its arsenal and store-houses, while the Varangian galleys were moored by the Tower of St Eugenius which also secured the southern end of the chain across the Golden Horn.

It should be said that at least one authority has suggested this episode as a 'borrowed tale' akin to the siege stories (a similar escape from the harbour at Syracuse being known from Roman times), but the authenticity of the saga account is too well supported for such doubt. Not only does the *Advice* confirm Harald's departure from Constantinople by stealth, but Snorri illustrates that stealth with detail so convincing as to indicate his original source having been the first-hand recollection of Halldor Snorrason who was certainly aboard the galley which brought Harald to Kiev on this first passage of his long journey home to the northlands.

Russia, 1042–1045

It was while on voyage up the Dnieper that Harald is believed to have composed sixteen strophes of verse recalling his Varangian exploits, each one ending with the same refrain: 'Yet the bracelet-goddess in Gardar still refuses me'.[13] Although most of these *Gamanvísur* have long since been lost, Snorri Sturluson does preserve one complete strophe which is quoted in his *Harald's saga* by way of conclusion to his account of the escape from Constantinople – and with a note identifying '*Ellisif*, the daughter of King *Jarisleif* in *Holmgarð*' as the 'goddess in Gardar' to whom all this poetry was addressed.

Whether or not these verses really were composed aboard ship – as they may well have been when they were evidently intended for presentation to the princess he was to marry shortly after his arrival at the Russian court – the lines preserved in the saga represent a fragment of immediately contemporary evidence containing more than one point of interest. First of all, they effectively discredit the earlier saga claim for his marital ambitions regarding the (presumably fictional) 'Maria', and also carry a curious echo of his revered half-brother Olaf, whose one recorded attempt at the skaldic art comprised similarly intended verses written for Ingigerd, the Swedish princess who was later to become the bride of Jaroslav of Kiev and the mother of his daughter, the Elizaveta known in the sagas, and presumably also to Harald, by her Norse name-form of *Ellisif*.

Elizaveta had been little more than a child, of course, when Harald set out for Byzantium eight years earlier and the marriage of any daughter of a Russian Grand Prince to a mere Varangian mercenary would have been virtually unthinkable anyway, but now an eighteen-year-old Kievan princess would represent an eminently suitable prospective wife for a wealthy Scandinavian prince whose ambition was turning towards kingship in the northlands. Just such a possibility may have been long in Jaroslav's mind, because he was in the habit of arranging politically strategic marriages for his offspring. His younger son Vsevolod was to be wed to a daughter of the Byzantine Monomachus family, while Elizaveta's two sisters made still more impressive marriages when they became the queens of Hungary and France. If Jaroslav had already recognised Harald's potential as a warrior king and suspected – or actually known – something of his ultimate ambition while he was still in Constantinople, it is not at all unlikely that the prospect of so prestigious a bride might have been offered to lure him back to Russia. All of which might be perfectly plausible and yet still does not explain why Harald was so anxious to leave imperial service or why he should have been refused permission to do so.

The homesickness implied in Snorri's claim that Harald was eager to see Norway again hardly corresponds to the apparent urgency of the situation and the further claim for Harald 'having heard' of his nephew Magnus adding the sovereignty over Denmark to his kingship in Norway clearly defies credibility. Magnus had remained in Russia while his father set out on the journey back to Norway which was to bring him to his death in battle at Stiklestad. Thereafter, the young prince stayed at Jaroslav's court until brought back to Norway as his father's successor in response to popular demand shortly before the death of Cnut in 1035. On the death of Cnut's son Hardacnut some seven years later, 'Magnus the Good' extended his sovereignty to Denmark, once again by apparent popular acclaim, and yet Hardacnut died in England – where he was buried at Winchester on 8 June 1042 – so it is scarcely possible that news of Magnus' succession as king of Denmark could have reached Constantinople until very much later in that year, by which time Harald had already made his escape to Kiev. The factor of most ominous significance in the sphere of Russo-Byzantine affairs at just that time is nowhere mentioned in the sagas and yet could only have had its own crucial bearing on Harald's situation because, by the spring of 1042, Jaroslav was already advanced in building the warfleet with which he was planning to launch an expedition against Constantinople in the following year.

According to Michael Psellus, Byzantine military intelligence would seem to have known something of these suspicious developments in Kiev even while Michael IV was still alive, although the brief but disruptive reign of his successor and the cataclysm surrounding his deposition must have proved a serious distraction from the forward planning of imperial defence policy. Even so, there is every likelihood that anxious fears of impending Russian hostilities lay behind his successor emperor Constantine's refusal of permission for Harald to leave Constantinople, and especially so when he would surely make his way directly to Kiev. To allow a widely experienced officer of the Varangian Guard to share his inside knowledge of the deployment and weaknesses of Byzantine forces with a likely aggressor would have been incautious to the point of irresponsibility, so the emperor's response to Harald's request for leave cannot be considered either unreasonable or unjust. In fact, it was particularly astute because Harald must have maintained contact with Jaroslav throughout almost all his years in imperial service if – as the saga claims – he had been sending his plunder 'in the care of trusted men to *Holmgarð*' and into the Grand Prince's safe-keeping. Such 'trusted men' would have been accomplished in evading the scrutiny of Byzantine officialdom – not least when the export of gold and currency from Byzantium was forbidden – and thus equally qualified for service as trustworthy message-bearers.

So too, it would surely have been similarly 'trusted men' arriving in Constantinople with the annual trading fleet in the summer of 1042 who brought Harald the tidings which called him back to Russia, and the most likely reason for that urgent summons would have been Jaroslav's requirement for detailed military intelligence to guide his planning of the intended assault on *Tsargrad* (as *Miklagarð* was called by the Rus). All historical opinion is agreed that Harald was gone from Constantinople by the time the Russian expeditionary force appeared in the Bosporus (presumably the later spring or early summer of 1043), so his date of departure is usually placed between the second half of 1042 and the earlier months of the following year – and yet, when other salient factors are brought into consideration, the date of his return to Russia might be fixed more precisely still. Not least among those factors is another threat which was about to be presented to the new emperor, and this one posed in the formidable form of Georgios Maniakes.

While in exile on Lesbos Constantine Monomachus had enjoyed the company of his long-standing mistress, a granddaughter of Bardas Sclerus who had been the second pretender (alongside Bardas Phocas) challenging Basil II at the time of his formation of the Varangian Guard in the later 980s. This lady was soon to follow her lover to the capital where Zoe would seem to have had no serious objection to sharing her new husband and so it was that the 'Sclerena' (as she is said to have been universally known) became a fixture in court circles. Outside the palace confines, however, the Sclerena became widely unpopular, although not so much in her own right as on account of her avaricious relatives who took every possible advantage of her new semi-imperial standing. Of these kinsfolk, it was her brother Romanus whose activities were to prove most disastrous for the course of Byzantine history, initially because his estates adjoined those of Georgios Maniakes in Anatolia where the two men had become bitterly hostile neighbours.

Since his restoration by the former emperor and subsequent return to Italy in April 1042, Maniakes had suppressed a revolt in Apulia with a devastating, but nonetheless effective, campaign of appalling savagery before he once again fell prey to typically Byzantine political intrigue when the Sclerena's brother contrived to have the general recalled and replaced – or would have done so had Georgios not refused to submit to a second dismissal from imperial favour. The officer sent to Italy as his replacement was seized upon arrival, disgustingly tortured and summarily executed. Having firmly asserted himself in command, Maniakes led his troops across the Adriatic in the early spring of 1043 and began his advance upon the capital until confronted by the greatly superior numbers of an imperial army near Ostrovo in Macedonia. Maniakes had his army acclaim him emperor before the battle began and Psellus describes his defiance in the front line of the first onslaught against the enemy lines: 'Thundering out commands as he rode up and down the ranks, he struck terror into the hearts of all who saw him, while his proud bearing overwhelmed our vast numbers from the very outset. Circling around our legions and spreading confusion all about, he had but to attack before the ranks gave way and the wall of troops pulled back.' At which point the battle-god who had favoured him on so many fields would seem to have turned away at just the same moment a thrown lance found its mark and delivered his death-wound to the mighty Maniakes. Decapitated on the battlefield, the head of the greatest Byzantine soldier of his time was brought back to the emperor in Constantinople, where it was paraded around the Hippodrome by the returning army and impaled high on a spike in full view of the populace.

While the annals assign no precise date, the death of Georgios Maniakes is usually and reliably placed in February/March of 1043, but what can be said with greater certainty of his last battle is that the imperial forces sent against him did not include Harald with his Varangians. Had it been otherwise, the saga-makers would have made every imaginable claim for Harald's achieving ultimate victory over the greatest personal enemy of his career in imperial service; and if he was not with the emperor's army in that battle then he had most certainly made his escape from Constantinople before February 1043. The long voyage across the Black Sea and up the Dnieper was hazardous enough in any season, but in the winter months it would have been a venture of utter folly, so Harald's journey from Constantinople to Kiev can be placed with all possible confidence in the autumn of 1042.

Particular attention must be paid to the date of events through this passage of Harald's warrior's way as a precaution against the misleading chronology of the saga narrative. Snorri's casual assignment of events to 'that winter' or 'the following spring' gives the impression of Harald having spent barely a year in Russia and yet some three full years must have passed between his arrival at Kiev in the autumn of 1042 and his departure for Scandinavia which could not have been made before the later autumn of 1045. While there is no absolute certainty that Snorri is to be trusted when he tells of Jaroslav having given Harald his daughter in marriage in the winter following his return from Constantinople, there is no real reason to doubt him in this instance. So the wedding to the princess Elizaveta was probably consecrated around the time of the winter festival which is more closely related with the feast of Epiphany in the Orthodox calendar and might be dated – although still with due caution – to the earliest weeks of the year 1043. Snorri's saga goes on to quote a half-strophe from the skald Stúf which speaks of Harald's marriage having brought him 'gold aplenty as reward [presumably a generous dowry] and a princess too' – and one whose distinguished parentage (of the Rurikid line and the Swedish royal family) would have conferred its own measure of new prestige upon a man with his own ambitions on kingship.

For Jaroslav, on the other hand, his immediate return on investment of that dowry would have been the detailed military intelligence Harald had brought with him along the east-way, because his predominant concerns in the new year of 1043 must have centred on plans for the great expedition he intended for the coming summer. Even though events in Byzantium had been moving on apace in Harald's absence, he would surely have had a useful working knowledge of the numbers and deployment of Byzantine land forces around the capital and elsewhere across the empire, although it would have been some months yet before he learned of the fate of his old enemy *Gyrgir*. The item of most immediate concern to Russian tactical planning and the one on which Harald may very well have been able to offer valuable information was the disposition of the imperial fleet, because its great warships armed with the empire's celebrated secret weapon of 'Greek Fire' represented Constantinople's first line of defence.[14] If, for example, Harald could report the empire's naval forces being 'below strength [with] the fireships dispersed at various naval stations', then he would have supplied the most reliable intelligence because those details are quoted from Psellus' account of shortcomings in marine defences available to the emperor when the Russian fleet did appear in the Bosporus. Sadly for Jaroslav, however, no military intelligence reports could have warned him of the sudden Black Sea storm which would seem to have been the decisive factor in the crushing defeat of his great enterprise.

Despite the inevitable discrepancies between accounts of the same event preserved in the Russian *Primary Chronicle* and the contemporary Byzantine record – as set down by Psellus and the annalist Cedrenus – all those sources agree on the outcome having been a disaster for the Rus. The strength of their fleet, led by Jaroslav's son Vladimir of Novgorod and an experienced *voevodo* by the name of Vyshata, is estimated at some four hundred ships (of a type resembling the Scandinavian longship, but reflecting Slavic influence in its broader beam and more heavily timbered hull), most of which were destroyed by a combination of storm at sea and enemy incendiary assault.

Psellus writes proudly of the emperor's assembly of an impromptu warfleet – three 'triremes' (or *dromoi*) with incendiary siphons aboard, some transport vessels and old hulks made as seaworthy as possible – to present 'the barbarians' with the semblance of a defensive naval cordon. He tells of the Byzantine warships engaging with the enemy fleet and throwing it into disarray with Greek Fire just before the onset of a hurricane force easterly completed the work of destruction. Yet his story is so suspiciously reminiscent of the defeat of a Russian attack of a hundred years before, when an earlier emperor achieved unexpected triumph with a similar scratch naval force, that the *Primary Chronicle* might be thought more trustworthy when it describes a storm playing havoc with the Russian fleet on the sea-crossing from the Danube to the Bosporus before fourteen Byzantine warships emerged to drive off such vessels as were still capable of flight.

Nonetheless, the Greeks did not have everything go their way. When Prince Vladimir's own ship was crippled, he and some of his *druzhina* managed to escape to the Bulgarian shore aboard another, presumably one of those which had survived the initial maelstrom well enough to be capable of destroying four enemy vessels off the Thracian coast. Vyshata, however, was less fortunate, because it was he who took command of those warriors who had managed to get ashore and led their retreat overland until it was cut off by Byzantine troops. Those not slain were taken prisoner, many of them said to have been mutilated in captivity, and three years were to pass before negotiations secured the return of Vyshata and his fellow survivors to Russia. While Cedrenus' claim for fifteen thousand Russian corpses washed up on the Bosporus shore is clearly a gross exaggeration, grievously heavy casualties must have been suffered when the *Primary Chronicle* admits barely six thousand survivors from a force which had set out with more than ten thousand fighting-men, of whom some number are said both by Russian and Byzantine sources to have been Varangian mercenaries. If so, then this was to be the last occasion on which Jaroslav is known to have employed the Varangians who had for so long been his principal source of mercenary recruitment, as they had for his father before him.

This year of 1043 can be seen as a landmark in the military history of the Rus – and on two counts. Not only does it effectively represent the end of the long-standing tradition of *Varjazi* mercenaries serving as the sword-arm of Russian princes, but it also marks the end of an era in Russo-Byzantine relations because Jaroslav's venture into the Bosporus was the last of a long history of Russian assaults on Tsargrad, of which the first is said to have been launched by Oleg, a kinsman of the founding dynast Rurik, in 860. Yet the question remains as to why Jaroslav made the attempt in the first place. His motive is said by the Byzantine sources to have been the death of a Rus merchant – 'a barbarian nobleman' according to Psellus – in a market brawl in Constantinople, which would seem to have been a mere pretext for an invasion which had been at least two years in the planning, even though Cedrenus tells of a demand for compensation in the sum of 3lb weight in gold for every man in the Russian fleet. Psellus, on the other hand, notices at least one Russian ship laden with a 'rampart', presumably meaning some structure intended for assault on city walls and yet those surrounding Constantinople had withstood such attempts by Persians, Avars and Arabs – as well as Rus – for more than half a millennium and it is almost inconceivable that Jaroslav actually intended the seizure of the city.

No less puzzling is the fact of the expedition being launched at the same time as Jaroslav's magnificent Hagia Sophia – the largest surviving Byzantine-style church of the eleventh century, even decorated with inscriptions in Greek rather than Church Slavonic, and unrivalled as the most visibly imposing feature of a far wider Russian cultural flowering – was under construction in Kiev. Interestingly, the authors of a highly respected recent history of early Russia have found no 'necessary contradiction between the demonstratively Constantinopolitan style of Jaroslav's public patronage and his campaign against Constantinople in 1043', going on to suggest his entire cultural programme having been directed *against* Constantinople as an assertion of Kievan equality and a reaction against Byzantine 'imperial pretensions'.[15] In fact, there is much in Psellus' account to support that explanation, especially when he refers to the expedition as the 'rebellion' inspired by the furious rage harboured by a 'barbarian race for the hegemony of the Romans'.

A closely similar view underlies the suggestion made by another historian, and one of pre-eminent authority, that 'it is quite possible that Psellus was alluding to the traditional Byzantine claim to political sovereignty over Russia'.[16] Thus Jaroslav's enterprise of 1043 must be seen as an extravagant gesture in defiance of imperial influence north of the steppe, and its apparent contradictions as a reflection of the paradox attendant upon the man himself. The 'Jaroslav the Wise' surrounding himself with 'the sweetness of books' while ushering in the 'Golden Age of Kiev' was the same Jaroslav Vladimirovich who had succeeded his father, 'Vladimir the Saint', as supreme ruler of the Rus only after two decades of bitter internecine warfare which had left all but one of his brothers dead – usually in violent circumstances – and the one survivor consigned to incarceration. His first importance in these pages, though, lies in his far-reaching influence on a future king of Norway, because there will be a number of occasions throughout the course of Harald's reign when the man called *Jarisleif* by the saga-makers can be recognised as his principal exemplar in the art and practice of kingship.

It is unfortunate, then, that the saga record preserves so little detail of the three years Harald spent in Russia before making his return to Scandinavia. Snorri Sturluson records the marriage to the princess Elizaveta, of course, but he would seem to know nothing else of his activities through this period other than his gathering together all the gold and treasure he had sent ahead from Byzantium into the celebrated hoard 'greater than had ever been seen in the north in one man's possession'. Snorri makes so many references to Harald's treasury that his claims cannot have been without a substantial core of truth – especially when they have been supported by archaeological evidence of coin finds in Scandinavia – and yet it is still curious that the *Morkinskinna* or *Fagrskinna* versions of the saga have nothing to say on the subject.

While considering the saga accounts of Harald in Russia, it should be noted that they all identify Jaroslav's capital as *Holmgarð* – by which, of course, is meant Novgorod and it is true that Novgorod had formerly been his preferred power base, even after the agreement with his brother Mstislav had granted him Kiev. On (or even shortly before) Mstislav's death and most evidently after his own decisive defeat of the Pecheneg siege in 1036, Jaroslav moved to establish Kiev as his new capital. Thus it would have been to Kiev rather than Novgorod that Harald had sent his profits from the east into Jaroslav's safe-keeping and in the orbit of the Kievan court that he would have spent the greater part of his stay in Russia after his return from Constantinople.

Nonetheless, he eventually would have had to make his way to *Holmgarð* because Novgorod lay on the route to Staraja Ladoga from where he was to take a ship across the Baltic. In fact, Harald must have spent some time in the north of Russia because it was there that he would have assembled the ships and fighting-men to accompany his return to Scandinavia.

There can be no doubt that news of his return from Byzantium would have been carried northwards long before he left Kiev, while stories of his exploits in the east had assuredly reached Russia long before he did and had already begun to build a reputation which was to attract some numbers of professional warriors seeking to share in such profitable battle-glory. Despite the doubtful authenticity of some of the saga stories, the fact of their being so numerous and so enthusiastically endorsed by the skalds can only confirm the genuine substance of a remarkable military record. So, too, their emphasis on Harald's guile and resourcefulness would have had a particular appeal to the Scandinavian military mind-set, while a Russian warrior would have been most impressed by what he heard of Harald's prominence in the imperial guard, his brushes with Maniakes and his part in the downfall of an emperor. There is every likelihood, then, of Slavic Rus, and perhaps even Finno-Ugrian, warriors having been included with Scandinavians in the force he was to raise in Novgorod where talk of his coming would have been abroad before the arrival of the man himself. Rumours of his looking to recruit mercenary forces and of the abundant treasury with which he would be ready to pay for them would have offered a welcome prospect in Varangian circles – and especially since Jaroslav's relocation of his power base to the middle Dnieper had so diminished his formerly voracious appetite for northern mercenaries.

However elaborated those rumours of Harald had become in the course of repeated and ever more enthusiastic retelling, the eventual arrival of the man himself can only have fulfilled their promise. If any in Novgorod still remembered the fifteen-year-old princeling of some fifteen years before, they would scarcely have recognised in him the full-grown man returned from the east with his own *druzhina* of battle-hardened veterans from the Varangian Guard at his back and a heavy purse of Byzantine gold at his belt. Now into his thirtieth year, Harald would have appeared very much as Snorri describes him in the saga: 'Handsome and of distinguished bearing, with a fair beard and long moustaches [as was the Slav-influenced fashion among east-farers]. One eyebrow was slightly higher than the other. His hands and feet were large and well proportioned.' Even though it is hardly possible that Harald was as tall as the five ells claimed by Snorri (a figure probably construed from the 'seven feet of earth or as much more as he is taller than other men' said to have been promised him by the English Harold before battle was joined at Stamford Bridge), he evidently was a man of towering physique, whose appearance would have been enhanced by the splendid Byzantine apparel and richly decorated weaponry and war-gear he had brought back from Grikaland.

In Novgorod and Ladoga, he would also have been ideally placed to hear the latest word from around the Baltic and with especial interest when it bore on his nephew's warfaring. Thus he would have already learned of Magnus' devastating defeat of the Wends and of his having made Svein Estridsson his Danish jarl ('just as Cnut the Great had set Jarl Ulf, his [Svein's] father as chieftain over Denmark while he himself was in England', according to Magnus' saga in *Heimskringla*) – at least until Svein rose up in arms to assert his own claim to the kingship of Denmark.

In the autumn of 1045 Magnus inflicted a decisive defeat on his Danish rival in battle off Helganess on the eastern coast of Jutland, Svein took flight to Sigtuna where he found refuge at the Swedish court and Harald evidently decided it was time to make his move. Snorri's saga quotes a strophe from the skald Valgard of Voll who had been with Harald since Miklagard and now sailed with him across the Varangian Sea . . .

> Laden with the richest cargo, you
> launched your swift ship, Harald,
> carrying gold from Gardar –
> hard-won with honour – westward.
> Through storm and gale you steered,
> sturdy chieftain. Ships wallowed
> deep until at last, through thinning
> spindrift, you sighted Sigtuna.

III

Hardrada

Scandinavia, 1045–1065

Harald's voyage from Russia to the Scandinavian mainland in the later autumn of 1045 was a sea-crossing of some 400 miles and little more than a week's duration – even when allowance is made for the 'storm and gale' recalled in Valgard's verse, yet it represents a passage of such significance in his warrior's way as to be considered a 'sea-change' in the fullest sense of that term. Throughout the previous ten years 'we can be sure he spent most of the time with harness on his back' (to borrow Gwyn Jones' evocative turn of phrase), '. . . [as] a professional who fought in any theatre of war to which his employer sent him'.[1] Now he was a warlord in his own right, with a reputation and a treasury which were already assuming legendary proportions, and driven by the ruthless ambition for which history would remember him as Harald Hardrada.

It can only have been that ambition – as yet, of course, cloaked with his characteristic guile – which had brought Harald to the court of the Swedish king Onund Olafsson at Sigtuna and to his first encounter with the man whom the saga calls by his patronymic name-form of Svein Ulfsson. 'Harald and Svein were greatly pleased to meet as they were related by marriage' – as, indeed, they were when Harald's Russian wife was a daughter of Onund's sister Ingigerd and Svein's mother Estrid was half-sister to Onund's father, Olaf.

From this point onwards in the saga narrative great attention is paid to kinship by marriage, and necessarily so because it formed a complex network of relationships crucial to the course of political history in early medieval Scandinavia. Indeed, Svein's own claim on the Danish kingship derived from his mother who was a full sister to the mighty Cnut (as well as half-sister to Olaf of Sweden), and his father, Ulf Thorgilsson, had been the jarl entrusted with his realm of Denmark while Cnut himself was most concerned with his new kingdom in England. By way of surety for his jarl's good behaviour, Cnut kept Ulf's two sons with him as hostage and so Svein passed his younger years at the English court. While his brother Beorn stayed on as an earl in England, Svein was drawn back to Scandinavia and, at some point after his father's assassination at Roskilde around the year 1028, he returned north to spend some twelve years in the service of his cousin Onund in Sweden.

Throughout most of those years, Svein must have been watching and waiting while kingship in Denmark passed first to Hardacnut (Cnut's son by his Norman queen Emma) and then, after Hardacnut's death, to the Norwegian Magnus Olafsson. Whether or not there really had been an agreement between Magnus and Hardacnut to the effect that whichever of them survived the other should succeed to his kingdom and Svein honoured that agreement when he submitted to Magnus and became his jarl in Denmark (as the sagas claim), the Danes were apparently content to accept the son of Olaf the Saint as their overlord. Yet Svein himself was not long to share such contentment and soon enough found sufficient support to challenge Magnus in arms. Saxo Grammaticus claims Magnus defeated Svein on land and at sea in Jutland, while Snorri tells of Svein's defeat in three battles, the last of them fought off Helganess and resulting in Svein's flight back to the court at Sigtuna shortly before the arrival there of Magnus' uncle Harald, who was likewise in search of a kingdom.

So it was that the two would have found themselves with rather more in common than kinship by marriage and their discussions through long winter nights at the Swedish court would seem to have been passed in formulating the plan of action they were to launch in the coming spring. Snorri tells of all the Swedes having been Svein's friends by reason of his kinship to their royal house and of their becoming Harald's friends too, although more probably attracted by the reputation of a wealthy and battle-glorious warlord, as is implied by the skald Thjodolf's strophe quoted in the saga and telling of Harald's 'gold-laden ship from the east . . . oaken keel parting the billows; since that time, Olaf's kinsman, all the Swedes did aid thee'. Thus the 'large force' with which Svein and Harald launched their raiding cruise around Denmark in the spring of 1046 would have mostly comprised Swedish ships crewed by Swedes of viking inclination when it sailed down the east coast of Sweden to bear west around the coast of Skaane and strike at the islands of Zealand and Fyn – as recorded, presumably again at first-hand, by the skald Valgard in his three strophes quoted in the saga.

Valgard exults in wolves battening on the battle-slain in Zealand, bright fire burning houses and barns south of Roskilde, helmets tested and ornate shields shattered on Fyn island, and 'chains chafing the flesh of chattel maidens' as they are dragged to the ships. All of this was the stock-in-trade of the skald as war-poet, of course, and yet for Harald this ravaging of Denmark must have been his practical introduction to the viking raiding for which his countrymen had long been notorious at home as well as abroad. Unlike his sainted half-brother, who had been taken aboard his first viking cruise at the age of twelve, and for all his own wide-ranging education in the way of the warrior, Harald's only comparable earlier experience would have been the attacks on corsair shore bases in which he had engaged as a newly recruited Varangian mercenary with the Byzantine fleet in the Mediterranean some twelve years before.

For all the detail of plunder and slave-taking preserved in Valgard's verse, the principal purpose of this campaign against the Danish islands in the spring of 1046 was intimidation, firstly of the islanders themselves, intending to cow them into submission to Svein's claim to kingship, and secondly of Magnus, when it threw down a newly reinforced challenge to his sovereignty over Denmark. While that was clearly Svein's motive, Harald's interest in the expedition is less apparent because he had no claim on Danish kingship in his own right or he would have been recognised by Svein as a rival rather than an ally. Harald's sole claim to kingship at this time lay in Norway and so his purpose in terrorising Magnus' Danish subjects can only have been a demonstration to his nephew of his return to the northlands as a force to be reckoned with.

By 1046 Magnus Olafsson – said by Saxo Grammaticus to have been called 'Magnus the Good' by the grateful Danes, while Snorri credits the cognomen to the skald Sigvat – had been king of Norway for more than a decade. As a five-year-old child, he had been left in the care of Jaroslav in Novgorod when his father returned to Norway on the death-journey to Stiklestad in 1030, and was 'not yet eleven' (on the evidence of Arnor Jarlaskald) when he was brought back to Norway in 1035.

Having earlier promised lordship of his new Norwegian kingdom to both Kalv Arnason and Einar Tambarskelve, Cnut had decided to place his own young son Svein in the kingship even before Olaf came back from Russia – and indeed, had told Einar as much in England, prompting Einar to delay his own return home until after the blood-fray at Stiklestad. Thus it was in the respective capacities of boy-king and regent that Svein Cnutsson and his mother Ælfgifu (Cnut's English wife, called *Alfifa* in the Norse) came to Norway from Denmark in the later summer of 1030 at the beginning of a five-year reign remembered almost exclusively, at least in the saga histories, for the oppressive rule and penal taxation which were to become so intolerable that their Norse subjects eventually drove them out.

There is widespread doubt among historians as to the reliability of the saga-makers' claims, not least because such policies would have been ultimately self-defeating when they could only alienate a subject people who had recently shown themselves capable of disposing of their own legitimate king. The true situation was more probably one of powerful native lords increasingly resentful of the imposition of an Anglo-Danish child monarch (especially one accompanied by his English regent mother) when one of their own kind might be so easily called back from his Russian exile. Then there was also the sense of national and personal guilt surrounding the martyrdom of Olaf, whose cult had gained ground at an almost unprecedented pace, and so the recall of a son to reclaim the kingship torn from his sainted father might even be seen as an act of reparation – especially when Kalv Arnason accompanied Einar Tambarskelve to summon the young Magnus home from Novgorod.

The most interestingly detailed account of their mission is that preserved in *Orkneyinga saga* when it tells of Einar and Kalv confronted on arrival at Staraja Ladoga by Rognvald Brusason, who was only dissuaded from taking summary vengeance when he was assured of Kalv's repentance for 'his crime of killing King Olaf the Saint'. Learning of the reason for their coming to Russia, Rognvald accompanied the pair to Novgorod and their meeting with Jaroslav, who recalled what had befallen Olaf on his return to Norway and was thus unwilling to place the son at risk of any similar fate. Only when the Norse contingent swore solemn oaths of their good faith was Magnus given leave to return to his homeland – and with the added assurance of the trustworthy Rognvald as his escort.

Once Magnus was back in Norway and acclaimed as king of the whole country, *Orkneyinga saga* turns its attention to Rognvald who returned to Orkney around the year 1037 after he had had news of the death of his father, Jarl Brusi. For some eight years, Rognvald shared the jarldom with his uncle, the famously mighty Thorfinn, the two even going together on viking raids west-over-sea until they came into violent contention over Thorfinn's demands to add a greater share of the islands to his mainland possessions in Caithness. The saga tells of Thorfinn's victory at sea in the Pentland Firth followed by Rognvald's flight to Norway to seek assistance from Magnus and his return to Orkney with a force of Norwegian housecarls. Even that formidable reinforcement was unable to protect him when conflict with Thorfinn was renewed in a sequence of reciprocal house-burnings before Rognvald was slain on the isle of Papa Stronsay in the Yuletide season of 1046.

Throughout that same period, of course, Magnus reigned as king of Norway and, after 1042, of Denmark also. Curiously, some of the most closely contemporary evidence for his reign is to be found in another Orkney-related source, namely the praise-poetry composed by Arnor Jarlaskald on a visit to the Norwegian court, probably made in the spring of 1047. Snorri's *Magnus the Good's saga* quotes Arnor's verses on more than one occasion and they evidently represent a principal source for his account of Magnus' war on the Wends. Arnor acclaims Magnus as the 'scion of heroes, [who] harried the Wendish homeland', and yet would seem to make no specific reference to his attack on 'Jomsburg' (the fortress base of the doubtfully historical 'Jomsvikings', whose celebrity rests almost entirely on the fictional *Jomsvikinga saga*) claimed by the sagas. Adam of Bremen, on the other hand, records Magnus' laying siege to *Jomne*, 'the richest city of the Slavs' and this apparent confusion among the sources is most convincingly disentangled by Gwyn Jones when he identifies the 'Jomsburg/Jomne' stormed and burnt by Magnus in 1043 as Wollin at the mouth of the Oder, 'whose inhabitants, by now predominantly Wendish, but no doubt still retaining a Danish element more sympathetic to Svein [Estridsson] than to any Norwegian, had thrown off their allegiance [to Magnus]'.[2]

Magnus' most celebrated triumph over the Wends, however, was the battle fought on Lyrskov Heath (called *Hlyrskogs Hede* in the saga and located northwest of what is now Schleswig) where he was operating in alliance against a common enemy with his sister's Saxon husband Ordulf when the Wends invaded southern Jutland. He brought his fleet to Hedeby where his forces disembarked to join up with Ordulf's Saxons for an attack on the rear of the Wendish host and Snorri tells of Magnus inspired by a vision of his father the saint to throw aside his mail and lead the attack 'wielding the battle-axe *Hel* which had been Olaf's own' (a claim supported by Arnor's lines: 'With broad axe burnished and byrnie cast off, for battle eager, with both hands the haft of Hel he grasped'). With or without such supernatural assistance, Magnus' forces and their allies won a famous victory over superior numbers. Snorri's saga tells how 'it was said that there had never been so great a carnage in the northlands in Christian times as that of the Wends on Hlyrskogs Hede' and Adam of Bremen, who was writing within living memory of the battle, records fifteen thousand Wendish dead.

There is no reason, then, to doubt Magnus' record of genuine military achievement – not only against the Wends but also against Svein's challenge to his sovereignty over Denmark – and yet the enthusiasm for his personal battle-glory expressed across the full range of sympathetic sources might still be read as an attempt to compensate for a shortfall in his warrior reputation, and most especially by comparison with that of his east-faring uncle. Magnus had acquired his kingship of Norway and of Denmark by invitation not conquest, while he had been a mere child sheltering in Russia when his uncle was shedding blood beside Olaf on the battlefield at Stiklestad.

All of which needs to be borne in mind when Snorri's *Harald's saga* tells of Magnus having returned to Norway after his victory off Helganess and there learning of his uncle's arrival in Sweden to forge an alliance with the man he thought to have so recently and so decisively defeated. In the following spring Magnus is said by the saga to have raised a levy of troops in Norway and to have mustered a great army even before he had news of his Danish subjects submitting to Harald and Svein's onslaught on Zealand and Fyn. Snorri once again takes the opportunity to report Harald's reputation – 'so much taller and stronger than most men, and so shrewd that he won the victory wherever he fought, and so rich in gold that no-one had ever seen the like of it' – which was doubtless already well known to Magnus and his court. While a quoted strophe from the skald Thjodolf exults in the prospect of 'death-dealing Magnus from the northward mustering his roller-horses [warships], whilst from the southward Sigurd's son makes ready his sea-steeds [ditto]', wiser counsel in Norway feared grievous consequences throughout the northlands if Olaf's son and brother were to make war upon each other and proposed instead that emissaries be sent with speed and in utmost secrecy to Denmark where trustworthy friends could be found to open negotiations.

The proposed terms of reconciliation – a half-share in the kingship of Norway and an equal apportionment of their combined treasury – were probably what Harald was hoping for and certainly the best he could reasonably expect, so word of his inclination to acceptance was brought back, under the same cloak of secrecy, to Norway. Evidently Harald now had what he wanted and so could dispense with Svein, yet it would be hardly seemly for a saga-maker to impute such casual treachery to his hero and so Snorri contrives an anecdote fully typical of northern tradition as his device of justification. While in conversation together one evening with drinking-horns in hand, Svein inquires of Harald which of all his treasures he most greatly values. Harald declares it to be his banner, the famous Land-ravager said to bring victory to the man before whom it is borne in battle and which has been of that same service to him ever since he came by it. Svein professes scepticism and refuses to believe any such tale before Harald has carried the banner to victory in no less than three battles against his nephew. To which Harald counters that he knows full well of his kinship with Magnus and, indeed, of no reason why they might not yet enjoy a more congenial meeting than the current state of contention.

Not unexpectedly, this exchange engenders mutual suspicion, and on Harald's part to the extent of leaving a log in his usual bed aboard ship while choosing another sleeping-place for himself. In the dark of night, an unknown man finds his way on to the ship to strike at Harald's bed with a great axe which is discovered fixed deep in the log before dawn on the following morning. It is clearly time to flee such a treacherous ally and Harald immediately summons his own men to put to sea under cover of darkness and row north along the coast until reaching the place (presumably around the Vik) where Magnus is encamped with his forces. Another strophe quoted from Thjodolf tells of a joyful reunion between the two and confirms Magnus' offer to share his kingdom with his uncle.

The saga narrative continues now with two anecdotes seemingly intended to illustrate the agreed division of Magnus' kingship and Harald's wealth. In the first of these, Magnus comes to his uncle's camp and distributes gifts of garments, gold and weaponry to the attendant warriors before inviting Harald to choose between two proffered reed-straws. When the choice is made, Magnus gives it into his uncle's hand and with it 'half of Norway, together with the dues and duties of all estates within it', yet retaining the royal precedence in protocol for himself whenever the two are together.

All of which being gracefully accepted, the new joint-kingship is announced to a public assembly on the following day and celebrated with a banquet which provides the setting for the second of Snorri's anecdotes. To this lavish feast Harald brings his vast wealth, carried in great chests which are emptied out on to a vast ox-hide on the floor and from this he takes up a piece of gold as large as a man's head, inviting Magnus to produce gold of his own to compare with it. The best he can offer is the golden ring about his own arm, which Harald considers a meagre token of the wealth of a man who holds two kingdoms and adds the provocative suggestion that there are those who would even question his claim to that small item. When Magnus insists on his undeniable right to an arm-ring given him by his father, Harald counters that Olaf had originally taken the ring from his own father, Sigurd Syr. A strophe from the skald Bolverk celebrating the 'close accord reached peacefully' between those kinsmen and predicting strife for 'the usurper Svein' is placed as the conclusion to Snorri's anecdote, yet it cannot disguise the first trace of rancour introduced into the relationship between the two kings of Norway.

According to Snorri, the two spent the winter on tribute-collecting circuits (an activity long since familiar to Harald) throughout the Upplands and northward to Nidaros and the Trondelag. Some of these were conducted together, others separately and Snorri tells how each also kept his own separate court. Yet they were together in the same hall when they received a visit – recorded in *Morkinskinna* – from the skald Arnor who had come from Orkney bringing two praise-poems he had composed in their honour. Arnor first recited his *Magnusdrápa*, obviously one he had prepared earlier since it appears to have been largely concerned with Arnor's own experiences with the Orkney jarls before celebrating Magnus in its concluding strophes. Even then, when Arnor declares that no king will be so great as he before the sky is rent asunder, his lines seem to be merely recycling closely similar terms of acclaim previously addressed to Jarl Thorfinn – but such must very often have been the way of the working skald on tour. Magnus was sufficiently impressed to express his appreciation with the gift of a gold arm-ring, while Harald, possessed of his own special expertise in the skaldic art, judged the verses addressed to Magnus quite superior to Arnor's *Blágaladrápa* ('Lay of the Black Goose' and perhaps a kenning for the raven on the battlefield) composed in his own honour. Nonetheless, he similarly rewarded the skald with a gold-inlaid spear on receipt of which Arnor promised to compose a memorial lay if he should outlive him – and, indeed, so he was to do some twenty years hence.

'It was not to be long, though,' according to Snorri, before the two kings were at odds, as is demonstrated in his saga by an anecdote telling of their two fleets assembled to collect tribute from Denmark and both at sea heading for the same unspecified destination. As it happened, Harald put his ships into harbour before Magnus' arrival and chose to moor them in the royal berth customarily reserved for his nephew's vessels. So affronted was the younger king by this disregard for protocol that he ordered his warriors to arms. Feigning alarm – 'Nephew Magnus is angered!' – Harald commanded his own ships to be cut loose from their moorings and only afterwards came with a warrior retinue aboard Magnus' ship where the two engaged in another exchange of taunts. The resemblance to that earlier dispute over choice of camp-site on campaign with Georgios Maniakes is so striking as to suggest the story (interestingly omitted from versions of the saga found in *Morkinskinna* and *Flateyjarbók*) as another example of a formulaic device serving to illustrate a relationship between co-rulers which really had begun to founder.

Indeed, Snorri virtually confirms as much when he suggests this being just one example of many similar disagreements between the two whose difficult relationship was being further aggravated by rival court factions. None of which seems to have greatly hampered the royal progress to Denmark, where Svein Estridsson, who had been collecting tribute from the Danes while the two kings were otherwise engaged through the winter in Norway, made a swift departure to Skaane on learning of the Norwegian fleet's approach. His absence enabled an apparently uncontended circuit of Denmark for Harald and Magnus who spent the greater part of the summer taking the submission of their Danish subjects before they came to Jutland in the autumn and it was there – 'at a place called Suderup' in the last week of October – that Magnus fell sick and died.

While the vision of his sainted father which attended Magnus' passing is recorded in full detail with dialogue by the saga, greater historical importance can be attached to the account of the death-bed bequest of his Danish kingdom to Svein and prompt despatch of a kinsman to inform Svein of these last wishes. To Harald, of course, Magnus bequeathed his share of the kingship of Norway, thus tempting suspicion as to the true cause of death and the possibility of his uncle having had some part in it, yet nowhere in the sagas, nor in the more formal histories, is there even the faintest hint of such guilt on Harald's part. Had there been any such rumour, however doubtfully founded, Adam of Bremen and other sources unrelenting in their hostility to Harald would most certainly have seized upon it and so his succession as sole king of Norway was evidently accomplished in all innocence, even though it would soon bring him into contention with the formidable Einar Tambarskelve.

Now some sixty-five years of age, Einar 'Paunch-shaker' had been prominently engaged on all sides of the struggle for power in Norway through almost half a century. Renowned as the strongest man and finest archer in the northlands, he had fought beside Olaf Tryggvason when the kingdom fell from his hand at the battle of Svold in 1000, and yet was still held in such high regard by the victorious Jarl Erik Hakonsson of Lade as to be given the jarl's sister Bergljot in marriage. High-born and wealthy in his own right, Einar was endowed by the jarls of Lade with such great landholdings in Orkadal that he was to become the most powerful man in the Trondelag.

When Jarl Erik followed his brother-in-law Cnut to England in 1012, he appointed Einar as guardian (and effectively regent) for his teenage son Hakon who was to govern western Norway in his stead, while his brother Svein remained jarl of the eastern provinces. Young Hakon was driven out to join his father in England as soon as Olaf Haraldsson returned to make his bid for kingship of Norway in 1015, so it was Einar who stood beside Jarl Svein in resistance to this new King Olaf, and it was Einar's grappling-hook which pulled Jarl Svein's ship to safety when Olaf triumphed at the battle of Nesjar in the following year. The two subsequently made their escape to Sweden where Svein died in that same autumn and Einar stayed on for some six years until making his peace with Olaf and returning to the Trondelag where he was restored to his own lands and to those of his wife's dowry. In about 1023, however, Erik died in Northumbria (where he had been Cnut's earl since 1016) and news of his death may very well have prompted Einar's journey to England where he was made welcome not only by his nephew Hakon but also, and with especial generosity, by the great Cnut himself who was probably already planning to move against Olaf in Norway.

In the event, of course, Olaf played directly into Cnut's hand when he allied with Onund of Sweden to launch an expedition against Denmark. Probably apprised of Cnut's intentions and feeling himself under no obligation to his Norwegian king, Einar absented himself from Olaf's enterprise and stayed at home to await developments. There he was well placed to welcome the arrival of Cnut's agents who came with gifts and promises to grease the slope of Olaf's descending fortunes in the aftermath of the battle of Holy River, and so he was to be again in the following year of 1028 when Cnut himself arrived to lay all Norway in his power. The flight of Olaf into exile in Russia and the return of Hakon as Cnut's jarl in Norway placed Einar firmly in the ascendant with the assurance that he and his son Eindridi were to be the most powerful men in the kingdom excepting only Jarl Hakon.

Thus when Hakon was drowned at sea, Einar had every expectation of succeeding him as jarl over Norway, even travelling to England in high hopes which were to be dashed, of course, when Cnut announced his intention to replace Hakon with his own son by his English wife. Evidently feeling no great urgency to make his own return to Norway, Einar was still out of the country when Olaf returned from Russia to meet his death at Stiklestad and when he did come home he found himself recognised as a great power in the land, a position he was able to further secure by his encouragement of the already burgeoning cult of Olaf the Martyr. Having placed himself in the forefront of the resentment building up against young Svein and his mother Alfifa, Einar was the natural choice of leader for the diplomatic mission which brought Magnus Olafsson back from Russia and, true to the oath he had sworn before Jaroslav in Novgorod, Einar gave his unswerving support to the new king throughout all twelve years of his reign – and, indeed, even after his death.

Harald's own response to the sudden demise of his nephew clearly sprang from ambition rather than sentiment. The saga tells how he considered Denmark also to be part of his legacy due from Magnus and so summoned all the warriors together, announcing his intention of going in force to the Vibjorg *thing*, and of having that great assembly acclaim his kingship of the Danes before proceeding to subjugate the whole country. With the full support of his forces, he intended to ensure Norwegian sovereignty over Denmark for all time, but that support was to be denied him on the instigation of Einar Tambarskelve who makes his first appearance in *Harald's saga* with the declaration that his own first duty was to bear King Magnus' body to its final resting-place before fighting wars in pursuit of another king's domain. It was better, he believed, to honour Magnus in death than any other king alive and he proceeded to array the body in fine robes and lay it out in clear view from Harald's ship.

All the men of the Trondelag followed Einar and most of the other Norwegians followed them to make ready the fleet for the solemn journey home. Finding himself now with no army at his command, Harald had no option but to return with them to Norway, yet no sooner had he put into the Vik than he set out westward on a royal progress, summoning assemblies in every province to acclaim his kingship over all the land, while Einar led the Trondelag contingent home to bury Magnus in St Clement's church where his father Olaf already lay enshrined. At which point in the saga narrative, Snorri pauses to enter his own obituary expressing full agreement with those of all the earlier sources in commemorating the nobility, courage and generosity of 'the most popular of kings, praised by friend and foe alike'. Presumably those former foes included Svein Estridsson who had been about to abandon his claim to kingship of

Denmark when he was brought news of Magnus' dying wish that he should inherit the kingdom and also of the entire Norwegian host having now left the country. Vowing that so long as he should live he would never again flee the kingdom, Svein raised a force in Skaane to accompany his own royal progress accepting submission of his people.

By the following spring, then, there were two claimants convinced of their right to kingship of Denmark, and one of them already assembling the forces with which to assert his claim because Harald is said by the saga to have called a levy throughout Norway, mustering half those ships and men to sail south and spend the summer plundering and burning Jutland. Snorri quotes a half-strophe of Harald's own composition, telling of his ships lying in *Gothnafjord* (now Randersfjord) while night-linened ladies lulled their husbands with song, and completes it with a half-strophe by Thjodolf promising to cast anchor further southward the following year. A further quotation, this one from the skald Bolverk describing 'the sea-steed, plunder-laden . . . on the darkling deep', apparently celebrates the same expedition, and lines ascribed to a lesser-known Icelandic skald called Grani exult in vengeance taken on the daughters of one Thorkel Geysa. These women, who had earlier mocked Harald's threat to Denmark, were carried off from their father's burning farmstead to the ships and returned only on Thorkel's payment of a huge ransom.

Thjodolf's lines foretelling repeat performances 'further southward next summer' are borne out by the saga when it goes on to record Harald's leading another such expedition against Denmark in the following raiding season and in every subsequent summer for almost a decade and a half. 'Each year the Danes trembled' according to the skald Stúf, and yet Svein had sworn that he would never relinquish his rightful claim and neither were his people ever to accept Harald as their king. After the raid of 1048, Svein threatened to launch his own fleet against Norway and there wreak the same havoc Harald had been inflicting on Denmark, unless he would agree either to a peace treaty or to a battle which would finally decide the dispute.

The challenge was to meet in battle on the Gaut Elf river (which marked the borderline between Norway and Danish territory on the Scandinavian mainland) in the following summer and both kings spent the winter preparing their ships and men for the contest. In the event, Harald brought his forces to the appointed place only to find Svein's fleet lying away to the south off Zealand. Perhaps suspecting that Svein had lured all the Norwegian forces into the Kattegat so as to leave Norway itself defenceless against his own fleet, Harald sent the greater part of his bonder levy home, while leading a select force made up of his own hird, his lendermen and the bonders with homes nearest to the Danish border on a raiding foray south of the Skagen headland to Thy province and across Jutland to plunder the great trading township of Hedeby. All of this is confirmed by the saga's quotation of verses attributed to the skald Stúf and Thorleik the Fair, an Icelandic skald visiting Svein Estridsson's court, but perhaps most vividly and certainly most immediately by lines attributed to an anonymous Norse warrior who tells of standing on the northern extremity of the town's rampart before dawn and watching 'high flames up out of houses whirling'.

Gwyn Jones suggests that destruction of Denmark's principal marketplace 'may appear a self-strangling exercise for a man ambitious for the Danish throne', before adding that 'burning towns came naturally to Harald . . . and if we can trust to Snorri the expedition of 1049 had terror and loot as its primary objectives'.[3] Having plundered Hedeby and left it aflame, Harald's fleet of sixty ships was sailing northwards laden with booty when Svein appeared on the coast of Thy with a large force and a challenge to do battle onshore. Realising his own crews were hopelessly outnumbered, Harald replied with a counter-challenge to a sea-fight (this exchange confirmed by a strophe from Thorleik quoted in the saga). By now it would seem to have been getting late in the day and a change in the wind left Harald's ships lying off the island of Læso where thick sea-fog came down as night fell.

As the sun rose on the following morning, however, its light picked out the approaching dragon prows of a huge Danish fleet and Harald ordered his men to take to the oars and put out to sea, but their ships were waterlogged and heavy with the plunder from Hedeby while the enemy fleet was already threatening to overtake the best efforts of their oarsmen. So a new order was given to throw some plunder overboard to hinder the enemy's progress by tempting them to retrieve abandoned booty from the water. Determined not to be cheated of his advantage by such a ruse, Svein urged his ships on in pursuit and Harald ordered heavier items of cargo thrown overboard to lighten the load and increase the speed of flight, but the enemy fleet was still gaining on them and it was then that Harald came up with his master-stroke of throwing Danish captives overboard. When he saw his own people floundering in the waves, Svein could do no other than break off the chase to let his crews rescue as many as possible of their countrymen from the water – and allow most of the Norwegian fleet to make their escape. Thus deprived of what might have been a decisive victory, Svein saved at least some face when he came upon just seven enemy vessels, manned by levied bonders and lagging behind the main fleet off Læso. Snorri's story concludes with a quoted strophe from the skald Thorleik (in Svein's service, of course) mocking the bonders as they begged for quarter and offered ransom, presumably to be paid out of plunder taken on the raiding, in exchange for their lives.

While there is no doubt as to the historicity of Harald's onslaught against Hedeby in 1049 – and especially when archaeological evidence confirms the burning of the town – the account of his fleet's escape as preserved in the sagas depends largely on two strophes of Thorleik's verse. It is curious, then, that Saxo Grammaticus records a suspiciously similar encounter, also dated to 1049 but located on the Djurså river, where Svein had managed to muster an army against the raiders, but one scarcely adequate either in numbers or experience to face a battle-hardened enemy. So terrified were they of the approaching Norwegians that the Danes jumped into the river rather than face the oncoming foe and, indeed, many of them were drowned. Saxo was the son of a distinguished Danish military family, so there is reason to respect his authority in this instance and yet it is possible that his account refers to a quite different incident, even though it seems unlikely that such an extraordinary encounter would have passed unnoticed by Harald's skalds and thus escaped the attention of the saga-makers.

This regular raiding of Denmark apparently continued, presumably on an annual basis, for another thirteen years and yet it takes up very little further space in the saga record. In terms of strictly military history, the 1050s might even be considered the least interesting decade of Harald's warrior's way if his transition from Varangian mercenary to Scandinavian warlord resulted in little more than a reversion to the piratical custom of his viking forebears.

In which case, his years of experience in Russia and throughout the Byzantine Empire would seem to have made the least impression on his early performance as a warrior king and yet their influence is rather more evident in other spheres of his governance. His fiscal policy – assuredly inspired by the Byzantine example – is credited with developing a true coin economy in Norway and archaeological evidence from coin-hoards attests the numerous mints established during his reign. The famous wealth he had brought back from the east was quite certainly the source of the Byzantine coins struck for emperors from Basil II through to Constantine IX and imitated on Danish currency of the eleventh century. Of which the out-standing example is a Danish silver penny of Svein Estridsson dated to *c.* 1047 and carefully copied from a rare gold *histamenon* of Michael IV, part of a limited issue and thought to have reached Scandinavia in Harald's treasury where it was probably a part of his reward for services rendered on the Bulgarian campaign of 1041.[4]

Similarly also, his network of contacts in Russia must have facilitated the expansion of Norway's trade along the east way in his reign and the example of the Russian traders he had known in Novgorod and Kiev may well have inspired the expansion of Norwegian trading around the North Atlantic. Into that context must be placed a curious remark made by Adam of Bremen in his *Description of the Islands of the North*. Describing the frozen sea 'beyond Thule [Iceland]', he writes of 'Harald, the well-informed prince of the Norwegians, [having] lately attempted this sea. After he had explored the expanse of the Northern Ocean in his ships, at length there lay before his eyes the darksome bounds of the world's edge and by retracing his course he barely escaped the vast pit of the abyss in safety.'

The skaldic verses which represent immediately contemporary evidence for Norsemen reaching the North American continent have been dated to the early eleventh century and Harald's contact with Iceland would assuredly have kept him informed of exploration to Greenland and beyond, so it is not impossible that he might have been tempted to follow in the wake of the Vinland voyagers. Had he actually done so, of course, his skalds would have surely celebrated the adventure and yet no such verses have survived even long enough to reach the attention of the saga-makers. Thus Adam of Bremen's claim for Harald's North Atlantic venturing rests entirely upon his own authority and yet his writings demonstrate a well-informed interest in the subject and so cannot be dismissed entirely out of hand.

It is in the ecclesiastical orbit, however, that the eastern influence is best recorded and here the saga account of Harald's church-building at Nidaros is not only rich in detail but reliably supported by more recent archaeological investigation. Snorri tells of Harald having completed construction of the church dedicated to Olaf by Magnus but left unfinished at the time of his death, and building two churches of his own, one dedicated to St Gregory beside his royal residence on the banks of the River Nid and a St Mary's church (interestingly bearing the same dedication as the earliest Varangian chapel in Constantinople) on the site where Olaf's remains had lain through the winter following his martyrdom.

There is every reason, of course, to assume Harald's genuine interest in memorials to his kinsman Olaf, who was already effectively established as Norway's patron saint and whose cult was ever more widely revered throughout the Scandinavian world within a few decades of his martyrdom. Yet it would be fully characteristic of Harald to have had a more political motive when every opportunity of association with the saint would more securely establish himself as a worthy successor in the kingship. In so doing, he would surely have been inspired by the example of Jaroslav and particularly by his magnificent Hagia Sophia which Harald had seen under construction in Kiev and in which he would have recognised a reflection of the prestige of the Grand Prince no less clearly than a monumental dedication to the Holy Wisdom.

While the reverence of Olaf as saint and martyr had finally established Christianity in Norway by the mid-eleventh century, the Christian tradition with which Harald himself would have been most familiar after spending so much of his adult life in Russia and Byzantium would have been the eastern Orthodox faith, so it is unsurprising that he invited eastern churchmen to his Norwegian court and arranged for them to visit Iceland also. Their presence in Scandinavia evidently incurred disapproval not only from the archbishop of Hamburg (which met with a typically defiant response), but evidently also on the part of the papacy itself when a papal legation was sent in protest to Harald's court and promptly thrown out. All of which would very well correspond to the closing line of the account of *Araltes* in the *Book of Advice to an Emperor* in which he is complimented on having 'maintained faith and friendship towards the *Rhomaioi* [the Byzantines] when he was ruling in his own land'.

Curiously, Snorri makes no reference to eastern churchmen in Iceland, but he does pay full tribute to Harald as 'a great friend to all Icelanders', telling of his sending four ships with cargoes of flour to a famine-stricken Iceland (thus dating the voyage to 1056) and of his gift of a bell for the church at Thingvellir. It has been suggested that Harald's generosity to the Icelanders was still more generously repaid by the accounts of him in Icelandic sources, and it may well have been so, especially in view of his patronage of so many court-poets from that country. This was very probably what Snorri meant by 'his great many acts of generosity to the people who stayed with him', and yet the only Icelanders mentioned by name in this passage are Harald's long-standing lieutenants, Halldor Snorrason and Ulf Ospaksson.

Both had served with Harald throughout most of his time in Byzantine service and both returned with him to Norway. Ulf came of an old Icelandic family (ultimately descended from Ketil

Bjornsson, called 'Flatnose', a Norse king in the Hebrides in the mid-ninth century whose offspring were among the earliest settlers in Iceland) and was a nephew of Gudrun Osvifsdottir, heroine of *Laxdœla saga*. His remarkable loyalty to Harald through some three decades in his service was justly rewarded in Norway where he was appointed the king's marshal, made a lenderman in the Trondelag and given Jorunn, daughter of Thorberg Arnason, as his wife. Snorri makes particular mention of Ulf's shrewd judgement, which is most evident in military matters and even to the extent that had he not died so early in the year 1066 Harald's warrior's way might not have come to an end in the manner that it did.

Ulf's comrade-in-arms, Halldor Snorrason, was a man of very different personality. Snorri tells of his huge build and powerful strength, yet frankly admits his personality to have been 'blunt, outspoken, sullen and obstinate'. Clearly Halldor was never going to be the most diplomatic of courtiers and so it is hardly surprising that some five years at the Norwegian court were to prove quite long enough and sometime around 1051 he returned to Iceland where he lived to a great age on his farm at Hjardarholt enjoying celebrity as a famous storyteller. Even while in retirement in Iceland, Halldor would still seem to have been in contact with Harald, even though his departure from the Norwegian court is said to have involved a dispute with the king over payment due (according to the *Tale of Halldor Snorrason* in *Morkinskinna*), a tradition not unconnected with Harald's increasingly imperious conduct reported in the saga. Even his favourite skald told how the king would brook no opposition to his demands and Snorri quotes a full strophe from Thjodolf telling how 'neither could the king's own men go against his wishes'.

If it was this aspect of his regal personality which prompted Adam of Bremen to call Harald a 'tyrant' and allowed later historians to endow him with the cognomen *harðraði* – whether translated as 'hard counsel' or as 'ruthless' – the same autocratic mind-set was to prove his first line of defence against the hostile native elements who had challenged Norwegian kings throughout the first decades of the eleventh century and brought down his half-brother Olaf as they had Olaf Tryggvason before him. The focal point of that hostility still lay around the Trondelag, long the heartland of the jarls of Lade and where now Einar Tambarskelve, himself son-in-law to the mighty Jarl Hakon, represented their effective successor in all but title. Although most often hostile and only nominally conciliatory to Olaf, Einar had reclaimed the kingship of Norway for Olaf's son in 1035 and remained staunchly loyal to 'Magnus the Good' thereafter, yet he clearly had no similar regard for his successor (even though Einar's son Eindridi was married to a daughter of Harald's sister, Gunnhild).

Skilled in law-dealing, Einar took any and every opportunity to speak for the Trondelag bonders against the royal officers at assemblies, even in the presence of the king himself. That attitude of defiance soon developed into a policy of deliberate provocation as the saga tells of his building 'a great following of men on his estates and bringing a still greater force with him when he came to Nidaros'. On one occasion, he is said to have brought eight or nine longships with a force five hundred strong which he boldly disembarked and marched through the town in full view of the king's residence. This scarcely veiled challenge prompted Harald to compose some lines of verse proclaiming his response to 'the mighty chieftain who means to fill the throne-seat':

> Einar with his flailing blade
> will drive me from my kingdom
> unless he is forced to kiss
> the axe's thin-lipped edge.

Here, then, was a king who intended to take no prisoners and awaited only the opportunity to arrange the axe-kissing he had promised in his poetry.

While there is no doubt as to Harald having arranged the killing of Einar, and of his son Eindridi with him, the saga record supplies two quite different accounts of how it happened. The version found similarly in *Morkinskinna* and *Flateyjarbók* tells of Einar being invited to a feast at Nidaros where he falls into a drunken sleep while a skald is celebrating the king's adventures. Harald has a kinsman suddenly wake him with a straw applied to his nostrils and in a state of embarrassment so acute that Einar takes revenge by killing the offender the next morning, providing the king with just reason to put both him and his son to death.

The alternative version of the story is found in Snorri's *Heimskringla* and independently in *Fagrskinna*, suggesting its likely origin in Norwegian (as distinct from Icelandic) tradition. The tale itself is of some more convincing character too, telling of a man in Einar's service, and standing high in his favour, caught thieving in Nidaros. When the accused was brought to face justice, Einar accompanied him with a heavily armed retinue to take the fellow away from the court by force. Confrontation with the king was becoming unavoidable now and mutual friends sought to arrange a conciliatory meeting between the two. Trusting in his son's kinship by marriage to the king's family as his own safe conduct, Einar arrived at the royal residence, but left Eindridi outside in the courtyard with others of his company while he entered alone, only to find himself trapped in a darkened chamber where Harald's warriors fell upon him and hacked him to death. Hearing the sound of weaponry, Eindridi rushed in to his father's aid, but was likewise struck down and fell dead beside Einar's body. Harald's housecarls formed up outside the entrance to forestall any attack by Einar's retinue, but there was no such attempt now that the Trondelag men were without a leader, so the king marched with his retinue to a ship moored on the river and was rowed away down the fjord.

When the news was brought to Einar's wife, Bergljot, she cried out for vengeance: 'Were Hakon here, those who killed my son would not now be pulling in safety downriver.' Hakon was the son of Ivar the White, a lenderman in the Upplands whose mother was also a daughter of the great Jarl Hakon and thus sister to Bergljot. If there was a man most able, and even obliged, to avenge Bergljot's husband and son it was this Hakon, a direct descendant of the jarls of Lade and said by the saga to have surpassed all others in Norway at that time in his courage, strength and accomplishment. Even while Einar and Eindridi were buried near to the tomb of Magnus in

St Olaf's church in Nidaros, so great a hostility to Harald was abroad among the men of the Trondelag that there was already talk of armed revolt.

The king's form of response on this occasion was to be diplomacy, so he was in need of an emissary well placed to deal on his behalf and the man he chose was Finn Arnason. Second son of the powerful lenderman Arne Armodsson, Finn had remained staunchly loyal to King Olaf, following him to Russia and returning to stand in the front rank of his forces at Stiklestad. Whether or not he had fled back to Russia after the battle and afterwards returned to Norway with Magnus is left unclear by the saga record, but now, almost thirty years after Stiklestad, he was established as a lenderman in Austratt (north-west of Trondheimfjord) and as a figure of great standing in Harald's kingdom. Snorri tells of the king's great affection for Finn and his brothers and (with just one significant exception) there is no reason to doubt him, not least by reason of the bonds of marital kinship. Not only was Finn's wife the daughter of Harald's brother, Halfdan, but Harald had himself recently formed a close relationship with Finn's niece.

According to Snorri, Harald had been 'married again' in the winter of 1047/8, this time to Thora, a daughter of Finn's younger brother, Thorberg Arnason. There is no question of the historicity nor, indeed, the intimacy of Harald's association with Thora because she was to become the mother of his two sons – and ultimate successors – Magnus and Olaf, but its legitimacy as a 'marriage' is utterly suspect when there is nowhere any indication that Harald's marriage to his Russian queen had been dissolved and when Ellisif was not only still alive but was to outlive her husband. The true situation, then, can only have been that Thora had become Harald's concubine within months of his full accession as king of Norway. Again it might be possible to detect a Byzantine exemplar because Harald would surely have known of the tripartite arrangement between Constantine Monomachus, the empress Zoe and the Sclerena, and yet the one highly probable reason for his taking a second 'wife' may well have been the hope of securing a male successor.

The precise dates of birth of his offspring are nowhere recorded, but his two children fathered upon Ellisif were both daughters – Maria and Ingigerd – and it is fully possible that both had been born before his 'second marriage' to Thora, by which time Harald had been married to Ellisif for some five years and the urgency of producing a male successor must have been a matter of increasing concern to him, because longevity was not commonly characteristic of warrior kings. His half-brother Olaf had been just thirty-five when he was killed in battle, Olaf Tryggvason only about thirty when he fell to his death at Svold and even Cnut had not yet reached the age of forty at the time of his death. Harald was now already a year or two into his thirties and evidently lost no time in fathering male offspring upon Thora when his first-born son, Magnus, was old enough to go to war with his father in the year 1062. Neither was formal legitimacy of birth any essential qualification for succession in Norway in those times, if only on the evidence of his predecessor, Magnus, having been born to Olaf not by his queen, but by his 'hand-maid'.

Thus all the Arnason brothers were bonded to the king by ties of marital kinship, but Finn was by far the best placed to negotiate on his behalf with current dissident elements, firstly by reason of his own and his family's standing in the Trondelag, but also because of his old acquaintance with Hakon Ivarsson who had sailed with him on viking ventures west-over-sea several summers past. When Harald came to Austratt, the saga tells of Finn having welcomed him in good humour, although with the least formality when he chided the king as a 'great scoundrel'. If Finn were to go into the Trondelag and the Upplands as Harald's ambassador and there pacify men who hated the king so bitterly, he would want a reward for his service. Harald was prepared to grant any favour he chose and Finn asked that his brother Kalv be restored to his lands in Norway and given a safe conduct and the king's peace when he returned to live there again.

With whatever ultimate motive already in his own mind, Harald granted the favour requested and Finn went forth to accomplish his embassy with quite remarkable success. Accompanied by a retinue nearly eighty strong, he came to the Trondelag men and reminded them of the evil consequences which had befallen the land the last time they had risen in arms against their king. Warning against letting their hatred of Harald push them into the same mistake again, his oratory – and the king's promise to pay compensation for the killing of Einar and Eindridi – persuaded them to take no further action, at least until they heard of Hakon Ivarsson's response to the appeal made to him by Einar's widow, Bergljot.

Finn travelled on over the Dovre mountains into the Upplands where he first sought the advice of his own son-in-law, the jarl Orm Eilifsson, who was himself the son of a daughter of the mighty Jarl Hakon of Lade. Jarl Orm accompanied Finn to his meeting with Hakon Ivarsson and together they negotiated an agreement: Hakon would be reconciled with the king in exchange for being given King Magnus' daughter, Ragnhild, in marriage and with a dowry befitting a princess. Finn agreed to the proposal on Harald's behalf and returned to the Trondelag where the former unrest and rebellion had by now apparently subsided.

All of which would have amounted to precisely the outcome intended, had it not been for the proud Ragnhild's response to Hakon's suit and her insistence that a king's daughter could not accept a husband of lesser rank than that of jarl. Hakon could only bring his case to Harald who refused the request, because there had never been more than one jarl in the land at any one time since Olaf's reign and there would be no new jarl appointed while Orm still lived. Accusing the king of breaking his agreement, the furious Hakon stormed out of the court and took ship to Denmark where he was welcomed as a kinsman by Svein Estridsson (Svein's wife and Hakon's father both being Jarl Hakon's grandchildren) and placed in command of Danish coastal defences. Although generously endowed with estates, Hakon nonetheless chose to live aboard his warships the whole year round keeping guard against Baltic pirates. Meanwhile, Finn Arnason is said himself to have been angered because Harald had broken his own agreement made in good faith with Hakon, but it was to be a far greater grievance against the king which would very shortly drive Finn also into exile in Denmark.

It might be helpful at this point to attempt a cautious alignment of the saga narrative with more reliable historical chronology, because Snorri provides very few indications of the date of events and tends, as on earlier occasions, towards misleading compression of the time-scale. In this instance, *Orkneyinga saga* supplies the most useful framework of reference, because it is from the orbit of Jarl Thorfinn that the infamous Kalv Arnason returns to make his first entry into Harald's saga. Kalv was last mentioned here when he travelled with Einar Tambarskelve to bring Magnus home from Russia in 1035. According to *Orkneyinga saga*, he had confessed his guilty part in the martyrdom of Olaf to Rognvald Brusason at that time and yet Snorri Sturluson's *Magnus' saga* appears to suggest that the young Magnus was not apprised of that confession and held both Kalv and Einar in high regard after his return to Norway. Indeed, the earlier years of Magnus' reign represented a new ascendancy for Kalv, who even assumed the role of foster-father to the young king, until a man from Værdal had occasion to inform him of Kalv's part in the battle of Stiklestad. When Magnus next met with Kalv it was at a feast held at the farm of Haug close by the battlefield and he took the opportunity to invite his foster-father to ride with him to the place of martyrdom and 'see the marks of what befell there'. Kalv was apparently expecting the worst, because he had already ordered his servant to load his ship in readiness for a swift departure, and he flushed deep red at Magnus' suggestion, but the king would accept no prevarication, even issuing a command. Having ridden to the place of martyrdom, the two dismounted and Magnus asked Kalv to point to the exact spot where Olaf had been slain. So he did with his spear-point and Magnus next asked where exactly he himself had stood at that moment. When he admitted to having stood then where he stood now, Magnus saw how the dying Olaf would have been within range of Kalv's axe. Challenged face to face at the very spot, Kalv still denied his guilt before leaping to his horse and riding away. By nightfall, he was aboard ship and sailing out of the fjord under cover of darkness on voyage to find refuge in Orkney with his kinsman Jarl Thorfinn (whose wife, Ingibjorg, was a daughter of Finn Arnason).

174

It is at this point that the *Orkneyinga saga* narrative can supply its evidence as to dating, because it claims that the cost to the jarl's household of accommodating Kalv and his retinue was the reason why Thorfinn demanded a greater share of the jarldom. Expecting imminent armed conflict with his uncle who was already assembling forces from Caithness and the Hebrides, Rognvald sailed for Norway to seek assistance from King Magnus. On his return to Orkney he brought with him a substantial and well-equipped army provided by Magnus and also a message for Kalv Arnason, promising him the king's pardon if he would support Rognvald against Thorfinn. When the dispute came to battle at sea in the Pentland Firth, Kalv's six large warships stood off from the action, but only until Rognvald began to get the upper hand and Thorfinn called out for assistance. Presumably, Kalv could hardly refuse his kinsman in such extremis and brought his ships against the smaller craft in Rognvald's fleet, swiftly clearing their decks. At which point the Norwegian crews cut their vessels loose from the lashings and took flight, thus depriving Rognvald of the greater part of his forces and ensuring certain victory for Thorfinn.

'That same night', according to the saga, Rognvald again sailed east to Norway and there told Magnus of the outcome of the battle. He is said by the saga to have stayed only a short while in Norway before sailing back west-over-sea with a retinue of Norwegian housecarls. On landfall in Shetland he learned that Thorfinn was in Orkney in company with only a small force and so Rognvald seized the opportunity for a surprise attack. Although caught quite unawares and finding his house aflame, Thorfinn broke his way through a wooden wall, carrying his wife Ingibjorg out of the burning building in one of the saga's most famously celebrated escapes. His chance for revenge came early in the Yuletide season when Rognvald, believing Thorfinn to have been killed in the fire, was on the small isle of Papa Stronsay collecting malt for the winter feasting. Thorfinn's reciprocal surprise attack put yet another house to the torch and slew Rognvald's Norsemen and yet Rognvald himself managed to get away, but only to be caught and killed while hiding among the rocks by the shore.

When Thorfinn sailed to Norway in the following spring in an (ultimately unsuccessful) attempt at reconciliation with Magnus, he found the king ruling jointly with Harald, so his visit can be securely dated to the earlier months of 1047. Thus Rognvald's death, his own two voyages to Norway and the intervening sea-battle in the Pentland Firth must all be similarly assigned to the year 1046, which would place Kalv Arnason's confrontation with Magnus and his flight from Norway to Orkney fairly safely in the year 1045, or just possibly in the previous autumn, when Magnus would have been at the peak of his ascendancy and well placed to confront the man who had slain his father.

The demise of Rognvald Brusason left Thorfinn with supreme power over the jarldom and *Orkneyinga saga* tells how 'Kalv Arnason never left his side'. Indeed, Kalv had already been placed in lordship over the Hebrides by Thorfinn 'to ensure his authority there' and there is every reason to believe he was so assigned because these *Suðreyjar* (as the Western Isles are called in the saga) were most often governed by the Orkney jarls throughout the first half of the eleventh century. Yet it would seem that his former land-holdings in Norway represented the more attractive prospect for Kalv, because Snorri tells how 'he made ready to leave at once and sailed east' as soon as he had news of the favour granted to his brother Finn by Harald. On his return and as promised, Kalv was restored to all the estates and revenues he had enjoyed under Magnus and bound himself 'to perform all services required of him by King Harald for the good of the kingdom'.

Just such a service was to fall due in the following spring when the king raised a levy for his annual raiding expedition around Denmark and assigned Kalv to command of the ship's crew which was to make the first landing on Fyn island. With the assurance that Harald would swiftly bring his main force up in support, Kalv led his men ashore into the attack, but encountered such fierce resistance that they were swiftly overwhelmed and he was just one of the many Norwegians cut down by pursuing Danes as they fled back to their ships. Presumably having seen Kalv slain on the sand, Harald's purpose was accomplished and he brought the main force ashore to advance inland for the serious business of plundering with fire and sword.

While a half-strophe by the skald Arnor and quoted by Snorri must be accepted as closely contemporary evidence for Harald having 'dyed crimson his flashing blade on *Funen* [Fyn]', the incident is nonetheless strikingly reminiscent of that siege where the Varangian officer held back while Halldor's company suffered the heat of the fray (and Halldor himself that famous wound to his face), only coming up in support when the plundering was at hand. This would seem to have been a tactic long favoured by Harald and here deployed again to take his ultimate revenge on the man he may actually have seen deliver Olaf's death-wound at Stiklestad more than twenty years before. Kalv's brother Finn certainly believed it so and is said by the saga to have been filled with hatred for the king, convinced that Harald had 'not only contrived Kalv's death, but also deliberately deceived Finn into tempting his brother back to Norway so as to bring him within the king's power'.

Harald let people say whatever they would, while refusing to confirm or deny any allegations – and yet 'the king was very pleased with the outcome of events', according to the saga and fully confirmed by the strophe which he composed at the time:

> Now I have done to death,
> – driven to it was I – and
> laid low two of my liegemen,
> eleven and two I remember.
> Men must guard against
> the guileful toil of traitors;
> great oaks are said to grow
> up out of acorns small.

So bitterly angry was Finn Arnason that he took his leave of the kingdom and sailed south to Denmark where he was welcomed by Svein Estridsson who eventually appointed him jarl of Halland and charged him with the defence of that border country against Norwegian attack.

177

The two subsequent chapters in Snorri's saga have less bearing on Harald himself, being concerned with the viking adventures of his nephew Guthorm whose sphere of activity lay around the Irish Sea with its base in the city of Dublin, but they nonetheless supply a valuable point of chronological reference. Of key importance in that respect is Guthorm's expedition with *Margad* which led to a falling-out over shares of plunder and culminated in the killing of his fellow raider, because the 'Margad' of the saga has been identified as Eachmargach, the Hiberno-Norse king of Dublin known to have been killed in 1052. Thus when Snorri places the death of 'Margad' in the summer following Kalv's death, the attack on Fyn island can be safely assigned to the year 1051 and Kalv's return to Norway to the previous year, 1050. The saga tells of Kalv's returning as soon as he learned of the favour his brother had secured from Harald, so Finn's embassy to the Trondelag and to Hakon Ivarsson in the Upplands can be similarly dated to 1050 and the killings of Einar Tambarskelve and Eindridi placed earlier in that same year or, just possibly, in the latter months of 1049. Within that same time-frame, Hakon Ivarsson's angry departure to Denmark and entry into Svein Estridsson's service must also be placed in 1050.

While the true date of Hakon's return to Norway is left uncertain in the saga narrative, the circumstances which brought it about provide the subject of a colourful anecdote. Although endowed with fine estates by Svein, Hakon still chose to live 'both winter and summer' aboard his warships as, indeed, befitted the man charged with defence against Baltic piracy. In the event, however, it was upon this policing duty that his career in Denmark was to founder when Svein's delinquent foster-son and his warband launched a campaign of viking brigandage which created havoc around the country. Protests brought to the king by victims of these predations were referred on to Hakon who hunted the fellow down, cleared his ships in a fierce sea-fight and delivered his head to the king at dinner as evidence of his own efficiency. Shortly afterwards, Hakon received a message assuring him that while Svein wished him no harm, the same could not be said of his victim's kinsfolk and he would be best advised to leave the country at once. So it was that Hakon Ivarsson came home to Norway – and with fortuitous timing because Jarl Orm had recently died, thus leaving a vacancy for a new jarl in the Upplands to which Hakon was duly appointed, Harald proving as good as his word on this occasion at least and the princess Ragnhild likewise when she consented to become Jarl Hakon's wife at last.

The compressed chronology of Snorri's saga narrative places the full story of Hakon's Danish exile and homecoming before the account of Kalv Arnason's return and demise, thus distorting a more realistic sequence of events. If Hakon truly had stayed aboard his warships 'winter and summer', it is hardly possible that he could have left Norway in umbrage before Kalv's arrival in the later months of 1050, become established in Svein's service and then overreached himself in time to return to Norway before Kalv was killed on Fyn some time in the summer of 1051. It would be more reasonable, then, to sacrifice the convenience of the saga-maker's storytelling and propose Hakon's homecoming, appointment as jarl of the Upplands and marriage to Ragnhild somewhat later in the 1050s – although quite certainly before the year 1062 when he makes his next and most significant appearance in the saga as the hero of the great battle on the River Nissa.

Although Snorri claims that Harald continued his raiding of Denmark 'every summer' after his succession to the kingship, the saga describes no further raids through a full decade after the attack on Fyn island in 1051. Exactly ten years, in fact, because the next account of such an expedition is quite firmly placed in the summer of 1061 and after Harald's 'founding' of the town of Oslo on the northernmost shore of the Vik estuary (now Oslofjord). The key importance of Oslo – at least, as suggested by the saga – would seem to have been as a forward base for the assembly and provisioning of the fleets about to sail for Denmark or held in ready proximity against Danish attack. The fleet of 1061, however, was made up of lighter craft manned by very much smaller forces than the full battle-fleet levied in 1049. The reason for this more modest operation would appear to have been the expectation of little, if any, resistance – even though fairly effective opposition had evidently been ready to resist the landing on Fyn island in 1051. It is, of course, possible that the raid on Fyn was planned in full knowledge of the hostile reception it was to encounter and with the deliberate purpose of committing Kalv Arnason to a suicide mission, and yet the expedition of 1061 would seem to have been caught unawares on Jutland where 'the inhabitants mustered forces and defended their homeland'.

Unprepared for so serious a confrontation, Harald sailed on into Limfjord to begin raiding settlements along its banks, but wherever his forces landed they came up against determined opposition – and then his spies brought news that Svein had arrived at the mouth of the fjord with a large warfleet. Fortunately for the Norwegians, the enemy pursuit was delayed by the narrow channel into Limfjord which allowed entry for only one ship at a time, so Harald sailed up to a wider point where just a narrow strip of land lay between the fjord and the North Sea. Waiting until nightfall, the Norwegian craft were brought on to land, unloaded of their plunder and carried across to the seashore where they were loaded up again and ready to put to sea by dawn.

Having escaped Svein's fleet, Harald's ships sailed homeward past Jutland while he swore that he would bring a bigger fleet and greater forces the next time he came to Denmark. Indeed, the story may well have been included in the saga purely by way of prelude to the events of the following year culminating in the epic sea-battle on the Nissa. All through the following winter of 1061/2 while Harald was at Nidaros, his new warship was being built at Eyrar and this was a vessel to rank with the very greatest launched in the northlands, even with Olaf Tryggvason's famous 'Long Serpent' described in his saga as the 'best-fitted and most costly ever to be built in Norway'. In fact, Harald's ship would have been marginally larger than Olaf's, built with thirty-five pair of benches when the 'Long Serpent' had thirty-four. Thus driven by seventy oars, it is described by the saga as much broader in the beam than the usual warship and so is thought to have been of a type called the *búz*, its design based on that of a large sea-going merchant vessel but adapted for the purpose of warfare. As flamboyant as it was

180

formidable, its bows were inlaid with gold, its prow surmounted by a dragon's head and its stern-post by the monster's tail – these latter features inspiring the skald Thjodolf to an abundance of dragon imagery when he celebrated the ship in verse.

That same winter Harald issued a challenge to Svein to meet him in battle on the Gaut Elf river in the coming spring and thus resolve which of them was to be king of both countries. Preparation of his forces was already under way and a full levy of all Norway brought together a great army, but the final flourish was the launching on to the Nid of Harald's new capital ship, described – at first hand – by Thjodolf as 'floating, with flaming mane and its sides all gilded, the dragon'. It would appear that Thjodolf accompanied his king when the fleet sailed, if only on the evidence of no less than six of his strophes quoted in the saga and describing the voyage south from Nidaros to the Vik where a storm blew up, scattering the ships to find shelter in the lee of islands and the safety of Oslofjord.

As soon as the weather improved, the fleet formed up and sailed on to the Gaut Elf, only to discover that Svein's ships and men were lying off to the south of Fyn and the Smalands. Once again, Harald is said to have assumed his old enemy was avoiding battle and so sent his 'bonders' levy' home, thus reducing his fleet to 150 ships which he took 'raiding far and wide' along the coast of Halland. Coming into Laholms fjord, however, he sighted Svein's fleet numbering some three hundred vessels and thus representing twice the strength of his own. It must be said that Snorri's repetition of this same formula does little to support the credibility of his saga as historical record, and yet his source of information in this instance is impressively reliable when the figures are derived from poetry (*Nisavísur*, or 'Nissa river verses', of which as many as seven strophes survive) composed by the skald Stein Herdisason who was an eye-witness to the battle aboard Ulf Ospaksson's ship.[5]

The size of the enemy fleet so alarmed some of the Norwegian warriors that they urged Harald to pull back, but the king remained quite determined and his address to the troops is preserved in another strophe from Stein Herdisason: 'Rather than flee shall each of us, unfaltering, fall dead heaped upon the other.' At which his fleet drew up into battle array with Harald's great dragon-ship at the centre and Ulf's vessel alongside, while the Trondelag contingent lay on one side and Jarl Hakon Ivarsson's flotilla on the other. Svein brought up the Danish fleet, including no less than six jarls among its commanders, and he set his own ship to face Harald's with Finn Arnason beside him. Now all the ships in the central battle lines of both sides were roped together, but Svein's fleet was so great in number that many vessels could not be lashed into his main formation and so were left free to engage with the enemy as their skippers felt inclined. Similarly on the Norwegian side, where Hakon Ivarsson's flotilla was left untied and also free to engage with individual enemy craft, as indeed they did and with great success in clearing every ship that they were able to grapple.

The manoeuvring and manhandling of so many oar-driven warships cannot have been easily or swiftly accomplished, and so it was late in the afternoon of 9 August 1062 by the time the fleets engaged around the mouth of the Nissa. Much of the saga account of the fighting relies on descriptive skaldic verse – two strophes by Stein Herdisason, two and a half strophes by Thjodolf, who was apparently also in attendance, and a single strophe by Arnor Jarlaskald who was almost certainly far away in Orkney while the battle was fought. As might be expected, they all tell of fierce fighting by heroic warriors on both sides and yet also securely confirm all the points of detail in Snorri's narrative (for which, of course, they provided the principal source).

The opposing formations, each of them apparently roped into a huge fighting-platform, seem not to have reached the stage of hand-to-hand action for some time, probably because they were made up of the largest high-hulled vessels, and so the lengthy opening phase of the conflict was conducted with projectile weaponry, with Harald himself wielding his bow for hours on end on the evidence of Thjodolf's lines: 'All night long, Norway's lord let arrows fly from yew-bow to shining shields.' The free-ranging craft on both sides were better able to engage, of course, and it was in this sector of the fighting that Hakon Ivarsson is said to have most excelled himself. Danish ships tried to keep out of his path, but Hakon kept up the pursuit, clearing the decks of ship after ship until a skiff found its way through the mêlée to summon him over to a flank of Harald's formation which was giving way under pressure and taking heavy casualties. Rowing to that sector of the action, Hakon attacked with such ferocity that the Danes fell back, and so he continued to fight all through the night, somehow always managing to be wherever there was the greatest need of his assistance.

Before the night was over the principal Danish formation finally broke up into flight and Harald was able to lead his men aboard Svein's capital ship, clearing its deck so thoroughly that the only members of its crew left alive were those who had jumped over the side and been lucky enough to be hauled aboard other ships as they fled the carnage. Svein's banner was down now and no fewer than seventy of his vessels cleared, while all the rest of his ships and men were in flight, with the notable exception of Finn Arnason, Svein's jarl of Halland but now an old man with failing eyesight, who had stayed till the very last – 'in mid-column fighting, too proud to flee' according to Thjodolf – and was finally made captive. Yet there was nowhere any sign of the king himself.

While Harald and his ships rowed off in pursuit of the escaping enemy, Jarl Hakon stayed with his ship which was so densely surrounded by damaged and deserted craft that he could scarcely force his way out through the tangle of ship-timber, and it was then that a small boat rowed up alongside and a tall stranger wearing a heavy cowl called out, asking for the jarl by name. Hakon was helping tend the wounds of one of his warriors and turned to ask who it was that called him. 'This is *Vandrað* (a cognomen used elsewhere in the sagas for one in difficulties) who wants to speak with you,' adding in a whisper, 'I would accept my life from you if you would grant it me.' Hakon called men to take the fellow aboard a skiff and serve as his safe conduct past Norwegian vessels, then to take him ashore to a named farmer who was to give him a horse and his son to go as his escort. They did just as they were bid and delivered the stranger to the farmer who likewise followed Hakon's instruction, although the farmer's wife was less welcoming. On learning the outcome of the battle, she expressed little surprise because she knew the Danish king Svein to be a coward as well as lame. Hakon's men took their boat and returned to the ships, while 'Vandrad' went on his own way, but there is a further point of particular interest in Snorri's anecdote, because the skeleton of Svein Estridsson – exhumed and scientifically examined in more recent times – has shown that, if not actually lame, he certainly would have walked with a limp.

Meanwhile, Harald had abandoned pursuit of the enemy and was back aboard Svein's ship sharing out the spoils, quite certain now that the Danish king must be dead elsewhere or drowned overboard when his body was nowhere to be found on deck – and it was only afterwards that he learned of Svein's reappearance on Zealand where he was gathering together his surviving troops. More immediately though, Harald had a prisoner of war to deal with because Finn Arnason had been brought before him. With the mocking complaint that the Norwegians would now have the nuisance of dragging an old blind man around with them, he asked Finn if he was ready to ask for his life to be spared.

'Not by a dog like you!' 'Then perhaps by your kinsman Magnus?' Harald's son (by Thora and thus Finn's great-nephew) was in command of one of the Norwegian warships, but Finn would not ask it of a puppy. 'Will you accept it from your niece, Thora, for she is here also?' 'Ah! Then it is no wonder you fought so lustily if the mare was with you!'

Harald spared Finn's life, of course, and kept the old man with him for a while until his surly temper became so very wearying that he was given leave to return to his king Svein and put ashore on Halland. Harald then sailed north to Oslo and it was there he passed the winter.

What had befallen in the battle was the talk of his court throughout that winter of 1062/3. Surely the skalds celebrated the king's victory, but when the warriors spoke of what they had seen it was generally agreed that Hakon Ivarsson had been the bravest, the shrewdest and the luckiest of the heroes, even to the point where it was said that it was he who had really won the battle.

Hakon himself, meanwhile, had returned to his jarldom of the Upplands before winter, but his exploits on the Nissa were still the most popular topic of conversation in Oslo in the following spring when someone recalled speaking with the men who had ferried 'Vandrad' ashore and declared Hakon's luckiest escapade to have been his rescue of Svein Estridsson. Just one remark among many passed over the drinking horns, of course, but the saga quotes a proverb in the northlands to the effect that 'Many are the king's ears' and, indeed, the story was very soon brought to Harald, who assembled a troop of some two hundred housecarls to ride out to the Upplands that very same night. Even then, it would seem that Hakon's luck still held, because a friendlier soul bribed a farmer to hasten ahead of the king and warn the jarl of his coming, so when Harald reached Hakon's house he found it empty. The warning had been brought to Hakon late in the night, yet there was just enough time to see all his valuables hidden safely away in the woods before he and his retinue took horse over the border into Sweden. There he was welcomed by King Steinkel (who had succeeded Onund-Jacob in 1056) and stayed with him at court into the summer.

Harald having returned north to pass the summer in Nidaros, Hakon was able to return to the Upplands in his absence and when the king returned south in the autumn Hakon crossed back again into the Swedish province of Vermaland where Steinkel had endowed him with the lordship. So it was that when Harald's officers were despatched to the Upplands that winter for the customary collection of revenues, the Upplanders refused payment, saying they would gladly pay their taxes but only to their own jarl Hakon.

As it happened, the king had greater affairs of state on hand in the winter of 1063/4, because emissaries were already in negotiation with Denmark. After some fifteen years of battle and raiding, both peoples now wanted peace and pressure was growing upon their kings to come to some form of settlement. Thus in the spring of 1064 Harald and Svein arrived, each with his own force of ships and men, at a pre-arranged meeting on the Gaut Elf river where, after lengthy and tortuous argument, a treaty was eventually agreed. Each king was to hold his own kingdom within its own ancient borders, no compensation was to be paid for injuries and depredations suffered through the long years of conflict, prisoners were to be exchanged and the kings were to remain at peace as long as they both should live.

Curiously though, Snorri is alone among the saga-makers in setting out so much detail of the peace-making and the six strophes of verse which he quotes in support of his account are suspiciously attributed to an anonymous skald. Still more curiously, Saxo Grammaticus' history supplies no account whatsoever of any treaty, recording only that Svein rebuilt his forces for the defence of Denmark after the defeat of 1062, while Harald's ambitions were already being drawn in other directions. There is no doubt that a settlement of some kind was reached and almost certainly in 1064, when Snorri later dates the treaty between Harald and Svein to the second year after the battle on the Nissa which had been fought 'fifteen years after the death of King Magnus [in 1047]'.

In fact, a peace settlement had become the only realistic option on both sides, because the wasteful warfare which had drained the resources of two nations for a decade and half had achieved nothing. Even though Svein had lost every battle he fought and despite all the intimidation of Harald's relentless raiding, the Danes had remained loyal to their king for more than twenty years and left not a trace of doubt as to the man whom they preferred as their ruler. As to Harald's own intentions, it has been suggested that Saxo is correct and that he may already have been thinking of further-flung conquest, but the immediate course of events would indicate his concern more urgently focused on the rumbling dissension within his own kingdom and the threat still posed by the last representative of the line of an ancient enemy. The same Hakon Ivarsson who had become the effective figurehead of dissension in the Upplands was the great-grandson – and, indeed, the very namesake – of the mighty jarl of Lade who had ruled Norway for fully twenty years before the advent of Olaf Tryggvason.

Harald returned to Oslo after the peace-making and passed the summer there while his officers went again into the Upplands and were again refused their dues, payment still being held back for the return of Jarl Hakon who was said to have already assembled a great force of Gautlanders. That news apparently prompted Harald to action and by the end of the summer he had sailed to Konungahella where he assembled a fleet of light craft to carry his troops up the Gaut Elf river. Snorri tells of these vessels being hauled ashore and carried overland around the waterfalls (now called the Trollhätten Falls) as the expedition made its way upriver – a passage which would have been reminiscent for Harald of the Dnieper rapids on his voyage to Miklagard some thirty years before – and thus they eventually came to the wide expanse of Lake Vanern. Rowing eastward across the lake, Harald came ashore on the far side and there learned of Hakon's whereabouts, but the jarl had already had word of the Norwegian advance and was bringing a sizeable force of Gautlanders to meet it, apparently expecting to repel a plunder raid.

Harald left his ships at the mouth of a river and a company of warriors there to guard them, before leading the greater strength of his troops overland. The saga tells of the king and some of his officers on horseback, but most of his warriors going on foot, as they made their way through woodland and marsh overgrown with brushwood until reaching a ridge of higher ground from which they could see Hakon's forces on the far side of more marshy ground. Now within sight of each other, both armies formed up into battle array, but Harald ordered his men to stay on the higher ground and wait to see if the enemy meant to attack. 'Hakon is a very impetuous man.'

Although Snorri writes of Harald having set out on this expedition in late summer, it would seem to have turned into later autumn by the time the armies met, because the saga account has the battle fought in frosty weather with light flurries of driving snow. Up on their higher ground, the Norwegians sheltered behind their shields, while Hakon's 'lightly clad' Gautlanders, likewise ordered to hold back and await Harald's move, were feeling the chill of the day. All of which would seem to have been included in Harald's tactical plan, when his warriors suddenly leaped to their feet, raising a war-whoop and beating their shields. The headman of the Gautlanders (whom Snorri styles their 'Lawman') had tethered his horse to a stake which was torn from the ground and hit him on the head when the animal bolted at the sound of the shouting and shield-beating.

At this the Lawman galloped away while Hakon had his banner brought forward, signalling the Gautlanders to advance across the marshy ground towards the Norwegian position atop the ridge, but as soon as they reached the foot of the hill Harald's men came down on them in a headlong charge. While some of Hakon's men fell under the impact and were slain, the rest of them took flight, but there was little point in pursuit because it was now evening and Harald had taken possession of Hakon's banner, which is said to have formerly belonged to King Magnus. The battle of Vanern was over and Harald had the victory, but as it was to be his last battle fought in Scandinavia, it might be worth a little more attention than it is generally offered by historians and particularly in terms of military detail.

By the mid-eleventh century, European influence had become more evident on Scandinavian battlefields and the better equipped Swedish warrior, although armed with the traditional sword and shield, may have worn a helmet of the conical Norman design with a nasal guard (although possibly of German manufacture) and been armoured in ring-mail, while the humbler 'lightly clad' fighting-men who apparently made up the majority of Hakon's force would have been without mail armour and dressed in woollen hats, tunics and straight trousers. Their fairly basic armament would have certainly been a 'flat', all-wooden slightly curved bow of the characteristic northern type, with a simple spear for hand-to-hand combat and a leather-faced round wooden shield hanging from a sling around the upper body. The majority of Harald's warriors would have been more heavily armed housecarls, wearing helmets of spangenhelm construction similarly fitted with a nasal guard and worn with a mail byrnie. Some of their swords and shields may have reflected eastern design, so wooden shields of longer Slavic rectangular style could have been found alongside the traditional heavy wooden disc type and some swords with single-edged blades showing the influence of the steppe warrior and the Byzantine armoury. Thus equipped, the impact of a downhill charge by battle-hardened warriors thrown against the lighter-armed and effectively unarmoured Gautlanders would been have very much as it is described in the strophe from Thjodolf quoted in the saga: 'Fallen the flocks of Steinkel's followers; sent straight to *Hel*.'

Snorri does supply a telling tailpiece to the battle of Vanern in his description of the Norwegian march back to their ships, when a man suddenly jumps out of the woodland to spear the warrior carrying Hakon's banner and seize it from his hand. To which Harald responds with the shout 'The jarl still lives! Bring me my coat of mail!', but the man has long disappeared into the brush, so the march continues on its way back to the boats – and Hakon Ivarsson has just made his last appearance along Harald's warrior's way.

It remained only to deal out retribution to the recalcitrant Upplanders and so, in the winter following his defeat of Hakon (1064/5), Harald embarked on a circuit of tribute-collection with menaces, which must have been long familiar to him ever since his first winter in northern Russia. He chose to move first against the bonders of Romerike, charging them not only with refusing payment of lawful taxes but also with support of the king's enemies. Some were ordered to be maimed, others to be killed and the rest to have their property seized. Through the next twelvemonth the king moved on to Hedemark, inflicting similar destruction to that dealt out in Romerike, afterwards with fire and sword to Hadaland and finally to Ringerike, all of this confirmed by three strophes from Thjodolf telling of Uppland farmsteads left derelict and empty. Yet there is a note of irony which cannot pass without notice, because Ringerike had been the small kingdom of Harald's own father, Sigurd Syr, and so it would almost seem as if his time in the northlands had come full circle by the ending of the year 1065.

IV

Stamford Bridge

England, 1066

Within eighteen months of the peace settlement with Svein of Denmark – according to Snorri's saga and a quoted strophe from the skald Thjodolf – Harald's campaign of intimidation against the Upplanders had brought about their full submission and when Hakon Ivarsson disappeared into the Swedish woodland after the battle of Vanern the long-standing challenge from the dynasty of Lade melted away with him. The rumbling dissension in the formerly troublesome Trondelag had been stilled for most of fifteen years and, so too, the death of Olaf had been avenged when Kalv Arnason was sent to his death on Fyn island, bringing to an end a blood-feud unsatisfied for two decades and, at the same time, fulfilling Olaf's prediction as to the future character of his half-brother: 'You will be vengeful one day, my kinsman'.

By the end of the year 1065, and for the first time in twenty years, there would seem to have been no reason why the fifty-year-old Harald should not have passed the Yuletide season undisturbed by the preparation of a campaign planned for the coming spring – and yet, by March of the following year, he was mustering his armies and assembling his fleet for an invasion of England. Just how long he might have had ambitions in that direction has been a subject of speculation among historians even since the time of Saxo Grammaticus – and, of course, will bear further consideration here – yet the sagas make no reference to the prospect of such a conquest until the arrival of a visitor to his court in the early months of 1066. Nonetheless, the short passage of chronological summary placed after the conclusion of the Uppland campaign is followed by a discernible pause in the narrative before Snorri launches into his own version of events in England during the early 1060s.

He tells how 'Edward Æthelredsson' was accepted as king by the English on the death of his half-brother Hardacnut and of Edward's marriage to 'Edith, the daughter of Earl Godwin Wulfnothsson'. Although English by descent and the son of a South Saxon thane, Godwin had stood high in Cnut's favour and already begun his rise to prominence by 1018, when he is thought to have returned with the king to Denmark and there been married to Gyda (or *Gyða*), the sister of Jarl Ulf Thorgilsson who was himself the husband of Cnut's sister Estrid and, of course, the father of her son Svein. Already made an earl by that time ('earl', or *eorl*, being the English form of the Old Norse *jarl*, and a title introduced into England during Cnut's reign), Godwin's lordship was extended to the earldom of all Wessex by 1020 and he had become one of the most powerful men in the land by the time of Cnut's death in 1035, thereafter playing an important and often contentious role through the reigns of the three successor kings until his own death in 1053.

The sole significance of this Earl Godwin in the saga, of course, is as the father of the two men destined to be of such ominous significance along the final passage of Harald's warrior's way, and it is to the brothers Harold and Tostig Godwinson that Snorri next turns his attention. As the eldest surviving son, Harold succeeded to the earldom of Wessex on his father's death and was to establish himself and his family as a still greater power in the land, while his younger brother Tostig was to become earl of Northumbria when Siward, a Danish warlord thought to have first come to England in Cnut's following, died in 1055 leaving a young son Waltheof who was not yet of an age to succeed to his father's earldom. Thus by the later 1050s, virtually all the land of Edward the Confessor's kingdom – excepting only the earldom of Mercia – lay within the grasp of the Godwinsons and remained so until the autumn of 1065 when the Northumbrians, weary of the heavy taxation demanded by Tostig (largely for his personal benefit) and the equally heavy-handed manner of its collection, rose in revolt. Tostig himself, always an especial favourite of the king, was with Edward and his court at Oxford on 3 October while the Northumbrians were declaring him an outlaw, slaying every last one of his housecarls, and seizing all the contents of both his armoury and his treasury at York.

The man they invited to take over his earldom was Morcar, the younger brother of Edwin who had quite recently succeeded their father Ælfgar as earl of Mercia, and so it was with the new earl Morcar at its head that a great host of insurgent northerners marched south to Northampton where Earl Edwin was to bring a Mercian contingent to join their advance. In the event, they were met at Northampton by Harold of Wessex ready to negotiate on behalf of King Edward. Recognising the risk of disastrous civil war, he acceded to their preferred choice of earl and persuaded the king to ratify his decision, which Edward was to do on 1 November before bidding farewell to Tostig and lading him with wealth before his departure into exile at the court of his wife's kinsman, Count Baldwin of Flanders. In fact, this parting from Tostig was to be the last public act of Edward's reign, because the Confessor soon afterwards fell ill and passed from this life on 5 January. On the following day, Harold Godwinson was consecrated king of England.

If Tostig expected the new king's first priority to be the restoration of his brother to his earldom or, at the very least, his recall from exile, he was to be disappointed because Harold's first public act following his succession would seem to have been his wedding ceremony. Having already fathered a number of children on his mistress, the woman whom Harold now chose to marry was not only the widow of the Welsh king Gruffydd ap Llywelyn (on whom the Godwinson brothers had jointly inflicted a decisive defeat just three years before), but also the sister of Earl Edwin of Mercia and Earl Morcar of Northumbria. Presumably the king's choice of bride was driven by the imperative of national unity, when this marriage served to link the noble houses of Wessex and Mercia, but to Tostig it can only have added a high varnish of insult to painfully recent injury. Thus deprived of any prospect of restoration in England, Tostig's fury evidently drove him to seek an ally in support of his cause, but it is at this point that the various sources of historical record prove less than helpful. He is said by Orderic Vitalis – an English-born chronicler living in Normandy and writing in the second quarter of the twelfth century – to have first approached Duke William of Normandy, but this claim is unsupported by any other source and given little, if any, credence by later historians.

A quite different first line of approach on Tostig's part is suggested by all the Scandinavian sources, Snorri Sturluson's *Heimskringla* foremost among them. In fact, there is good reason to accept at least the substance of Snorri's account of events in his *Harald's saga* because, although clearly inaccurate on some points of detail, its proposal of Tostig's journey from Flanders to Denmark, by way of Frisia, in order to seek the support of his cousin Svein Estridsson has the full measure of plausibility. The close kinship between the two is beyond question – Tostig's mother Gyda and Svein's father Ulf having been brother and sister – and the practicality of the journey itself is hardly in doubt, even in the earlier months of the year when it could have been made overland on horseback over flat coastal country. Snorri's detailed presentation of their conversation at the Danish court can only have been of his own reconstruction and yet corresponds perfectly well to the wider scheme of things while being fully in character on both parts: Tostig pleading his case and Svein responding with the generous offer of a home and a jarldom in Denmark, although unwilling to provide the military support requested. He had enjoyed just two years of peace after enduring some fifteen years of hostility from his warlike neighbour in Norway, and was too well aware of his own limitations 'to vie with the prowess of my kinsman, King Cnut' by attempting a campaign of conquest in England. Bitterly disappointed by his cousin's refusal, Tostig announced his intention to 'find a friend in a less likely quarter' and Snorri records that 'the two parted on less than cordial terms'.

Following his departure from the Danish court, Tostig is said by the saga to have travelled on to Norway by way of the modest sea-crossing through the Kattegat and into the Vik, whereabouts Harald Hardrada was still in residence at his winter court. While there is no evidence for any earlier contact between the two, Harald's reputation must have been no less famed in Anglo-Danish Northumbria than elsewhere in the Scandinavian world and so

Tostig would have been well acquainted with the warfaring prowess of Norway's king, if only from what he had learned in York. Indeed, just such is the indication of Snorri's form of words when he has Tostig tell Harald that 'all men know that no greater warrior than you has come out of the northlands'. As before at the Danish court, the saga's detailed, but still more expansive, account of the exchanges between these two can only be of Snorri's own reconstruction and yet, for all that, it is no less convincing both in character and in substance.

Tostig (whom Snorri erroneously describes as the eldest of the Godwinsons) is said to have told Harald of his banishment from England and his unsuccessful quest for an ally in Denmark which had led him to approach the 'greater warrior' in search of support for his claim on the English throne. The saga indicates Harald's initial reluctance on the grounds that Norwegians would be disinclined to make war on England under an English commander when 'people say that the English are not entirely trustworthy'. Tostig counters with a reminder of Harald's nephew Magnus having informed King Edward of his own claim to the kingships of both Denmark and of England under the terms of his agreement with Hardacnut. When Harald is sceptical, Tostig next asks why he does not hold kingship of Denmark as his predecessor Magnus had done, only to be assured that the Norwegians had 'left their mark on those [Danish] kinsmen of yours'. To which Tostig responds with the undeniably truthful statement that Magnus had won the support of the Danish chieftains (whereas Harald had all the Danes against him), but did not attempt conquest of England because its people all wanted Edward as their king. At which point, he offers his most tempting lure in the form of an assurance that most of the chieftains in England would be his friends and support him should he wish to attempt its conquest – paying off with the pointed comment that 'it does seem very strange that you should have spent fifteen years failing to conquer Denmark and yet now show such little interest when England is yours for the taking'.

Harald is said to have considered all this carefully, to have recognised 'the truth in Tostig's words' which led him to acknowledge his own 'great desire to win this kingdom'. Thereafter, the two spoke again at length and in detail before reaching their decision to invade England in the coming summer of the year 1066.

Having followed the template of Snorri's *Harald's saga* thus far in this chapter, it would be unjust to overlook the objections raised by very many scholarly historians to his account of Harald and Tostig, objections which amount to serious doubt that there was any such meeting between the two in Norway, or anywhere else in Scandinavia, in the early months of 1066. The first basis for these objections is the fact that the meeting is noticed almost exclusively in Scandinavian sources, the awkward exception being Orderic Vitalis, whose account bears striking similarities to those found in the *Ágrip*, in Theodoric's *Historia* and, most curiously, to the speeches recorded in the kings' sagas, among which, of course, Snorri's *Heimskringla* stands foremost here.

The historian Kelly DeVries offers an astute comment on the interpretation of these various sources by modern historians when he suggests that 'it is much easier to believe that the Norwegian invasion of England was Harald's scheme alone and that his alliance with Tostig Godwinson was an afterthought made only when the two met for the first time, probably in Scotland or Northumbria. . . . Simply declaring the saga accounts of this meeting to be fiction places a lot of belief in the accuracy of the other sources, most of which are silent about any of Tostig's movements not taking place in England.'[1] The obvious answer might be as straightforward as the quite different sources of information available to the various earlier authorities working in widely different locations or, put most simply, to ask how they might have known what they say they know.

For example, Adam of Bremen and Saxo Grammaticus, whose works represent the more formal historical record set down within the Scandinavian orbit, both seem to know of prior contact between Harald and Tostig, if not of its date or location, and yet there is no obvious reason why English or Anglo-Norman chroniclers should have had information about such a meeting, and especially so if the sagas are correct in locating it in Norway. Interestingly, though, one of the earliest versions of the *Anglo-Saxon Chronicle* (the 'C' manuscript of the Abingdon text) tells of Harald's fleet arriving at the mouth of the Tyne in September 1066 where it is joined by Tostig's ships 'as they had previously arranged', which would clearly indicate knowledge of an earlier contact between the two.

Some modern historians accept that such contact had been made, but by an emissary acting for Tostig rather than the man himself, even though there is no mention of such a go-between anywhere in the sources and it would have been quite uncharacteristic of the always deeply suspicious Harald to have planned such a momentous venture with an ally of whom he can have known very little, if anything at all, and had yet to meet in person. One factor possibly underlying the 'emissary theory' is that of the time required for Tostig to travel from Flanders to Denmark and Norway, then back to Flanders before launching his own (reliably recorded) raid on the Isle of Wight before the end of May or, at the very latest, in early June. Yet the four-month period available to him need not exclude any of those destinations when considered in the light of the saga evidence for seafaring, and especially when all the sea-travel involved would have been undertaken during the better weather of advancing spring.

All of which would have been familiar territory to a saga-maker and, not least among them, Snorri Sturluson. In fact and despite the late date of its composition, there is good reason to credit the substance of his account, even in preference to that of earlier sources. First of all, he offers none of the usual signals of his own doubt as to the accuracy of his information and, indeed, it would be utterly remarkable were he to describe an entirely fictional episode in such thoroughly convincing detail. The greater likelihood, then, might be that his saga account of the initial negotiations between Harald and Tostig had been informed by his own privileged access to Norwegian diplomatic circles when he was an honoured guest at King Hakon Hakonsson's court in 1218.

To dismiss all this Scandinavian evidence as total fiction would mean that the invasion of 1066 was entirely of Harald's own devising, and yet – despite widespread assertion to the contrary –

there is nowhere any indisputable evidence of such intention on his part prior to the early months of 1066 in which the saga places his meeting with Tostig. Indeed, an entry in the Worcester manuscript of the *Anglo-Saxon Chronicle* for 1048 (being the year after the death of Magnus had enabled his succession as sole king of Norway) records Harald's despatching assurances to King Edward of his peaceful intentions as regards England. It is true, of course, that his nephew had inherited a claim on the English kingship following the death of Hardacnut, but as Gwyn Jones points out, 'there is little evidence that Magnus seriously considered the conquest of England'.[2] Indeed, Edward had been unwilling to supply ships and men in response to a request from Svein Estridsson while he was in contention with Magnus, and it is most unlikely that Harald would have entertained any serious thought of conquest of England while Edward still lived.

The fragments of evidence picked out by all the historians taking a contrary view are associated with an attempt made by Ælfgar, father of the aforementioned Edwin and Morcar, to win back his earldom of Mercia from which he had been deposed earlier in the same year of 1058. Entries in the Worcester manuscript of the *Anglo-Saxon Chronicle*, the Irish *Annals of Tigernach* and a thirteenth-century recension of the Welsh *Annales Cambriae* have led to the widespread conclusion that Ælfgar and his ally Gruffydd ap Llywelyn secured the assistance (perhaps on a mercenary basis) of a Norwegian fleet at large in the Irish Sea at the time and under the command of Harald's eldest son, Magnus. This same conclusion has led to the proposal that such an expedition would have been sent under Harald's own authority and with the probable intention of testing the defences of the English coast, yet a closer examination of the evidence of those three sources would indicate nothing of the kind.

The 'pirate host from Norway' noticed in the *Anglo-Saxon Chronicle* is more meticulously described by the Irish annalist as 'a fleet [led] by the son of the king of the *Lochland* [Scandinavians], along with the *gallaib* [literally 'foreigners', but meaning Norsemen] of the Orkney isles, of the Hebrides and of Dublin', which would actually indicate an assembly of the same viking elements regularly found summer-raiding along the western seaboard. These same free-booters are recorded in employment as mercenary naval forces on a number of occasions through the eleventh and twelfth centuries and so their services would have been available to Gruffydd, who was well connected in the Irish Sea zone, as also to Ælfgar, who had similarly hired a dozen viking ships to force his return the last time he had been driven from his earldom. As to the commander of such a viking coalition, the person identified by Tigernach as 'the son of the king of the *Lochland*' could well have been the son of a Norse chieftain in the Western Isles (customarily styled *rig* or 'king' in the Irish sources). If his name really was 'Magnus, Harald's son' as is claimed by the Welsh annalist (but by no other source), it would be quite implausible to identify him with Harald Hardrada's son of that name by his Norwegian 'wife' Thora, because that Magnus could not possibly have been born earlier than 1047 (1049 being the more likely date indicated by the saga) and the claim for a boy no older than eleven placed in command of a viking fleet such as that described by Tigernach lies entirely beyond the bounds of credibility.

Thus it can be said that there is no indisputable evidence for Harald's planning a conquest of England prior to the spring of 1066 and everything to support Kelly DeVries' proposal of Tostig as 'the prime instigator' of the expedition which was to lead him to his death at Stamford Bridge in the September of that same year.[3] The question remains, however, as to how Tostig managed to persuade him – or how he persuaded himself – to undertake the English enterprise and, indeed, what it was that he hoped to gain from it.

This last question is perhaps the most easily answered, if only on the strength of the claim made in the *Ágrip* and by Theodoric's history (and also, indeed, by Orderic Vitalis) that Tostig offered Harald half of England, intending to rule the other half as his vassal (the submission of fealty being attested by Adam and Saxo, as also by two of the English sources). No such offer is specified by Snorri's account and yet it might be implied in Tostig's claim that the majority of English chieftains would be his friends and supporters, an assurance which Harald had little reason to doubt, at least in respect of the English north country, because he would always have known of York, which stood as the capital centre of Tostig's former earldom, as *Jorvik* and of its stature as a principal stronghold of the northmen west-over-sea through two centuries. Indeed, the old kingdom of Northumbria would still have been recognisable to him, if only in terms of cultural fusion, as an Anglo-Scandinavian province and the greater extent of the English territory formally recognised as the Danelaw since the second half of the tenth century. This, of course, had also been the earldom of which Tostig had been deprived scarcely six months before, so the very least achievement expected of their projected invasion was to reclaim Northumbria for its former earl who would thenceforth rule as the liege client of a Norwegian overlord. When his liegeman was also a scion of the current English royal house, the conquest of all England surely lay within reach – and it was that prospect which offered the irresistible lure to the 'vengeful' Harald.

Snorri tells of his thinking carefully over Tostig's proposal, recognising the 'truth in his words and realising at the same time his own great desire to win this kingdom'. When the mighty Cnut had won that same kingdom scarcely half a century before, England had represented his crowning achievement and yet it was one which his sons could not sustain. Assured that England was now his 'for the taking', Harald was presented with the opportunity to take his vengeance at last upon the man long since buried at Winchester but still bearing the ultimate responsibility for the death of Olaf in the battle he had contrived at Stiklestad. Harald's very last act before leaving Nidaros to join the great invasion fleet awaiting him in the Solund Isles was to open the saint's shrine and to trim his half-brother's hair and nails. While the saga does not record whatever words he might have spoken while standing alone in that silent place, it is hard to believe they did not include some form of promise made by an avenging kinsman.

Whether or not Tostig realised that he might have awoken Harald's thirst for vengeance, he surely intended the most flattering appeal to his warrior pride. So too, he would have been ideally placed to inform a realistic assessment of the opponent Harald could expect to meet in England, because Tostig had taken his own prominent part in his brother Harold's principal military triumph some three years earlier. Indeed, the Norwegian Harald may already have known something of the campaign launched against Gruffydd ap Llywelyn in 1063, when Tostig had brought a force out of Northumbria down to the Dee and there linked up with the fleet Harold had brought north round the Welsh coast from Bristol to drive Gruffydd into flight over the Irish Sea. Together the Godwinsons had inflicted such widespread devastation across Gruffydd's kingdom of Gwynedd and such grievous suffering upon its people that they rejected and put to death their own king when he attempted to return to his ruined domain later the same year.

News of this decisive destruction of a Welsh king long notorious for his raiding over the border may well have been brought to Norway by means of the regular traffic plying the sea-road linking Dublin with Scandinavia by way of the Hebrides and Orkney. No less likely is that Harald would have heard tales of the English Harold's later warrior service to Duke William in Normandy (reliably dated to 1064), because his Norman sojourn and his swearing of fealty to William was so well known to Snorri as to be recorded in remarkable detail in his *Harald's saga*. Harald assuredly knew at least something of William the Norman too, but it is unlikely that he would have been daunted by either of these men. Both were his juniors, Harold (born *c.* 1022) by at least six years and William (born 1028) by more than a dozen, and neither could boast a military reputation bearing any comparison to the one he had earned throughout three and a half decades of warfaring across the greater extent of the known world. For all Harald's undoubted appreciation of his own warrior fame, he was not spared a word of hard-headed caution from his old comrade-in-arms Ulf Ospaksson, who is said by the saga to have warned him to expect no easy conquest, by reason of 'the army called in England the king's housecarls and formed of men so valiant that one of them was worth more than two of Harald's best men'. Snorri emphasises the significance of this caveat with a strophe of verse which he attributes to the marshal himself (although perhaps more likely the work of Stein Herdisason, the skald closely associated with Ulf in life and the author of his memorial lay).

In fact, Ulf's advice would well correspond to the opinion of at least one modern historian who believes it 'likely that there was no force in Europe equal to the Anglo-Saxon *huscarls* . . . so well-trained that they were able [if only on the evidence of the Bayeux Tapestry] to use both the two-handled battle axe and the sword with equal dexterity'.[4] Ironically and as the name 'housecarls' suggests, this body of professional fighting-men had been introduced into the English military by Cnut when he became king of England in 1016, but fifty years later the ranks of the 'royal housecarls', and their counterparts in the service of the earls, were more often filled by warriors of native stock eager for the status associated with a warrior elite and, of course, the pay that went with it. Unlike the Scandinavian housecarl who was usually rewarded with land grants, his English equivalent had always been paid in cash, initially funded by a general tax specially levied for the purpose by Cnut, but later from the treasuries of the king and his earls after the tax had been abolished by Edward the Confessor.

While there was little difference between the essential weaponry of the English and Scandinavian housecarl – sword and shield, axe and spear making the complement in each case – there would have been finer points of variation reflecting different foreign influences. Just as the arms and armour of some Norwegian warriors might be expected to reflect the Russo-Slavic, or even Byzantine, characteristics brought home by the east-farers, and Germanic styles were more likely to be found among their counterparts in Denmark and Sweden, so the Anglo-Saxon (or, perhaps more accurately, 'Anglo-Danish') housecarl of the mid-eleventh century would reflect the Norman influence which had long since found its way into the English court and its military. His mail-coat extending to the knee (thus longer than the Scandinavian custom) and his helmet of a one-piece forging fitted with a nasal guard are two such examples, while his long kite-shaped shield, similar in design to those associated with the Norman knight, would be another. There was, however, something particularly significant about this fighting-man because – like the Varangian in Byzantium and the *galloglach* in medieval Ireland – he was similarly representative of the elite mercenary axe-bearing warrior type found right across the Scandinavian expansion in the early Middle Ages.

While Ulf's pessimistic comparison of English and Norwegian housecarls might be thought less than fair, it does serve to illustrate the international reputation of the foemen whom Harald was to face in England. So too, it reflects the wise caution characteristic of this old soldier who was sadly and deeply mourned by his king when he died in that same spring. 'There lies the man who was most faithful and loyal of all to me' are the words said to have been spoken by Harald as he walked from Ulf's graveside – and I can think of no other occasion where the saga record touches so convincingly on the core of human warmth beneath the mail-coat of the warrior king.

'In the spring' – according to the saga and apparently shortly after Ulf Ospaksson's passing – Tostig left Norway and sailed westward to Flanders, there to rejoin the men who had come with him into exile and the other troops who had since gathered to his cause out of England and from Flanders too. Having already agreed with Harald to mount their joint invasion later that summer, Tostig appears to have made the first move on his own account, crossing from the Flemish coast – 'with as many housecarls as he could muster', according to two manuscripts of the *Anglo-Saxon Chronicle* – to attack the Isle of Wight where he plundered provisions for his troops and funds for his war-chest. The early sources offer no indication as to why Tostig should have chosen to strike at the south coast of England, but it has been persuasively suggested that he specifically chose the Isle of Wight as his first target in emulation of his father, Earl Godwin, who had himself been briefly exiled to Flanders during Edward's reign and made his own successful return with a landing on the same island. It is no less likely, however, that the more general direction of his attack might have been chosen by Harald in Norway with the strategic intention of concentrating the greater strength of English forces in the south.

Just such was indeed the result of Tostig's sudden appearance on the Isle of Wight, because the English Harold was in London when he learned of the landing and – perhaps imagining that this was the first phase of the anticipated Norman invasion – urgently commanded a full-scale mobilisation said by the *Chronicle* to have 'assembled greater naval and land hosts than any king in this country had ever mustered before'. By this time, Tostig's fleet already had moved on to harry the Sussex coast and reached Sandwich, where he had occupied the town and was seizing ships and recruiting men (willingly or otherwise) to reinforce his Flemish forces, when news of the advancing royal army prompted him to put back to sea. Sailing up the east coast, he paused to raid Norfolk before entering the Humber estuary with a fleet numbered at 'sixty ships' by the Anglo-Saxon chroniclers. It would seem that this strength now included seventeen ships said by the twelfth-century verse chronicle of Geoffroi Gaimar to have been brought from Orkney by Copsi (or Copsig), one of the supporters who had earlier accompanied Tostig into exile, which had joined up with his fleet as it rounded the coast of Thanet.

It was with these quite impressive forces that Tostig came ashore on the south bank of the Humber to plunder and burn around Lindsey (modern Lincolnshire) until confronted by the Mercian and Northumbrian levies mustered against them by the brother earls Edwin and Morcar. Although the *Anglo-Saxon Chronicles* supply no detail of the engagement or its precise whereabouts, they leave no doubt as to Tostig having been convincingly defeated. Gaimar would appear to credit this victory to Edwin and his Mercians, while Morcar's Northumbrian forces remained on the north bank of the Humber to prevent the invaders crossing over into (what is now) east Yorkshire. Thus Tostig was driven back out to sea, where his forces were further reduced by the flight home of the Flemish contingent laden with their plunder. So it was with only a dozen ships that he made his way up the Northumbrian coast and into the Firth of Forth where he found refuge at the Scottish court in Dunfermline and there awaited the arrival of the very much greater fleet being assembled by Harald in Norway.

By way of a footnote to Tostig's unpromising overture to the greater enterprise, it is perhaps worth mentioning the reference made by the English chroniclers to 'a portent in the heavens such as men had never seen before', which remained visible every night for a week after its first appearance on 24 April. This phenomenon, called by some 'the long-haired star' and illustrated on the Bayeux Tapestry, was Halley's Comet and its practical importance here bears on the dating of Tostig's incursion which is placed by the *Chronicle* 'soon after' the passage of the comet and thus dated to May (or, perhaps just possibly, early June) of 1066. The greater significance of this comet for the chroniclers, of course, appears to have been as an omen and one impressively borne out by the subsequent course of events.

While there is no mention of the comet in the saga (and neither is there any account of Tostig's activities), other omens are described in such sinister detail as to cast the darkest shadow over Harald's fleet being brought together in the shelter of the Solund Isles. Snorri mentions very many 'dreams and portents' reported at this time, but selects just three for inclusion in his saga. The first of these was a nightmare which came to one Gyrth, probably one of Harald's own housecarls, who was sleeping aboard the king's ship when he dreamed that he saw a huge troll-woman (one of the monstrously ugly and invariably hostile giant race of northern mythology) out on one of the islands, with a knife in one hand and a trough in the other. As his dreamscape widened, Gyrth could see eagles or ravens perched atop every prow in the fleet as the gruesome giantess sang (in skaldic verse, of course) of the king being enticed west-over-sea to fill graveyards and of birds of carrion following in his wake to feast on slain seamen.

A troll-woman also appeared in a dream to another man as he slept aboard a vessel lying alongside Harald's ship, this one riding on a wolf with a dead warrior in its blood-streaming jaws and the English battle-array behind her against the skyline. As soon as the wolf had consumed the corpse, its grisly rider dropped another into its jaws while chanting a strophe foretelling reddened shields, fallen fighting-men and the doom awaiting Harald himself. Apparitions very much like these are found elsewhere in the saga literature – perhaps most vividly in its record of ominous supernatural experiences surrounding the battle of Clontarf where the Orkney jarl Sigurd was slain in Ireland in 1014 – and represent a legacy from the darker side of pagan antiquity still preserved in the literary Christian culture of thirteenth-century Iceland. The association of such traditions with Harald may not be entirely accidental, however, and especially in the light of Adam of Bremen's claim that he 'gave himself up to the magic arts'. In fact, Adam's remark most probably refers to nothing more sinister than Harald's accomplishment in the art of the skald which demanded of its practitioners an extensive knowledge of the ancient beliefs of the northlands to inform the imagery of their kennings. There is good reason – and, perhaps, on more than one count – to believe Harald well acquainted with Odin, the lord of battle among the old gods of the north. The last of the three apparitions described in Snorri's saga (and also included in the other collections) has no such pagan associations, however, because it concerns a dream – or, perhaps more properly, a vision – said to have occurred to Harald himself and in which 'his brother Saint Olaf' brought him a warning: 'Now I fear, great Harald, your death at last awaits you. . . .'

No 'dreams and portents', however disturbingly prophetic, could turn back the great enterprise now because the invasion fleet was ready and word had long since been sent through all the kingdom to summon up a 'half-levy of the whole army'. These terms 'levy' and 'half-levy' occur throughout the kings' sagas and yet there is still no full consensus in scholarly circles as to whether any such system of muster – of which there is no formal historical record until the twelfth century – was actually practised in the Scandinavian warfaring of Harald's time. While the forces raised by Svein Forkbeard and his son Cnut for their invasions of England certainly appear to have been of the order of national armies as distinct from viking warbands, one school of thought has still recognised them as an effective coalition of the king's own force (or *lið*) made up of his warrior retinue of housecarls (or *hirð*) with the semi-professional manpower of free farmers called bonders and those of his allied chieftains and client rulers, possibly drawn from a wider extent of the Scandinavian world.

The alternative view proposes a systematic levy (or *leiðang*) of ships and men, together with their weaponry and provisioning, called up by the king and supplied by his subjects on a proportional basis – such as that estimated for the early eleventh century in terms of three farmsteads required to supply one man with his war-gear and provisions. The terms of such a system, known only from later sources, provide for the mustering of a full levy for national defence, while only the half-levy was to be called up for a campaign of aggression such as Harald intended in 1066 and so Snorri's statement of his summoning 'a half-levy of the full army' would correspond to what is known of the *leiðang* in the twelfth century. Indeed, one Norwegian historian has even proposed this same *leiðang* as Harald's own innovation – to which Kelly DeVries adds an observation of particular relevance here when he suggests that 'it seems ludicrous to believe that someone like Harald Hardrada, who had served in what was probably the most organised army in the world at the time, the Byzantine army, would abandon such a logical notion once he had returned to Scandinavia'.[5]

None of which, unfortunately, is of very great assistance in attempting to estimate either the size of fleet or the numbers of fighting-men which Harald brought to England in the autumn of 1066. As to ship numbers, Snorri records it being 'said that the king had over two hundred warships as well as supply ships and smaller craft' assembled in the Solund Isles and his estimate is comparable (especially if reckoned in 'long hundreds') to the round figure of three hundred vessels in the *Anglo-Saxon Chronicles*, a total which must also include the reinforcements acquired on route, principally those known to have joined the expedition by the time it set sail from Orkney. Other estimates supplied in the English sources tend to range upwards from that figure and even so far as the total of 'five hundred great ships' claimed by the historian John (formerly known as 'Florent' or 'Florence') of Worcester writing in the early twelfth century, but the figure most widely accepted by modern historians would be around the three hundred recorded in the *Chronicles* and plausibly supported by the saga.

In the absence of any numerical estimate of manpower in the earlier sources, it has been upon a base-line of ship numbers that historians have attempted to calculate the strength of Harald's army of 1066 – and with an extraordinarily wide range of results. Such calculations are subject to many variables, of course, and not least that of the average number of warriors aboard each ship. Harald's capital ship at the battle on the Nissa was said to have been fitted with thirty-five benches which would have accommodated a crew of at least seventy oarsmen, in addition to a shipmaster or steersman and, presumably also, the king accompanied by his attendants. Snorri's claim for its quite exceptional proportions must be taken to mean that there would have been no other vessel of such size in the fleet which sailed from Norway in 1066 (if, indeed, the 'great dragon' was still in service at that time, because the sagas make no further reference to it after 1062).

In view of such variables, it is perhaps unsurprising that the estimated sizes of Harald's forces vary so very widely from as few as seven and a half thousand to the most ambitious estimate (at least, of which I am aware) placing it at eighteen thousand fighting men. While a figure in the region of nine thousand seems to be most often found in the general currency of modern accounts, a more detailed analysis has suggested a figure somewhere between eleven and twelve thousand, presumably including an essentially non-combatant component such as serving-men and boys.

As to the course followed by the fleet between its departure from the Solund Isles and its arrival off the Northumbrian coast, history depends almost entirely upon the evidence of the saga record, which is preserved in greatest detail by Snorri's *Harald's saga* and *Orkneyinga saga*. The first landfall was in Shetland – as was customary for Norse voyagers bound west-over-sea – whence the fleet sailed south, through the turbulent Sumburgh Roosts towards the Fair Isle and on to Orkney where it assuredly found moorings in the famous broad haven of Scapa Flow.

The jarls Paul and Erlend, sons of the mighty Thorfinn, had recently succeeded their father, who had died only a year or two earlier. They are said by *Orkneyinga saga* to have been good-natured and well regarded by their people, ruling as joint jarls rather than dividing up the islands and mainland territories between them. Having come awry with King Magnus by reason of a blood-feud arising out of the killing of Rognvald Brusason, Thorfinn is said by the saga to have returned again to Norway after Magnus' death and there made his peace with Harald, effectively acknowledging him as his overlord. So, when Harald's fleet put into Orkney on voyage to England in 1066, Thorfinn's sons and successor jarls would have been obliged to join their ships to his expedition – as, indeed, they appear to have done quite willingly. Neither would their Orkney contingent have been the only reinforcement waiting in Scapa Flow, because a Hebridean Norse adventurer by the name of Godred Haraldsson – but more usually remembered as Godred *Crovan* ('of the white hand') – is known to have fought at Stamford Bridge and would almost certainly have joined the Norwegian forces in Orkney, presumably in company with some number of other ships and warriors from the Isles and from Man.

When the fleet sailed out of the Flow to cross the Pentland Firth on voyage for England, Harald's queen Ellisif remained in Orkney, probably at Kirkwall, with her daughters and there awaited a husband and father whom they were never again to see alive. Presumably Harald had brought his queen and their daughters thus far west-over-sea so as to be nearer at hand to join him when he had won his new kingdom, and yet he had left his elder son Magnus with his mother, Thora, in Norway where he was to act as regent while his father was otherwise engaged upon the conquest of England.

Across the Pentland Firth now and rounding Duncansby Head, the fleet sailed down the east coast of the Scottish mainland until it reached the Forth. Two versions of the *Anglo-Saxon Chronicle* have been taken to indicate the Scottish court of Malcolm Canmore at Dunfermline as the place of Harald's first meeting with Tostig, who there 'gave him allegiance and became his man', but the evidence of the Abingdon 'C' *Chronicle* is probably to be preferred when it places their meeting at 'the mouth of the Tyne as they had previously arranged'. If so, then there is no reason to assume that Harald might have put into the Forth on an impromptu state visit to Scotland. In fact, the saga does state quite plainly that 'he sailed down the coast of Scotland and down the English coast' and there is a very practical reason why he should have done so, because the wind had thus far been with him, giving his fleet a good speed southwards from Orkney. That same wind was keeping William the Norman's invasion fleet bottled up at the mouth of the Somme and winds can change or simply drop away altogether, so there was everything to be gained by pressing on to the target zone in northern England.

If the same thought had also been in Tostig's mind, then he would have had reason to expect the timely arrival of the Norwegian fleet from Orkney and brought his own few ships out of the Forth to meet the Norwegian fleet at Tynemouth 'as they had previously arranged'. Harald cannot have been greatly impressed by the first sight of his ally's contribution to the enterprise, although the saga makes no mention of any such opinion and, indeed, makes no mention of Tostig at all until the expedition had sailed up the Humber and won its first battle. Only at that point is there entered a hasty reassurance – framed as if it were a mere detail which had slipped Snorri's mind – of Tostig having travelled north from Flanders 'to join King Harald as soon as he arrived in England'.

Snorri does have a full account, and one more detailed than in any other version of the saga, of the Norwegian progress down the Northumbrian coast to make its first English landfall in the district of Cleveland – probably disembarking at the mouth of the Tees – where a landing party is said to have ravaged the countryside without resistance. While this might be recognised as a 'run ashore' to replenish supplies after days at sea and in the way of the old viking *strandhögg*, the saga reference to Harald having 'subjugated the whole district' might equally be read to indicate it as an exercise in intimidation akin to his regular summer-raiding of the Danes. Unless the same raiding band stayed on shore to advance southwards overland, the fleet's next landfall would seem to have been made at Scarborough – a place-name originating as 'Skarthi's burg' and said to commemorate one Thorgil called *Skarthi* ('the hare-lipped') who had established his viking fortress there a full century before Harald's arrival – and this one is still more reminiscent of that earlier campaigning in Denmark. Meeting with determined resistance on the part of the townsfolk, Harald's weapon of choice on this occasion, as so often in the past, was fire and a great pyre was lit on the higher ground above the town, from which flaming logs were pitchforked down on to the roofs. Houses went afire one after another until Skarthi's old burg was so greatly damaged – even 'destroyed' according to the saga – that the raiders were able to descend upon it for the usual plunder and slaughter. Curiously, nothing of this is recorded in the early English sources and yet it is said still to survive as a horror story in local tradition.

'In this manner,' says the saga, 'King Harald subdued the country wherever he went.' So he was to do further down the coast in the district of Holderness, a place-name indicating the district as the domain of a *hold*, a title reserved for an important local magnate and evidently one with forces ready to meet the invader in arms when Snorri tells of Harald's men having defeated them in battle. The landing parties would have been back aboard their ships before the fleet rounded Ravenspur (now Spurn Head) to sail up the Humber estuary until it entered the River Ouse and there put into land at a place identified – but only by John of Worcester and his very early twelfth-century contemporary, Simeon of Durham – as *Richale* (now Riccall).

Harald was now within reach of his principal objective, because the Ouse flows through York, a city of some fifteen thousand households defended by such fortified walls as befitted the capital fortress of the vast Northumbrian earldom and yet still very much a trading centre of similar Scandinavian character to that of Dublin beyond the Irish Sea. Capture of York must have been the first major objective of the expedition, and certainly on the part of Tostig who would have known the city, its people and its surrounding shires very well since it had been his official power base for a full decade, thus raising the question as to why the invasion fleet should have come to rest at Riccall rather than pressing on up the Ouse, even to York itself. The most likely explanation would seem to be the presence of an element of the English fleet, or possibly the naval component of the Northumbrian earl's forces, which would appear – from a reference in the *Anglo-Saxon Chronicle* – to have been up the River Wharfe, where it might well have taken refuge on learning of the appearance of so great a Norwegian force approaching the Humber. It would seem, then, that Harald probably placed his own fleet at Riccall to trap these English ships in the Wharfe, while still enabling disembarkation of his troops at a point just some seven miles' march from the city.

It is possible, had he been so optimistic, that Tostig might have hoped to gain immediate entry to his former capital and the submission of its townsfolk on his arrival with an impressive Norwegian army. It is certainly no less likely that he would have given Harald just such an impression, and yet his own arrival off the Tyne with a mere dozen ships would not have inspired confidence in such assurances, especially when Morcar and Edwin had their combined forces within the city walls, presumably inspired with confidence after their success against Tostig in Lincolnshire. While the alarming news of this quite unexpected invasion had been despatched to Harold Godwinson as soon as the Norwegian Harald landed at Riccall, the great forces he had mustered against Tostig's earlier attacks on the south coast are known to have been disbanded on 8 September (and thus, according to John of Worcester and Simeon of Durham, only shortly before the Norwegian fleet reached Tynemouth).

Probably thinking that York was unable to hold out against the expected onslaught or siege long enough for a royal relief force to be assembled and to accomplish the long march north, Edwin and Morcar appear to have decided to march their forces out of the city and confront the enemy in open battle, possibly even in the belief that just such a strategy had more often favoured English than Scandinavian forces in the past. The saga seems to indicate Harald's forces disembarking from their ships at Riccall and almost immediately advancing along the road to York, but it is more likely that the landing of so many troops with their equipment and supplies from some three hundred craft would have taken rather longer, and that the advance along the Ouse would not have begun until at least a day or two after the disembarkation. Edwin and Morcar, meanwhile, had assuredly stationed a watch along the obvious route of approach while holding their forces in readiness for warning of the approaching enemy.

While so much of this preliminary detail is left obscure in all the sources, the account of the conflict itself as set out by Snorri in his *Harald's saga* is possessed of an unusual clarity. He is even able to agree with the English sources on the precise date of the battle when he assigns it to the 'Wednesday before Saint Matthew's Day' or Wednesday 20 September in the modern calendar. It is to just one English authority however – namely, the locally well-informed Simeon of Durham – that history is indebted for the specific location of the site of battle 'at Fulford near York on the northern bank of the Ouse'. The name Fulford apparently does mean 'foul ford' and is said by a local historian to refer to 'the foul or muddy beck which feeds into the river here',[6] yet in older times there were two Fulfords along this bank of the river, one of them called Water Fulford and the other Fulford Gate (or sometimes 'Gate Fulford') which has given its name to the battle fought along the stretch of riverbank known as Fulford Ings.

Simeon's use of the term 'northern bank' is somewhat misleading because it can only apply to the city of York rather than to the battlefield, which was clearly on the southern bank of the river as it flowed along the left of Harald's advance from Riccall. By the time his army reached the vicinity of the Fulford and had thus come within a couple of miles of the city, the Northumbrian and Mercian armies were formed up behind their shield-wall to block the invaders' path. Snorri tells how Harald drew up his troops across a broad front, with its left flank reaching down to the river and the other towards a dike (or ditch) which appears to have extended into a deep, wide swamp. Harald's standard was raised on the riverside flank 'where his forces stood thickest' while the thinner ranks of his less reliable troops (presumably those with Tostig) stood over by the dike.

The earls' forces took the initiative with a charge – made along the line of the dike and led by Morcar's standard – which drove into the right flank of the Norwegian line and apparently caused it to break up on impact. Whether this reflected the weakness of Tostig's contingent or represented a tactical feint typical of Harald's guile is uncertain, but it was that point in the battle which the king chose to order his left wing into an attack against the facing ranks of Edwin's forces. With his Land-ravager standard to the fore, the swerve of the Norwegian charge crumbled the enemy into disorder and a great many were slain even before they took flight, some along the riverbanks but most of them into the dike 'where their dead soon lay so thickly that the northmen could cross the waterlogged swamp dry-shod'.

Whether success came quite as swiftly as the saga suggests or only after the 'long contest' described in the English sources, it was still a truly historic triumph – not only the last of so many credited to Harald himself, but also the very last Scandinavian victory on English soil. It would seem, nonetheless, to have been won at no small cost when John of Worcester tells of Morcar's men having 'fought so bravely at the onset of the battle that many of the enemy were laid low', so it is very likely that Tostig's right wing would have suffered heavy casualties in Morcar's initial onslaught. Yet all the saga-makers are in error when they claim Earl Morcar to have been slain in the fighting, because he certainly survived the battle, probably by taking flight and perhaps to his own country of East Anglia where he was to reappear in 1071 and with his brother Edwin among the leaders of a revolt against the Norman conquest. The authority for this premature obituary of Morcar appears to be an oddly formed strophe quoted in the *Heimskringla* version of the saga where it is attributed to the skald Stein Herdisason, and so perhaps even the learned Snorri was misled in this instance by the acrobatic complexities of skaldic syntax. So too, it seems that misinterpretation of another line of verse might have led him to identify Morcar's brother earl Edwin as Waltheof, presumably meaning the son of the late Earl Siward of Northumbria. This strophe, quoted from an otherwise unknown and unattributed *Haraldsstikki*, tells of 'Waltheof's warriors by weapons slain, lying fallen thickly in the fenland', but does not indicate this *Wæltheow*

216

either as Morcar's brother or as an earl (even though he had been given an earldom in the Midlands). Yet Siward's son was certainly of an age to fight at Fulford and may well have done so – possibly among Edwin's Mercian contingent – because he is known to have fought with the English forces just a few weeks later at Hastings.

Neither of these two skaldic authorities quoted in the saga can be said with any certainty to have been present at the battle of Fulford, but there was one skald who is known to have accompanied the expedition to England in 1066 and he was, of course, Harald's favourite court-poet Thjodolf Arnorsson who composed his last known verses on the field of his king's last battle and is said by a credible Icelandic source to have been killed at Stamford Bridge.[7]

Not until the passage immediately following the account of the blood-fray at Fulford, however, does the saga find occasion to notice that Tostig had earlier joined the expedition and to add an almost apologetic note of the earl having taken part 'in all these battles'. It is also at this point in the narrative that Snorri makes his first reference to the place-name of Stamford Bridge (or *Stafnfurðubryggja*) when he tells of Harald's assembling his forces there while preparing to advance on York (apparently imagining Stamford Bridge on the Derwent some seven miles east of the city to have been very much closer to the fleet at Riccall).

The saga next tells of English friends and supporters of Tostig flocking to join the victorious army – 'just as Jarl Tostig had previously promised' – and of all the inhabitants of the countryside around the city offering submission to Harald after learning of the defeat of their 'powerful chieftains'. In fact, these few sentences must represent a summary of the invaders' activity during the three days following the battle, events which culminated in Harald's receipt of a message sent out by the inhabitants of York to offer – in the words of his saga in *Fagrskinna* – 'themselves and their town into his power'.

Agreement on the terms of submission was to be made at a meeting just outside the city walls on the following Sunday (24 September), to which Harald arrived accompanied by his whole army. Having demonstrated the potential of his military might, the king is said by the saga to have been given the allegiance of the townsfolk and 'the sons of their leading men' (a choice apparently guided by Tostig's local knowledge) as the customary hostages. In fact, these terms would appear to have been even more reasonable than indicated by the saga, because John of Worcester and Simeon of Durham tell of an exchange of hostages, a hundred and fifty being given over by each side. Such generosity would have been sensibly diplomatic on Harald's part, if his greater need was recruitment of local warriors to replenish the manpower thinned down at Fulford before moving south against the English Harold, and would also have been in Tostig's best interests if York was to be the capital of his earldom once again.

Of still greater value in explaining the subsequent course of this hostage exchange is the evidence of the Abingdon 'C' version of the *Anglo-Saxon Chronicle* because its indication of the Yorkshire hostages being delivered to Harald on the following day would imply their being gathered from the surrounding districts, the Wolds and the vales of Pickering and of York, as well as from the city itself. The best-appointed place of delivery from these different directions would have been the crossing over the Derwent where the old Roman roadways linking York to outer-lying centres of population at Bridlington, Malton and Thornton-le-Street all converged on Stamford Bridge.

Having returned with his army to the ships on the Sunday night, Harald rose on the next morning to breakfast in bright sunshine before dispersing his forces for the day ahead. One warrior out of every three was to stay with the ships and under the command of his son Olaf, his new marshal Eystein Thorbergsson, called *Orri* ('the heathcock'), and the two Orkney jarls, while the other two thirds of his army were to accompany him for collection of the promised hostages at Stamford Bridge. Taking up their shields, helmets, swords and spears, there seemed no need to burden themselves with the great weight of mail-coats on such a day and so their armour was left behind. The saga even describes the troops as 'very carefree' when they set out from Riccall that morning, because they were as yet entirely unaware that Harold Godwinson and his army, numbered by the chroniclers in the 'many thousands', was just seven miles away.

There is no precise indication of when news of the invasion reached the English king, whose greater concern as regards impending invasion from Normandy had kept him in the south while his northerly earls saw off the nuisance of his brother Tostig's raiding around the east coast, but he evidently moved with the greatest urgency as soon as he knew of the Norwegian landing at Riccall, summoning his housecarls and 'marching northward, by day and night' – according to the Abingdon 'C' *Anglo-Saxon Chronicle* – 'as quickly as he could muster his *fyrd*'.

This *fyrd* was the English equivalent of the Scandinavian *leiðang*, although much more reliably recorded and in detail before the mid-eleventh century. Put most simply, then, the *fyrd* was a levy raised on the basis of one man from every five hides (a 'hide' being the land necessary to support a household, varying between different parts of the country and so ranging between 60 and 120 acres). Although unarmoured and equipped only with such weaponry as the bow and the axe which otherwise served them as the customary tools of the countryman, the select *fyrd* – meaning those most usually called out and kept in some measure of military training – nonetheless represented a semi-professional fighting force forming the rank and file of an Anglo-Saxon army, while the mail-coated, sword-bearing housecarls were the real professionals who formed its true cutting-edge.

In all probability, the royal housecarls would have accompanied the king on horseback so as to make all possible speed on the long road to York. Some members of the *fyrd* may also have had horses to ride, but the greater majority would have been on foot and mustered to join the march as it passed through their shires. By whatever means the army travelled, it clearly managed a remarkable pace for almost 200 miles, because the king was already on his way when he had news of the earls' defeat at Fulford and yet had reached the Wharfe in time to spend the night of Sunday 24 September at Tadcaster. On the following morning, his troops made directly for York, where they would have been informed of the place of the planned hostage-collection and so marched straight through the city to advance on Stamford Bridge.

For whatever reason – possibly the belief that Harold was too far distant to present any immediate threat or perhaps sheer over-confidence in the wake of a decisive victory – the usually deeply suspicious Harald of Norway had neglected to post any watch on the main approaches to the city itself, because the sources are unanimous as to his being caught entirely unawares when a swelling dust cloud was seen in the distance from the ridge of higher ground where he stood with his men on the east bank of the Derwent. The saga tells of the sunlight picking out the gleam of shields and glint of mail through the rolling cloud, prompting Harald to ask of Tostig who this host might be. Admitting that it did indeed appear hostile, Tostig still hoped that it might be the approach of more of his friends seeking protection from the all-conquering invader, and yet the king chose to wait until more was known about this army. 'So they did' – according to the saga – 'and the nearer came the host, the greater it appeared and its glitter of its weapons sparkled like a field of broken ice.'

By this time Harald can have been in no doubt that this was the enemy host and surely led by the English king himself. Tostig's first thought was 'to turn and hasten back to the ships for the rest of the men and the weapons, and to put up a defence among them with the ships to prevent their horsemen riding over us', but Harald had another plan: 'We shall send three good warriors on the fastest horses, to ride with all speed to bring our men to come to our assistance at once. The English will have a hard fight of it before we are all brought down.' These two statements – probably true in substance, but otherwise of the saga-maker's own reconstruction – introduce a question which stands at the centre of the historians' debate about Stamford Bridge when it concerns the role of horses in the battle, not least as regards the sagas' claim for Anglo-Saxons fighting as cavalry.

It is usually assumed that northmen coming ashore from their ships to plunder inland would have simply seized any available horses to speed their progress and this was assuredly the case in the earlier 'viking' period, but King Harald was not embarked upon any such free-booting enterprise in 1066. This was a full-scale invasion akin to that in which he had served as a Varangian officer in the front line of Maniakes' landings in Sicily almost thirty years before. There he quite certainly saw the warhorses of the Tagmata being brought ashore from the imperial fleet, so Harald may have been seeking to emulate the Greeks if he shipped horses of a quality befitting a conquering king and his retinue aboard the fleet he brought out of the Solunds that autumn.

The supposed English cavalry of such concern to Tostig are another question entirely, and one which will bear further consideration shortly, but attention must first be paid to a feature of the opening phase of the battle which seems to have entirely escaped the notice of the saga-makers. Saxo Grammaticus agrees with all the other Scandinavian sources when he tells of the Norwegians having 'left off their armour' when leaving their camp, but stands alone in his assertion that their intention was to plunder the surrounding land, yet he would seem to have some support from Geoffroi Gaimar's reference to 'thieving cattle'. Kelly DeVries has linked these two references to the story found in some English chronicles and telling of a Norwegian contingent caught on the other side of the bridge when the enemy host appeared. His very convincing theory proposes some of the northmen having earlier crossed the river from Harald's position to replenish their provisions by slaughtering cattle grazing in the meadow on the west bank.[8] There is every reason, in that case, to believe that they would have been attacked by the first English arrivals, some attempting to take flight back across the river while others made a stand at the bridge, if only to buy more time for the main force to arrange its defensive formation. The heroism of one of these warriors – a burly axe-man who apparently had chosen to wear his byrnie that day – is celebrated by the twelfth-century historians Henry of Huntingdon and William of Malmesbury as also by an interpolation of the same date into the Abingdon 'C' *Anglo-Saxon Chronicle*, all describing how he held the bridge against the enemy, his mail-coat deflecting their arrows until a spear thrust from below finally dealt him his death wound and allowed the English free passage across the river.

Surprisingly, there is no account of this magnificent stand in any version of the saga, possibly because it simply went unnoticed by his comrades on the east bank who were more urgently concerned with preparation for battle, but if there is any truth in the story then Harald and his men owed no small debt to the time he bought for their formation into the shield-wall which was to long hold off the English onslaught. The sagas all describe the use of this characteristic defensive tactic, with Snorri supplying the most detail of a 'long and rather slender line, its wings bent back until they met to form a wide circle of even depth all round, with shields overlapping both before and above'. Harald was inside the circle with his standard and his warrior retinue, as was Tostig with his company and his own banner, but Snorri goes on to explain that the archers (who cannot have been numerous) were to remain inside the circle while the men in the front rank fixed their spear-shafts into the ground with the points levelled directly against oncoming cavalry, both the men and their mounts.

By this time Harold Godwinson had arrayed a 'vast army, of both cavalry and infantry', and the saga records the sequence of verbal exchanges which usually form a prelude to battle. The first of these occurs when Harald falls from his 'black horse with a blaze [on its nose]' while riding around the shield-wall and clambering swiftly back to his feet as he declares: 'That fall was the farewell to fortune.'[9] All of which is said to have been seen from a distance by the English Harold who asks of some Norse-speakers who were with him if they recognised the 'big man who fell from his horse, the man in the blue tunic and beautiful helmet' and is told that it was the king himself. 'What a large and formidable man he is! Let us hope now that his luck has run out.'

Now the saga tells of twenty horsemen riding out from the English host and up to (or at least within earshot of) the Norwegian lines. One of them asks whether Tostig is with the army and the man himself replies in the affirmative. The foremost of the riders presents him his brother Harold's greetings along with an offer of peace and all of Northumbria as well. Indeed, and rather than have his brother refuse to join him, he would even concede a full third of his kingdom. Tostig recalls his brother's very different attitude of the previous winter before asking what might be offered to King Harald Sigurdsson for all his endeavours, only to be told of the precise extent of England which was to be allowed the Norwegian Harald: 'Seven feet of earth or as much more as he is taller than other men.'

This reply is set down in slightly variant forms across the versions of Harald's sagas (excepting only that in *Morkinskinna* which records nothing of these preliminary exchanges) and with such close similarity as to indicate their having drawn it from a common source. If this, presumably Scandinavian and probably Norwegian, original represented an entirely fictional construction, it is one quite remarkable for its splendidly English resonance, and all the more so when it appears nowhere in the earlier English historical record. As so often on these occasions, if no such statement really was spoken at the time then there is every reason to feel that it ought to have been – even though no such eloquence was to sway Tostig, who compared the earlier 'treachery' of Harold his brother with the loyalty shown by Harald his ally, and declared their shared intention to win the realm of England by a victory or to die with honour in the attempt.

As the rider and his company rode back to the English lines, the Norwegian Harald asked Tostig if he knew 'the man who had spoken so well'. When told that it had been Harold Godwinson himself, the king said he wished he had known that earlier so as to ensure that 'this Harold should not live to tell of the deaths of so many of our men'. Tostig admitted to having expected as much and so to have revealed the identity of his brother would have effectively amounted to becoming his murderer. 'Rather that he should kill me than I him.' 'What a small man,' was Harald's comment on the English king as he turned towards his own warriors, 'but how well he stood in his stirrups.'

At which point in the darkening narrative, Snorri quotes a strophe said to have been composed by Harald at the time which tells of going 'forward into battle against blue blades, [while] my byrnie and all our armour lies with the ships'. Snorri takes this opportunity to describe the king's mail-coat as being so long that it reached below the knee (thus closer to the Norman style than that of the thigh-length northern byrnie) and nicknamed 'Emma' (perhaps as a satirical reference to Cnut's Norman queen and the mother of Hardacnut). Unhappy with his first 'poor verse', Harald attempts a more inspiring version which speaks of the 'Hild of combat [a kenning for one of Odin's valkyrie daughters, but perhaps alluding also to his own mother] who bade me hold my head high in bloody battle, when blades and skulls are clashing'. To which the skald Thjodolf adds his own strophe promising to guard the 'eaglet' princes who are destined to avenge 'hard-fighting, high-hearted Harald' should their father fall in the blood-fray now about to begin.

The course of the battle of Stamford Bridge as described in the sagas corresponds in most essentials to the traditional sequence of assaults on the shield-wall repulsed by arrow and spear until at last the defending formation breaks out in a charge and the day is decided by hand-to-hand combat. None of which would surprise the military historian were it not for the sagas' clear statement of the English attacking as cavalry, because while the Anglo-Saxon warrior is known to have ridden to battle on horseback he is always believed to have dismounted on reaching the field where he invariably fought on foot. Numerous contributors to a long-running scholarly debate have suggested various other battles as the model followed by the saga-makers, but it is the one fought at Hastings where Harold Godwinson was defeated and slain just nineteen days after his own defeat of Harald Hardrada at Stamford Bridge which is usually suggested as the likely exemplar.

The most unhelpful factor in this debate is the absence from other accounts of Stamford Bridge of any detail which might confirm or deny the saga-makers' version of events, and this has enabled the suggestion from at least one quarter that the saga version might, at least to some extent, be historically accurate. Nor can such a proposal be dismissed out of hand, because it is certainly not impossible that Harold Godwinson might have taken advantage of so many of his housecarls having been mounted for the northward march to order them into battle on horseback against a shield-wall such as he himself may not have encountered before. He might even have been inspired to do so by the Norman cavalry he would have seen while in service with Duke William some two years earlier – and yet cavalry warfare of the quality perfected by the Normans is a rather more sophisticated technique than simply fighting on horseback and it is inconceivable that Anglo-Saxon warriors armed to fight on foot as heavy infantry could have gone into battle on horseback with anything akin to the expertise of Norman cavalry highly trained to charge with couched lance in squadron formation.

Whatever might have been the source of the saga accounts, the suggestion of waves of mounted spearmen flung against a shield-wall flies in the face of everything that is known about Anglo-Saxon warfaring and so the most that might be allowed – if the saga-makers are to be given some benefit of doubt in the absence of any decisive evidence to the contrary – is the possibility of just some housecarls having led the English attack on horseback, even if not strictly as 'cavalry'. Nonetheless, the Norwegian defensive formation held firm and drove off each wave of assailants, although Snorri indicates mounted warriors riding in circles around a loose defensive formation and seeking for any openings into the ranks. After some duration of this onslaught – and probably very much later in the afternoon, because it is unlikely that the armies had reached the field before midday – there came the crucial moment when the shield-wall broke open to allow the headlong charge in pursuit of a retreating enemy.

Yet here the saga-makers are at variance, because Snorri indicates this as an unwise Norwegian response to a deliberately feigned retreat by the English intended to draw them out from behind a solid wall formed of iron, oak and muscle before turning around to unleash a maelstrom of spears and arrows against a headlong disordered pursuit. This proposal bears such a distinct similarity to the later course of battle at Hastings as to arouse suspicion and so the rather different interpretation offered by the other versions of the saga in *Morkinskinna, Fagrskinna* and *Flateyjarbók* – all of them indicating the sudden charge as a counter-attack against a particularly fierce mounted offensive around the defensive circle – is probably to be preferred. Understandably provoked by the sheer aggravation of relentless attack suffered in close and cramped formation, the northmen at last broke out of their shield-wall to launch a ferocious charge against an enemy thrown into sudden retreat 'and there was a great slaughter among both armies'. When the Norwegian king saw what was happening, he led his own retinue into the greatest heat of the fighting, much as Olaf had done at this stage in his own last battle. Quite unlike his half-brother, however, Harald was consumed by an uncontrolled warrior-fury – seemingly akin to that of the berserkers of viking legend – when he rushed ahead of his companion warriors, slashing with both hands so that neither helmet nor mail-coat could withstand his onslaught and all in his path fell back before him.

In the death-song he had promised to compose for Harald some twenty years before, Arnor Jarlaskald tells how 'Norway's king had nothing to shield his breast in the battling, and yet his war-hardened heart never wavered, while Norway's warriors were watching the bloodied sword of their bravest leader slicing down their foemen'. So perhaps it was just as he had always known it would be – with his battle-rage at white heat and no mail-coat to stem his stride nor shield-grip to hamper his wielding a weapon in each hand – that Harald Hardrada came at last to the end of his warrior's way, because the saga tells how it seemed that the enemy were about to be routed when the king was struck by an arrow in the throat.

'And this was his death-wound.'

There is no reason to doubt the wound-site, because the exposed throat and face offered the obvious target area for an archer aiming to kill a fully mailed warrior. The saga-maker may even have been right in believing the victory to have been within grasp when the king fell because a berserker charge must have been one of the most fearsome experiences of early medieval warfare. Even so, the odds were still stacked against a Norwegian victory when the northmen without armour or heavier war-gear had been caught entirely unawares by an enemy host of apparently superior numbers.

Beyond such straightforward pragmatic considerations, there is another factor of bearing and it lies in the claims made by the skalds and saga-makers for Harald's 'great victory-luck'. Indeed, the English Harold would seem also to have known of it, if he truly did suspect that it might be about to run out when he saw his enemy fall from a horse on that Monday afternoon – as did Harald himself, and at much the same time, when he spoke of a 'farewell to fortune'. Yet a skald steeped in the ancient legends of the northland might have read those same runes differently, because he would have known Odin as the least trustworthy of battle-gods who would sustain and shield one of his chosen through years of warfaring before suddenly failing him, and for no other reason than to summon another hero home to Valhalla.

On the field of Stamford Bridge meanwhile, the king was dead and his fall is said to have been followed by a lengthy pause in the fighting. Tostig still stood beside the royal standard in the place where the main force had earlier held their formation and there began to re-form the shield-wall while the skald Thjodolf – possibly already wounded and not long to outlive his lord – composed the grim lines of what was to be his last strophe:

> Upon evil days has
> the host now fallen;
> needless and for nothing out
> of northland Harald brought us;
> badly bested we are now
> and ended in the life of he
> who boldly bade us battle
> here in England.

It was then that the English Harold found his way towards earshot of his brother and again offered quarter both to him and to those survivors who stood with him. But the northmen shouted back that they would sooner die than yield and roared out their war-cry to begin the slaughter once again. It must have been during this phase of the battle – which cannot have lasted long with so few left alive to fill up gaps in the shield-wall – that Tostig was slain, although Snorri makes no further mention of him and the saga record of his fighting bravely until finally struck down is preserved only in *Morkinskinna, Fagrskinna* and *Flateyjarbók.*

Yet the blood-fray was still not done, because at this point Harald's marshal Eystein Orri arrived and with him a force of warriors who had remained at the ships that morning. These men had not left their armour behind, of course, and so were exhausted after running so many miles from Riccall in full war-gear, yet when Eystein found Land-ravager and raised it up again, they summoned up the energy to renew the onset with such greater ferocity that it was long remembered – according to the saga – as 'Orri's Battle'. As the heat of battle rose to match the heat of the day, many of Eystein's men are said to have thrown off the weight of their mail-coats, thus offering softer targets to the English blades that cut them down. 'Almost all the leading Norwegians were killed there.'

Those who survived apparently attempted to flee back to Riccall, because the Worcester *Anglo-Saxon Chronicle* tells of many killed by drowning or burning and indicates the English pursuit having extended even to an attack on at least some of the ships, which would well correspond to Snorri's statement that 'it had grown dark before the carnage was ended'. Nonetheless, there were some of 'the leading Norwegians' who had not fallen with Eystein, because other saga sources record that the young prince Olaf (who is known to have fought at Fulford) had stayed with the two Orkney jarls to guard the ships while Eystein answered the call to battle. Thus these three represented the surviving principals of the Norwegian army when, according to the same *Chronicle*, Harold Godwinson of England gave 'quarter to Olaf, the son of the king of the Norwegians . . . to the jarl[s] of Orkney and to all those who were left aboard the ships'. Harold Godwinson must have had more than enough of killing when, despite his best efforts at peacemaking, he had found his own brother's remains among the thousands lying on the battlefield at Stamford Bridge and afterwards arranged for Tostig's burial at York, but not so very long before he himself was to fall in battle at Hastings against the Norman duke to whom he was said to have sworn fealty two years earlier.

By which time, Olaf, Paul and Erlend had taken ship – or, more precisely, just two dozen ships, which are said by the *Chronicle* to have been all that were needed to carry home the survivors of the Norwegian army – from Ravenspur back to Orkney. There Olaf was reunited with his father's queen Ellisif and his half-sister Ingigerd, but alas not with her sister Maria, who is said by the sagas to have died on the day – and, indeed, at the very hour – when her father had fallen in battle.

The three of them passed the winter in Orkney and in the following summer returned to Norway where Olaf shared the kingship with his brother Magnus. On Magnus' death, just two years later in 1069, he succeeded as sole king of Norway and is remembered as *Olaf kyrra*, or 'Olaf the Quiet'. For whatever reason (unexplained in any of the sources), his father's remains were not brought back to Norway until later in the year following the battle, when Harald Sigurdsson was buried, according to his saga, 'at Nidaros in Saint Mary's church which he himself had founded'.

Land-ravager

AN AFTERWORD FROM WEST-OVER-SEA

Nothing further is told of Harald's famous standard in the saga after Eystein Orri had retrieved the banner from wherever it had been abandoned when Tostig was slain and raised it up again to lead his warriors in the last desperate stand remembered as 'Orri's Battle'. At which point *Landeyðuna* disappears entirely from the saga record and might be thought to have been lost for ever amid the blood-stained debris left lying along the bank of the Derwent water. Yet it need not be so, because there is reason to believe that the celebrated Land-ravager was not only rescued from the field of Stamford Bridge but eventually found its way to a westward region of the Scandinavian expansion where Harald himself had no occasion to travel but where his grandson, Magnus Olafsson – called 'Bareleg' on account of his adoption of the garb of the Gael – is well remembered as the warrior king who finally and formally claimed the Hebrides (or *Suðreyjar*) for Norway in 1098.

In the room thought to have been the original Great Hall of Dunvegan Castle on the Isle of Skye is displayed a broad fragment of textile known in the Gaelic as *Am Bratach Sidhe* (or 'The Fairy Flag') and long regarded as the most treasured possession of the Clan Macleod, whose principal stronghold this fortress is said to have been since the fourteenth century when the name Macleod made its first entry into the historical record. At least half a dozen stories are told of how this 'Fairy Flag' came into the possession of the Macleods of Dunvegan – some claiming it to have been a gift of the fairy folk (and, indeed, the bridge where that gift was made is clearly signalled to any modern visitor who might pass that way), while others say it was brought from the Holy Land by a clansman returning from a crusade. There are problems with both of these traditions, firstly by reason of the unreliable historicity of fairies and secondly because there appears to be no record of any Macleod known to have been on any of the crusades.

Another feature of the traditions surrounding this *Bratach Sidhe* is the belief in its power to save the clan in times of danger and Macleod chieftains are said to have twice unfurled the flag when hard-pressed in battle and thus to have won the victory. It is this claim – and the possibility of its association with the Fairy Flag long before it came into the hands of the Macleods – which points toward the genuinely historical proposal that *Am Bratach Sidhe* is, in fact, Harald Hardrada's *Landeyðuna*.

Clan Macleod has always been proud of its Gaelic-Norse origins and justly so because their line has been convincingly traced all the way back to Olaf Cuaran, Norse king of York and of Dublin, who died the 'straw death' in monastic retirement on Iona in 981. The *Leod* for whom the clan is named, however, was directly descended from the line of the Norse kings of Man and the Isles through one Helga 'of the beautiful hair' who was the sister of the same Godred Crovan who fought with the Norwegian army at Stamford Bridge and survived the battle to become the founding dynast of the royal house of Man.

The entry under the year 1066 in the thirteenth-century *Chronicle of Man* refers to the 'very great slaughter of the Norwegians' at Stamford Bridge and tells of 'Godred, called *Crovan*, son of Harald the Black from *Island* [thought to mean the Isle of Islay], fleeing from the rout' and making his escape (probably overland by way of North Wales or the Solway) to the Isle of Man. The saga account of the phases of the conflict would almost certainly indicate the 'rout' referred to by the *Chronicle* as 'Orri's Battle', in the course of which Land-ravager disappears from the historical record. If Godred had brought a banner, probably made of silk and assuredly of Byzantine origin, back from Stamford Bridge, he could very well have made a gift of it to his sister and assuredly also spoken of the legendary powers associated with its service as Harald's battle-flag.

All of which might be thought to correspond quite impressively to the proposal of Land-ravager having been handed down the generations of Helga's descendants even to the present Macleod of Macleod in whose castle at Dunvegan it is revered as *Am Bratach Sidhe*. Still more impressive, though, are the results of a modern forensic examination of the fabric of the Fairy Flag identifying it as a silk at least as old as the seventh century and of eastern origin, probably from Rhodes or possibly from Syria, both of which were sources supplying this greatly prized textile to the Byzantines.

If the Fairy Flag of the Macleods really is the same Land-ravager banner which Harald is said to have valued above all other treasures in his possession, then its location on Skye offers a quite remarkable coincidence, because to the south-east of Dunvegan stands the magnificent mountain range known as the Cuillin.

Once again, the claims of 'Celtic' tradition might stand accused of clouding the issue and not least through the efforts of Sir Walter Scott who played a great part in associating 'Cuillin' with the legendary Irish hero Cuchullain. In fact, the true origin of the name, alike to that of the other Cuillin on the neighbouring island of Rum, derives from the Old Norse – *kjolr* ('the keel') or *kiolen* ('high rocks') – and so the Cuillin of Skye can be said to share its name with the Kjolen range over which the young Harald Sigurdsson, having recovered from wounds suffered at Stiklestad, crossed from Norway into Sweden along that early passage of his warrior's way.

Genealogies

There is just one abbreviation: HH = Harald Hardrada

DESCENT OF HARALD HARDRADA AND HIS SUCCESSORS FROM HARALD FAIR-HAIR

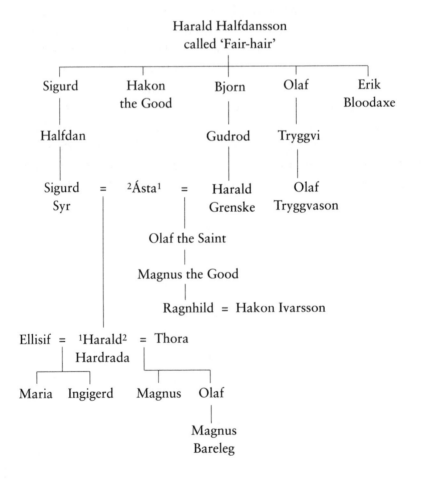

Harald Halfdansson
called 'Fair-hair'

Sigurd   Hakon   Bjorn   Olaf   Erik
          the Good   Bloodaxe

Halfdan   Gudrod   Tryggvi

Sigurd = ²Ásta¹ = Harald   Olaf
Syr   Grenske   Tryggvason

Olaf the Saint

Magnus the Good

Ragnhild = Hakon Ivarsson

Ellisif = ¹Harald² = Thora
            Hardrada

Maria   Ingigerd   Magnus   Olaf

Magnus
Bareleg

THE ARNASONS AND THEIR NETWORK OF MARITAL KINSHIP

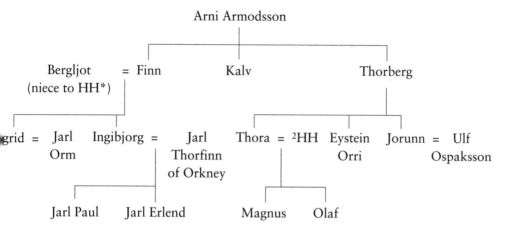

Arni Armodsson

Bergljot (niece to HH*) = Finn Kalv Thorberg

grid = Jarl Orm Ingibjorg = Jarl Thorfinn of Orkney Thora = ²HH Eystein Orri Jorunn = Ulf Ospaksson

Jarl Paul Jarl Erlend Magnus Olaf

* Bergljot's father was Halfdan, son of Sigurd Syr and Ásta.

THE JARLS OF LADE AND THEIR DESCENDANTS

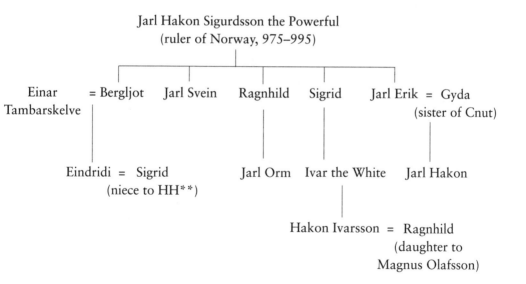

Jarl Hakon Sigurdsson the Powerful
(ruler of Norway, 975–995)

Einar Tambarskelve = Bergljot Jarl Svein Ragnhild Sigrid Jarl Erik = Gyda (sister of Cnut)

Eindridi = Sigrid (niece to HH**) Jarl Orm Ivar the White Jarl Hakon

Hakon Ivarsson = Ragnhild (daughter to Magnus Olafsson)

** Sigrid's mother was Gunnhild, daughter of Sigurd Syr and Ásta.

Notes and References

Introduction

1. Magnusson & Pálsson (ed.), *King Harald's Saga*, p. 31.
2. Turville-Petre, *Haraldr the Hard-ruler and his Poets*, p. 5.
3. Blöndal & Benedikz, *The Varangians of Byzantium*, p. 210.
4. Turville-Petre, *Haraldr the Hard-ruler and his Poets*, pp. 3–4.

Stiklestad

1. Turville-Petre, *The Heroic Age of Scandinavia*, p. 156.
2. Jones, *A History of the Vikings*, p. 382.
3. In the twelfth-century saga texts, however, Russia is identified by the later Icelandic name-form of *Garðaríki*.
4. While the saga actually specifies 'four hundred chosen men', such references are calculated in 'long hundreds', or 120 in modern reckoning, and so the reinforcement would have amounted to 480 of Onund's warriors. That same formula is applied here to all troop and ship numbers found in the saga texts, although such figures should usually be considered only as approximations.
5. Foote & Wilson, *The Viking Achievement*, p. 284.
6. 'Weapon thing' is one of many skaldic kennings for 'battle'.
7. Foote & Wilson, *The Viking Achievement*, p. 80.
8. Although usually translated as 'paunch-shaker', the original meaning may have been 'he who twangs the bow-string' and a reference to his part in the battle of Svold where the young Einar fought as an archer aboard Olaf Tryggvason's ship.
9. Thorstein's surname translates as 'knorr-maker', from the trading ship type known as a *knorr*.
10. Jacqueline Simpson (ed.), *The Olaf Sagas*, p. 381.
11. By 'the Finns' is meant the Lapps, who are also a Finno–Ugrian people.
12. Turville-Petre, *Haraldr the Hard-ruler and his Poets*, p. 10.

Varangian

1. Known in Russian as *Povest' Vremennykh Let*, a title literally translated as 'Tale of the Years of Time'.
2. Franklin & Shepard, *The Emergence of Rus*, p. 201.

3. Blöndal & Benedikz, *The Varangians of Byzantium*, pp. 54–5.
4. Her eldest sister, Eudocia, had long since become a nun, thus effectively renouncing her claim on succession.
5. Blöndal & Benedikz, *The Varangians of Byzantium*, p. 75.
6. *Ibid.*, p. 66.
7. Pritsak, 'Varangians', in Pulsiano (ed.), *Medieval Scandinavia: An Encyclopedia*, p. 689.
8. Gravett, *Norman Knight: 950–1204 AD*, p. 60.
9. Obolensky, *The Byzantine Commonwealth*, pp. 84, 160.
10. Norwich, *A Short History of Byzantium*, p. 222.
11. Blöndal & Benedikz, *The Varangians of Byzantium*, pp. 80–6.
12. *Ibid.*, pp. 97–8.
13. Harald's actual phrase is 'gold-[arm]ring *Gerðr*'; *Gerðr* being the name of the wife of the god Frey and used as a skaldic kenning to mean 'goddess' in the complimentary sense of the term when applied to a mortal woman.
14. 'Greek Fire' is thought to have been distilled petroleum thickened with sulphurous resin, which burst into flame on contact with enemy vessels and continued to burn on the water.
15. Franklin & Shepard, *The Emergence of Rus 750–1200*, p. 216.
16. Obolensky, *The Byzantine Commonwealth*, p. 225.

Hardrada

1. Jones, *A History of the Vikings*, p. 404.
2. *Ibid.*, p. 401.
3. *Ibid.*, p. 407.
4. Davidson, *The Viking Road to Byzantium*, pp. 221, 228.
5. If Stein's figures are given in 'long hundreds', as they probably are, then 150 Norwegian and 300 Danish ships would represent 180 and 360 respectively in modern reckoning, although such precision is of little bearing here.

Stamford Bridge

1. DeVries, *The Norwegian Invasion of England in 1066*, p. 238.
2. Jones, *A History of the Vikings*, p. 403.
3. DeVries, *The Norwegian Invasion of England in 1066*, p. 230.
4. *Ibid.*, p. 211.
5. *Ibid.*, p. 204.
6. Broadhead, *Yorkshire Battlefields*, p. 41.
7. Turville-Petre, *Haraldr the Hard-ruler and his Poets*, p. 17.
8. DeVries, *The Norwegian Invasion of England in 1066*, pp. 278–9.
9. There are different forms of translation of these words, but this (from DeVries, p. 284) is the most accurate.

Select Bibliography

Adam of Bremen, *History of the Archbishops of Hamburg-Bremen* (trans. F.T. Tschan), New York, 1959

Anderson, A.O. (trans.), *Early Sources of Scottish History AD 500–1286*, 1922, repr. Stanford, 1991

Anglo-Saxon Chronicle, The (trans. G.N. Garmonsway), London, 1972

Blöndal, S. and Benedikz, B.S. (trans. and rev.), *The Varangians of Byzantium*, Cambridge, 1978

Broadhead, I.E., *Yorkshire Battlefields*, London, 1989

Davidson, H.R.E., *The Viking Road to Byzantium*, London, 1976

DeVries, K., *The Norwegian Invasion of England in 1066*, Woodbridge, 1999

Foote, P.G. and Wilson, D.M., *The Viking Achievement*, London, 1980

Franklin, S. and Shepard, J., *The Emergence of Rus 750–1200*, London, 1996

Graham-Campbell, J. (ed.), *The Viking World*, London, 1980

Gravett, C., *Norman Knight 950–1204 AD*, London, 1993

Griffith, P., *The Viking Art of War*, London, 1995

Harrison, M., *Anglo-Saxon Thegn 449–1066*, London, 1993

——, *Viking Hersir 793–1066*, London, 1993

Heath, I., *Byzantine Armies AD 886–1118*, Oxford, 1979

——, *The Vikings*, London, 1985

Henry of Huntingdon, *The Chronicle of Henry of Huntingdon* (trans. T. Forester), 1853, repr. Lampeter, 1991

John ['Florence'] of Worcester, *Florence of Worcester: The History of the Kings of England* (trans. J. Stevenson), 1853, repr. Lampeter, 1988

Jones, G., *A History of the Vikings*, Oxford, 1984

Karasulas, A., *Mounted Archers of the Steppe 600BC–AD1300*, Oxford, 2004

Lang, D.M., *The Bulgarians from ancient times to the Ottoman Conquest*, London, 1976

Laxdæla Saga (trans. M. Magnusson and H. Pálsson), Harmondsworth, 1969

Lindholm, D. and Nicolle, D., *Medieval Scandinavian Armies 1100–1300*, Oxford, 2003

Nicolle, D., *Medieval Warfare Source Book: Christian Europe and its Neighbours*, London, 1998

——, *Armies of the Caliphates 862–1098*, Oxford, 1998

——, *Armies of Medieval Russia 750–1250*, Oxford, 1999

Norwich, J.J., *A Short History of Byzantium*, London, 1997

Obolensky, D., *The Byzantine Commonwealth: Eastern Europe 500–1453*, London, 1971

Orkneyinga Saga (trans. H. Pálsson and P. Edwards), London, 1978

Page, R.I., *Chronicles of the Vikings: Records, Memorials and Myths*, London, 1995

Psellus, Michael, *Fourteen Byzantine Rulers* (trans. E.R.A. Sewter), London, 1966

Pulsiano, P. (ed.), *Medieval Scandinavia: An Encyclopedia*, London and New York, 1993

Rumble, A.A. (ed.), *The Reign of Cnut, King of England, Denmark and Norway*, London, 1994

Russian Primary Chronicle, The (trans. S.H. Cross), Cambridge, Massachusetts, 1930

Simeon of Durham, *Simeon of Durham's History of the Kings of England* (trans. J. Stevenson), 1858, repr. Lampeter, 1987

Stenton, F.M., *Anglo-Saxon England*, Oxford, 1947

Sturluson, Snorri, *Edda* (trans. A. Faulkes), London, 1987

——, *Heimskringla* (trans. L.M. Hollander), Austin, Texas, 1964

——, *King Harald's Saga* [from *Heimskringla*] (trans. M. Magnusson and H. Pálsson), Harmondsworth, 1966

——, *Olaf Sagas* [from *Heimskringla*] (ed. J. Simpson and trans. S. Laing), London, 1964

——, *Sagas of the Norse Kings* [from *Heimskringla*], (ed. P. Foote and trans. S. Laing), London, 1961

Tale of Halldor Snorrason, The (trans. T. Gunnell) in *The Sagas of Icelanders* (ed. O. Thorsson), New York, 2000

Tale of the Story-wise Icelander, The (trans. A. Maxwell) in *The Sagas of Icelanders* (ed. O. Thorsson), New York, 2000

Treadgold, W., *Byzantium and its Armies, 284–1081*, Stanford, California, 1995

Turnbull, S., *The Walls of Constantinople AD 324–1453*, Oxford, 2004

Turville-Petre, G., *The Heroic Age of Scandinavia*, London, 1951

——, *Haraldr the Hard-ruler and his Poets*, London, 1968

William of Malmesbury, *History of the Kings before the Norman Conquest* (trans. J. Stevenson), 1854, repr. Lampeter, 1989

Wilson, D.M. (ed.), *The Northern World*, London, 1980

Index

240

Index

241